Praise for *The Virtual Handshake:*

"Today, everyone has to learn how to use technology to grow their network. The authors have written a groundbreaking book that shows very clearly the options available to anyone and how technology can be used to multiply one's reach. This is a major contribution to the way in which people do business."

—**Richard Guha,** Principal, The New England Consulting Group; former President, Reliant Energy Retail

"An important and timely read."

—**Gregg S. Robins,** Executive Fellow, NYU Stern School of Business; former Citigroup Business Head, International Personal Banking, Switzerland, Monaco & Luxembourg

"Authors David Teten and Scott Allen clearly practice what they preach, and have drawn on their own impressive networks to assemble a vast but well-organized and highly applicable set of recommendations for how to be successful in the emerging, networked world. This book will be an invaluable resource for anyone who wants to build their own network and/or to understand the growing importance of social capital."

—**Ben Dattner,** Ph.D., Adjunct Professor of Industrial and Organizational Psychology, New York University

"*The Virtual Handshake* is an invaluable wakeup call about how quickly things are changing and what you must do to become successful in this new world. More and more people are building relationships and transacting business using online networks. The new generation of people entering the business world (and many already in it) see the Internet as one of the most natural ways to build and maintain business relationships, and a whole new suite of capabilities is rapidly being developed to facilitate such interactions. As an executive, you are affected by the growth of this new medium whether you choose to fully utilize these new tools or not, because others will be using them to gain a competitive advantage. At a minimum, you must be aware of how your virtual image is being presented (and how to manage it), because it will increasingly be seen by people considering doing business with you."

—**Gerry Mintz,** former President, Gartner Executive Programs; Principal, Mintz & Partners, Inc.

"David Teten and Scott Allen have written a terrific book that, while remaining true to universal laws of business and social success, provides us with the knowledge and wisdom to succeed in the 21st Century. I greatly appreciate their sharing their expertise so completely and in such a way that anyone from the 'newbie' to the most experienced can come away with a practical and clear understanding of how this very important 'game' is played."

—**Bob Burg,** Author, *Endless Referrals: Network Your Everyday Contacts into Sales* and *Winning Without Intimidation: How to Master the Art of Positive Persuasion*

"*The Virtual Handshake* is an invaluable resource and insiders' guide for anyone who wants to proactively manage their business and personal relationships online. Don't go home without it."

—**Robert Labatt,** CEO, ezboard, Inc.

"This is a book that business executives should read. The authors show how communications technologies are allowing people to form lasting business relationships and personal networks. This goes way beyond just a tech-trend."

—**Michael Tanner,** Managing Director, The Chasm Group, LLC

" If you want to learn how to build powerful relationships, take this book off the shelf and buy it. This is *The Seven Habits of Highly Effective People* for the Internet. It is a nonstop flow of ideas which will help you to make more money, take your career into overdrive, and make you a far more effective person."

—**Chris Michel,** President, Military.com, largest military membership organization in the U.S.

"I really love it. It's frank, specific and useful, and that's what people need."

—**Thomas Power,** Founder and Chairman, Ecademy

"In a globally competitive world, a person's business network is the key to success. *The Virtual Handshake* gives readers tactics that provide immediate results and strategies for long-term, enduring success and value creation."

—**Adrian Scott,** Ph.D., Founder and CEO, Ryze

"This is easily the best how-to manual for online business networking. I recommend it to Contact Network customers, and to users of all online social networks."

—**Geoffrey Hyatt,** Founder and CEO, Contact Network Corporation

"The time I have invested in building a powerful personal network has been critical to my success. Doing it online has enabled me to leverage it even better. In fact, what made Cvent the industry leader in online event planning was my willingness to take a traditional business practice outside of historical boundaries. *The Virtual Handshake* is a distillation of insight into face-to-face and online networks that should have been made available years ago. *The Virtual Handshake* will open doors for you that you did not even know were closed."

—**Reggie Aggarwal,** CEO, Cvent

"*The Virtual Handshake* is a wonderful resource to improve your online business relation building. David Teten and Scott Allen provide hundreds of useful hints embedded in a strategic guide to enhance online social relations. Even considering myself as blogging and social software literate, I could find much advice and dozens of helpful links in this wonderful book."

—**Torsten Jacobi,** Founder of Creative Weblogging, Ltd.

"Suddenly the internet has given everyone access to the little black books of background and contact information that have traditionally been the exclusive currency of successful business people. *The Virtual Handshake* is the perfect instructional guide that actually shows people how to harness the incredible breadth and depth of information that's now available, and turn it into actionable tools for achieving business success."

—**Gary Halliwell,** President of Zoom Information Inc., formerly Eliyon Technologies Corporation

"As an entrepreneur, I am an ardent supporter of utilizing technology to be more effective in business. *The Virtual Handshake* provides the tools and tactics everyone would need to succeed in today's online business networks."

—**Chandra Bodapati,** Founder & CEO, eGrabber, Inc.

"This book couldn't be more timely. The World Wide Web is the perfect infrastructure for networking. The age we live in is all about global connecting. This fascinating and unique book gives us the directions to build and maintain that infrastructure and create global relationships. This is the way the world now works. Read this book if you want to work in it."

—**Michael Hick,** Author, *Global Deals: Marketing and Managing Across Cultural Frontiers*

"Long-distance relationships that I've created online have [been] a huge factor of the success of my books and speaking career. *This* is simply the only book I've seen that really shares examples, and teaches how we can create and manage those relationships most effectively."

—**Greg S. Reid,** Author, *The Millionaire Mentor*

"Contact management software is the foundation tool for managing a powerful network; social network software and other new technology tools are now becoming part of the way successful people are doing business. The clear logical reasoning of *The Virtual Handshake* helps people like me who like to know "why," not just "what." I've spent 15 years in the customer relationship management industry, and I still learned a boatload of valuable ideas from this extremely useful book."

—**Greg Head,** formerly General Manager, ACT!, Best Software's CRM division

"While most people recognize the value of networking, many are unable to achieve their desired results. This book outlines step-by-step processes that anyone can follow. It takes complex issues and breaks them into actionable items."

—**Andy Nunemaker,** CEO, EMSystem

THE Virtual
Handshake

THE Virtual Handshake

→ Opening Doors
and Closing Deals
Online

DAVID TETEN and SCOTT ALLEN

AMACOM

AMERICAN MANAGEMENT ASSOCIATION
New York | Atlanta | Brussels | Chicago
Mexico City | San Francisco | Shanghai
Tokyo | Toronto | Washington, D.C.

This publication is designed to provide accurate and authoritative information in regard to the subject matter covered. It is sold with the understanding that the publisher and author are not engaged in rendering legal, accounting, or other professional service. If legal advice or other expert assistance is required, the services of a competent professional person should be sought.

Library of Congress Cataloging-in-Publication Data

Teten, David.
    The virtual handshake : opening doors and closing deals online / David Teten, Scott Allen.
        p. cm.
    Includes bibliographical references and index.
    ISBN 0-8144-7286-9
    1. Business enterprises—Computer networks.   I. Allen, Scott, 1965–   II. Title.

    HD30.37.T48   2005
    650.1'3'02854678—dc22   2005002638

Printing number

10 9 8 7 6 5 4 3 2 1

The following trademarks are the property of their respective owners: About.com, AltaVista, aSmallWorld, ACT!, Always-On Network, Amaya, American Society of Association Executives, AmphetaDesk, AOL, Architectural Designs, Blogger, Bloglines, Brain Food, Classmates, Contact Network Corporation, Corp-Net, Creative Commons, craigslist, DanceTime Publications, Docusearch, Everquest, eWomenNetwork, Easytrieve, Ecademy, Zoom Info, Entopia, Fibre2Fashion, FirstGov, FreeConference.com, FreeConferenceCall.com, Friends Reunited, Friendster, Geocities, Google, Habbo Hotel, HotOrNot.com Huminity, iCohere, iVillage, ICQ, Intel, *KaZaA*, K-Collector, Knowmentum, kuro5hin Leverage Software, LiveJournal, LinkedIn, LinkSV, Lockergnome, Major League Baseball, Match.com, Media Bistro, Meetup, Military.com, Microsoft, Movable Type, Monster, Mozilla, Neopets, Networking for Professionals, NewsGator, NewsIsFree, Nitron Advisors, Circle of Experts, openBC, Open Directory, Powermingle, Procter & Gamble, Royal Dutch Shell, Ryze, SelectMinds, SilkRoad technology, Skype, Slashdot, Socialtext, Soflow, Spoke Software, SixDegrees, The Sims, The Square, Sullivan Executive, Tacit, Teten Recruiting, TrackBack, TypePad, Voiceglo, Visible Path, Wikipedia, WordPress, Xanga, Yahoo!, Zero Degrees.

DAVID TETEN: For my father, mother, dear wife, and sister.

SCOTT ALLEN: To my wife, Jayne, and my mother, Glennie, for their love and support; to my cousin, Melanie, for challenging me to maintain focus and integrity; and to my son, Jordan, for being a daily reminder of what's truly important to me.

Contents

Preface

Business is a social enterprise with
economic ends.—DANIEL P. BURNHAM

How can you open doors and close deals *online?* More generally, how can you use "social software"—blogs and other tools for building your network online—to become dramatically more successful in business?

Most professionals meet new people and maintain relationships the same way they did 50 years ago—with phone calls, letters, and face-to-face meetings. However, today you can use social software to build and leverage a much larger and more effective network. Even if you do not use these technologies yourself, your competitors do—to gain an advantage over you or, at a minimum, to learn more about you. Whether you choose to participate or not, social software *will* impact you. Eighty-four percent of U.S. Internet users have used the Internet to contact or get information from an online group—*more than have used the Internet to read news, search for health information, or to buy something.*[1]

We'll discuss how to use the new tools that have emerged in the last few years: blogs (Web journals), social network sites, relationship capital management software, and biography analysis software. We'll also discuss older tools, including contact management software, personal Web sites, e-mail lists, instant messaging, and Web conferencing. While you are probably familiar with some of this technology, most people are only using a small fraction of the power of these tools.

Our book is particularly relevant to people in roles that depend on relationships: professional investors seeking deals, CEOs seeking business partners, investment bankers seeking capital, salespeople seeking customers, and jobseekers searching for their dream job. We did not write this book for programmers. To master *The Virtual Handshake,* you only need to be sufficiently computer-literate to write e-mail and use the Web.

A few decades ago, when you joined a company you became a member of a network that could last for many years. Today, the average American has been employed at her job for only 4.0 years.[2] You cannot rely on your employer's network or your father's network; you have to build your own flexible, lifetime network.

However, this is not a book about "networking" in itself: how to win friends and influence people. We're not interested in socializing. Instead, we're interested in the **results** of your relationships: opening doors, closing deals, and your professional success. Whether your goal is a client, a new business partner, or a new job, you will achieve that goal through your network. We want to make sure that you achieve *your* goal.

How David Teten Ended Up Writing This Book

In 2001, I moved to New York and started looking for a new business opportunity. Or to use the technical term, a "job."

My timing wasn't very good. Everyone I knew seemed to be busy looking for a new job. While I was looking around, I created an informal mailing list for a dozen of my friends and acquaintances who were seeking new positions. I forwarded all sorts of job opportunities to the list.

As more and more of my friends lost their jobs in the postbubble trauma, more and more people asked to join my list. Soon, friends of friends, and then friends of friends of friends, asked to join the list also. I got to know a lot of unemployed people.

After a few months, some companies realized that I had a good mailing list and that I might be helpful in recruiting. Firms started to hire me to help them recruit new employees. As a result, I created a recruiting firm (Teten Recruiting), which specializes in using online networks to find high-quality candidates. Teten Recruiting grew to serve a range of customers, including multibillion dollar private equity funds, rapidly growing companies such as OfficeTiger, and large public companies such as American Real Estate Partners.

In 2002, while I was just getting my company off the ground, I met my wife online (at SpeedDating.com). Fortunately, she was willing to date someone self-employed (a technical term meaning, "not taking a regular salary"). If someone like me could find a woman online who was willing to marry him, perhaps there was something to the online dating industry after all.

In 2003, I saw a new business opportunity. I created Nitron Advisors, an independent securities research firm with a business model quite different from most other research firms. Our clients are typically hedge funds, private equity funds, and mutual funds. Nitron introduces our clients to executives, academics, scientists, and other industry experts who can analyze investment opportunities based on their experience on the industry's front lines. We use social software to help our clients interview and learn directly from these industry experts.

Today, both Nitron Advisors and Teten Recruiting are thriving and profitable. Both businesses grew from a free Yahoo! Group mailing list—a simple example of the social software that we discuss in this book.

I realized that just as online dating had become mainstream, more and more business relationships were also moving online. I became a little obsessed with the subject of online networks, and started writing this book. As I was beginning my research, I met my coauthor, Scott Allen, online in a Yahoo! Group.

How Scott Allen Ended Up Writing This Book

In 2000, I start getting e-mails and phone calls from recruiters who had heard my name from some former colleagues. Two telephone interviews and a few months later, I was working from home for Viador, a Silicon Valley enterprise portal software company. I was managing a team of other home-based consultants located throughout North America.

It was the heyday of the tech boom, and we needed warm bodies out in the field as fast as we could put them there. I had to hire most of them without ever meeting them in person. Sometimes *no one* from the company met them in person. A couple of them didn't work out, but most of them did, and I doubt face-to-face interviews would have prevented us from hiring any of the people who were not a fit.

E-mail and instant messaging were our primary means of sharing knowledge and collaborating. It's difficult to have a discreet phone conversation when you're on-site at a client. And it was often not a matter of talking to the *best* person, but to the best person *available*. This was easy to do with instant messaging, but nearly impossible via phone. Plus, instant messaging allowed us to more easily capture the conversation and share our solutions with the team.

I also started conducting a lot of our business development online. I frequently had to identify and build relationships with technology companies and implementation partners. A phone call or two was usually involved, but I typically both initiated and consummated the relationships via e-mail.

I found my next job through a more unusual channel. I followed up on a story in Jim Cashel's *Online Community Report* (OnlineCommunityReport. com), which led me to reconnect with some former coworkers and landed me a Vice President position with their startup, Mongoose Technology.

In January 2000, I met Cynthia Typaldos on the Communities of Practice Yahoo! Group, in the course of a discussion about what kind of electronic infrastructure was needed to support a robust virtual community. Mongoose Technology was planning to build or buy one. Typaldos was CEO of RealCommunities, which already had a community infrastructure under development and was looking for funding or a buyout. Within days, we had progressed in the conversation, done some initial investigation about one another's companies, and set up a face-to-face meeting. Within a couple of weeks, we were beginning due diligence for a seven-figure merger.

When I left Mongoose in 2002, I explored several possibilities for my next move, but the one that kept jumping out at me was social software—building business relationships online. This was just when Friendster was all the rage and LinkedIn and other business network sites were starting to gain traction. I knew that this wasn't just a passing fad. Meeting people online was something new to the general public, but was going to be an integral part of business practices within the next few years.

I started devoting myself to studying, practicing, and teaching people about building business relationships online.

How to Use This Book

We faced a dilemma in writing a book about such a fast-moving topic. We did not want it to be out of date six months after we wrote it. So we focus primarily on the timeless business and social practices that will help you build a powerful network. We do not discuss specific companies or technologies in depth, because of how quickly that material would become out of date. Please visit TheVirtualHandshake.com for specific, timely advice on how to use the latest tools. TheVirtualHandshake.com/directory includes free detailed profiles of the major companies and sites in this space.

Whenever 🦾 appears in the margin, visit our Reader's Guide (TheVirtualHandshake.com/guide) for more information on the topic listed. After you answer a quick question to prove that you own a copy of this book, you will see extensive resources that update and expand on the book, along with coupons for some of the companies that we discuss. We also suggest you subscribe to our blog and our free e-mail newsletter. You will receive additional information, success stories, and recommended sites that will keep you on track to making the best use of online networks.

Our site also contains links to discussion groups where you can meet other people interested in this topic and discuss how you can use these tools to become dramatically more successful.

We recommend visiting the sites that we mention at the same time as you read this book. You will get much more from our research by playing with the sites that we mention. The best way to learn is to teach. We also encourage you to spread the word to your friends about how useful these tools can be. If you give them a copy of the book, we won't complain.

We expect that the tools in this book will allow you to become a far more successful person. They have worked for us in our businesses, in writing this book . . . and in David's case even for finding him a wife. *They will work for you too.*

We very much value your feedback; please contact us at Handshake@Teten.com and Scott@TheVirtualHandshake.com

David Teten and Scott Allen
April 10, 2005

Part **I**

Building Relationships Face to Face and Virtually

→ The Internet? Is that thing
still around?—HOMER SIMPSON[3]

Who Do You Know?

> The biggest mistake is believing
> there is one right way to listen,
> to talk, to have a conversation—
> or a relationship.—DEBORAH TANNEN,
> *YOU JUST DON'T UNDERSTAND: WOMEN
> AND MEN IN CONVERSATION*[4]

The 18th-Century Internet

In 1765, a small group of businessmen/inventors in Birmingham, England, formed a discussion group. They called it the Lunar Society, because they met every four weeks during the full moon so they could see their way home following their late-night discussions. The Lunar Society's distinguished membership included James Watt, inventor of the modern steam engine, and Josiah Wedgwood, founder of the Wedgwood china company. Other members were some of the most renowned inventors, manufacturers, scientists, engineers, and physicians of the day. Their personal interests varied, but they came together to talk with other equally learned and creative men. Initially, they discussed the application of technology to business, but their conversations quickly expanded to include science, literature, philosophy, and politics. Some historians credit this group with helping to launch the Industrial Revolution.[5]

The Lunar Society also routinely invited visiting businessmen, dignitaries, and politicians to attend meetings. As founding members moved away from Birmingham, they continued to participate through mail. So did many of their visitors, including such luminaries as Benjamin Franklin and Thomas Jefferson.

Although the core group was founded in Birmingham, the members quickly learned the value of continuing their dialogue between meetings and in extending their reach beyond their local community. Never larger than fourteen members, approximately half attended any one meeting. However, the volumes of letters they wrote to each other—predecessors of e-mail—carried the conversation beyond the walls of their meeting place.[6]

From the Eighteenth Century to the Twenty-First Century

The spirit of the Lunar Society still lives; they just discuss stocks now.

The Value Investors Club (ValueInvestorsClub.com) is a highly exclusive virtual community for discussion of value-based investment ideas and special situations (corporate spin-offs and recapitalizations). "VIC" only has 220 members, with a ceiling of 250 members. Because of its exclusivity, the members have a chance to build relationships with a group of senior professionals who would otherwise be inaccessible to them.

Hedge-fund managers Joel Greenblatt and John Petry of Gotham Capital founded VIC in 1999. Joel Greenblatt teaches securities analysis at Columbia Business School and wrote *You Can Be a Stock Market Genius*. Gotham Capital is a very successful hedge fund that returned 50 percent a year during the decade that it managed outside capital.

The requirements for entry are twofold:

1. **Write an "A+" description of an investment idea in keeping with the site's investment style,** which uses the approach of Warren Buffett and Benjamin Graham. VIC receives approximately 100 member applications per month, of which only approximately 1 in 15 is accepted.

2. **If you are accepted, you must provide between two and six investment ideas per year.** The reason for the six-idea maximum is that VIC only wants your very best investment ideas. The club management pays a $5,000 reward every week to the member with the top investment idea.

Because of this quality backing and organization, the site's members are approximately half professional investors and half serious amateurs. This is a much higher ratio of serious professional investors than you will find on almost any other investing discussion site. The Albourne Village (Village.Albourne.com) is one of the few other virtual communities where serious institutional investors congregate.

Each idea contributed by participants is rated by the community members. The conversation on VIC tends to be very high-quality and focused, because members want to sound intelligent while talking in front of their peers. VIC does eject a small percentage of the participants each year, almost always for failure to contribute enough good ideas.

The real-time discussion is only available to members. People who register with a name, e-mail, and a few other pieces of personal information can see the information with a 45-day delay. Unregistered guests have a 90-day delay.

The most unusual design feature of the site is that information flow is centralized in Greenblatt and Petry. All participants use pseudonyms for screen names. Only Greenblatt and Petry know people's real names, contact details, and employers. Participants cannot send private messages to one another. Therefore, participants cannot attempt to recruit other participants for their firms or even set up face-to-face meetings. Instead, they must return to VIC to benefit from participation in this exclusive community.

Greenblatt and Petry have a very reasonable argument for this unusual centralization of information. They built and manage the community for free. They want to retain the intellectual and social capital in the community.

Gotham has spent a significant amount of time and money to develop and run VIC; the weekly prizes alone cost $260,000 per year. However, both Gotham and its participants get more than enough value from the site to make it profitable to maintain.

The fact that VIC will spend significant money to attract members—or that others will pay significant money to join an online community—is proof that people value online networks. Ecademy, another virtual community, recently introduced Blackstar Life Membership. For just a $4,500 one-time fee, you receive a lifetime membership, plus some exclusive coaching, introductions, and other services. While that might seem exorbitant, apparently many people think it's a bargain; some 3,000 of Ecademy's 47,000 members have already applied.

How people build relationships has not changed fundamentally since the days of the Lunar Society. What has changed is the medium; more and more of our conversations are virtual. Academics and researchers have been heavy users of e-mail lists and virtual communities since 1971.[7] People started using those technologies for dating and gaming soon thereafter.

The mainstream business community is now starting to use online social networks. Forty-four percent of U.S. Internet users—53 million Americans—have taken the first step to creating a virtual presence by "contribut[ing] their thoughts and their files to the online world through building or posting to Web sites, creating [Web journals], and sharing files."[8] Those 53 million have opened the door to a virtual handshake.

Like most consultants, we love bullet point lists. To structure our discussion, we will first outline the Seven Keys to creating and maintaining a powerful network (Part I):

→ your **Character,**

→ your **Competence** to do what you claim you can do,

→ the **Relevance** of the people you know,

→ the **Strength** of your relationships,

→ the **Information** that you have about people,

→ the **Number** of people you know, and

→ the **Diversity** of your network.

Part I is the more academic part of our book, but we think it will give you the framework necessary for our later arguments. In Part II, we discuss "social software," a general term for Web site and software tools which help you to discover, extend, manage, and/or leverage your social network. Specifically, we discuss some of the latest new tools, including blogs, social network sites, relationship capital management software, and biography analysis software. We also discuss more traditional tools: personal Web sites, e-mail lists, instant messaging, Web conferencing, virtual communities, and contact management software.

We move on to discuss online etiquette, managing the e-mail deluge, putting your best foot forward online, and safety and privacy concerns (Part III). After that, we will walk you through how to use the Seven Keys to a powerful network online (Part IV). Lastly, we will explore how to use these tools for finding a job, marketing, sales, business development, and volunteering (Part V).

By learning and using the Seven Keys to a powerful network, you can dramatically increase both the quality and quantity of your network. We emphasize that we do *not* encourage you to spend all your time at a computer and not meet people face to face. Social software not only opens new doors for building relationships online; it also makes the traditional process of meeting people face to face dramatically more efficient.

Robert Putnam, a Harvard University political scientist, famously argued in his 2000 book *Bowling Alone* that the average American's social capital has declined steadily since the 1960s. Social capital refers to the collective value of all social networks (who people know) and the inclinations that arise from these networks to do things for each other ("norms of reciprocity").[9] For example, Americans spent two-thirds as much time on informal socializing in the late 1990s as they did just three decades earlier. He links this decline to a decrease in children's welfare, neighborhood safety, economic prosperity, health, and even democracy.[10]

We believe that one of the few ways that we as a society can rebuild our social capital is by using online networks. We focus in this book on how you can improve your business network. More bluntly, *we will help you to make more money.* But in doing so—in building business relationships with more people—you will also help to rebuild some of the social capital that our society has lost.

Your network equals your success.

An excellent overview book for traditional networks is University of Michigan Business School Professor Wayne Baker's *Achieving Success Through Social Capital.* Baker summarizes the empirical evidence for the many benefits of social capital to people and to enterprises:[11]

→ **Getting a job:** More people find jobs through personal contacts than by any other means.

→ **Pay and promotion:** People with rich social capital are paid better and promoted faster at younger ages.

→ **Influence and effectiveness:** People who are central in an organization's networks are more influential than those in the periphery.

→ **Venture capital and financing:** Seventy-five percent of startups find and secure financing through the informal investing grapevine: the social networks of capital seekers and investors.

→ **Organizational learning and doing:** As much as 80 percent of learning in the workplace takes place through informal interactions.

→ **Word-of-mouth marketing:** Advertising increases awareness of products and services, but personal referrals and recommendations are extremely influential in the decision to purchase.

→ **Strategic alliances:** The more strategic alliances a company creates, the more alliances it is likely to create in the future.

→ **Financial stability:** Bankruptcy is less likely for firms with well-connected executives and board members, even when considering many other explanations.[12]

→ **Democracy:** Robert Putnam found in his 25-year study of democracy in Italy that those regions with rich social capital enjoy stronger economic development and more responsive local governments than those regions with poor social capital.

In addition, extensive studies in psychology and medicine also demonstrate that social capital can improve your personal quality of life:

→ **Happiness:** A stronger social network leads to greater happiness and a greater sense of meaning.

→ **Health:** Robert Putnam writes, "People who are socially disconnected are between two and five times more likely to die from all causes, compared with matched individuals who have [strong] ties."[13]

A high level of social capital is critical for your professional and personal success.

The Ties That Bind

All of your relationships fall into two loosely-defined buckets, strong ties and weak ties:[14]

1. **Strong ties.** Your strong ties are your family, close friends, and close professional colleagues. They are long term and high reciprocity; you help them and they help you.

2. **Weak ties.** Your weak ties are usually short term and instrumental; you interact with them for a specific purpose. These ties often end when the relationship has served its purpose. You may not interact with these ties regularly, but they are important for giving you access to remote information and opportunities. The manager of your corporate mailroom is likely a weak tie to you. You interact with her only because you need something from her (e.g., you need your package weighed).

Everyone else in the world falls into two other buckets:

1. **Latent ties:** Ties with people with whom you have no relationship today, but with whom it would be relatively easy to start relationships. If you graduated from Princeton in 1992, and you see that Winthrop Smithers (Princeton 1993) just got a job in your industry, he is a latent tie. You can easily approach him; you have people and a subculture in common. Anyone two degrees away from you (a friend of a friend) is also a latent tie.[15]

2. **Strangers:** As American humorist Will Rogers said, "A stranger is just a friend I haven't met yet."

Whether someone is a latent tie depends on three factors:

1. **How densely interconnected is the common network?** In other words, do you know people in common? Because the Princeton graduate does not want to look unfriendly to your mutual friends, he is inclined to be responsive.

2. How exclusive is your common network? The harder a club is to enter, the more tightly bound the members will be.

3. Are you of a similar status? If you are a partner at a law firm, a partner at a similarly prestigious bank is likely to see you as a peer and be responsive.

According to anthropologist Robin Dunbar, the human brain is hard wired to handle a maximum of approximately 150 active social connections.[16] In addition to time required to maintain those relationships, they occupy space in our mind even when we are not in contact with them. Fortunately, social software allows you to develop a much larger network of weak and latent ties.[17]

We recommend building a portfolio of both strong and weak ties. Although your weak ties can produce great value, it is typically the strong ties that provide you with a sense of companionship, comfort, and security. However, stronger does not mean better or more valuable. Strong and weak, in this context, simply refer to different types of relationships.

THE STRENGTH OF WEAK TIES

Many people intuitively believe that they will most likely get their next client or next job through their strong ties, not their weak ties. However, this is not necessarily the case. Stanford Professor Mark Granovetter emphasized the importance of weak ties in his seminal book, *Getting a Job: A Study in Contacts and Careers* (1974).[18] His research showed that weak ties were disproportionately more effective for finding jobs than strong ties. Those weak ties are particularly important for low-income or low-social-status people to advance.[19]

One possible reason for this is that most people have more acquaintances (weak ties) than friends (strong ties). A more subtle reason for the importance of weak ties is flows of information. Your strong ties tend to be similar to you and often share a similar network. However, your weak ties differ from you on two levels. First, a weak tie is probably different from you as a person, perhaps working in another industry or living in another city. Second, a weak tie's own network is different from yours, and therefore she has access to different information flows.

For example, you do not speak Korean, but went to school with Kim, a Korean-American woman. Kim has a brother who works for a Korean company expanding in the United States, which needs to hire someone with exactly your skill set. Kim is far more likely to know of this opening than you are. Almost the only way you will land that great job with the Korean company is through Kim. Of course, strong ties often win out over weak ties. Just hope that Kim isn't applying for the job too!

2

The Seven Keys to a Powerful Network

> The whole value of the dime is in knowing what to do with it.—RALPH WALDO EMERSON, LECTURE TO THE MERCANTILE LIBRARY ASSOCIATION, BOSTON, 1844

To explain the Seven Keys to a powerful network, we will analyze a simple example. Let's assume that you are a lawyer living in Los Angeles, and you have a very simple network of three people: Armand, Brenda, and Chaim. You know that your billing is driven by who you know. *What exactly is the value of your network?*

In Table 2-1, the Seven Keys provide a powerful social network to analyze your network. To define our terms more formally, we will explain them using two people: "You" (the center of the network) and "Acquaintance" (your friend, neighbor, coworker, or any other person you know).

Five of the keys measure the relationship between You and your Acquaintance:

Character: Your integrity, clarity of motives, consistency of behavior, openness, discretion, and trustworthiness. This is driven by the reality and the appearance: the real content of your Character, and what each Acquaintance thinks of your Character.

Competence: Your ability to walk your talk; your demonstrated capability. It includes functional knowledge and skills, interpersonal skills, and judgment. Similarly, this is driven by both the real level of your

TABLE 2-1. The Seven Keys to a Powerful Network

1. Your **Character**	Armand and Chaim all think of you as a trustworthy, high-Character person. However, you have been late for several lunch appointments with Brenda and tend to gossip about various common friends with her. As a result, she thinks of you as unreliable and of mediocre Character.
2. Your **Competence**	Armand, Brenda, and Chaim all know that you are an excellent lawyer. You have high perceived Competence.
3. **Relevance** of the people you know	Armand and Brenda work for ExxonMobil Corporation, a potential client for your legal services. They are high Relevance. Chaim is an unpublished fiction writer, so he is low Relevance as a potential client.
4. **Information** you have about your network	You have current work and home telephone and e-mail information for Armand, Brenda, and Chaim. In addition, because you see Armand and Chaim so often, you have current Information about their moods, how happy they are in their jobs, and all sorts of other useful background information.
5. **Strength** of your relationships	You went to school with Armand and Chaim and have been close friends with them ever since. You go out once a month for dinner, so you have a high Strength relationship with them. You only see Brenda about twice a year; that relationship is low Strength.
6. **Number** of people in your network	You only have three people in your network, a very low Number.
7. **Diversity**	Armand, Brenda, and Chaim are all of a different religious and cultural background than you. However, the three also all live in Los Angeles, and Armand and Brenda both work for the same company. On the whole, you have a modest level of Diversity.

Competence and by what each Acquaintance views as the level of your Competence.

8━┳ **Relevance: The Acquaintance's value to You,** defined as the Acquaintance's ability to contribute to your own goals. The Acquaintance's Relevance is driven by the value of the Acquaintance's own network.

☞ **Information: The data that you have about the Acquaintance.** First are the basic coordinates: e-mail address, phone numbers, family Information, and so on. Also invaluable is Information about his professional background, how his career is advancing, what coworkers say about him, what his likes and dislikes are, and so on.

☞ **Strength: The closeness of the relationship between You and your Acquaintance.** This reflects the degree of trust and reciprocity between you.

The last two keys measures the size and the diversity of your network:

☞ **Number: How many people you know directly,** including both strong and weak ties.

☞ **Diversity: Heterogeneity of your network** by geography, profession, industry, and hierarchical position. In addition, your network should ideally be Diverse by age, sex, ethnicity, political orientation, and so on.

Please see Appendix A for a mathematical model for the Seven Keys. We based this seven-part structure on our review of relevant academic research. However, we will not attempt to quantify how to measure and weigh each key. Academics have done relatively little research on the exact valuation of personal networks.[20] It would be very difficult to quantify each key, and it is not necessary for our purposes. Plus, too much math would hurt sales of this book.

As an absolute rule, credibility—your Character and your Competence—must underlie your network. A massive network will not aid you if you are selling an inferior product or trying to[21] get a job for which you are unqualified. In fact, a big network will rapidly become a liability, as too many people will be aware of the inferior goods you are peddling. No matter how much your friends like you, they will not recommend you for a job if they see that you are consistently unethical, tardy, sloppy, or otherwise unprofessional.

The ideal network has a large Number of heterogeneous people who think highly of you and with whom you are well bonded. This principle explains the value of Outward Bound expeditions, Ropes Courses, and other similar wilderness retreats. These programs all promote quick bonding between participants (immediate Strength), partly by placing people in a hazardous new environment in which they must rely on each other.

Traditionally, power in a company came from your title or formal authority. But in today's networked, ad-hoc organizations, power can come from many sources, including how well connected you are both within and outside the organization.[22]

Quality or Quantity?

Consider two extremes. Stefan, a German dentist, has spent his whole life in Munich. He spends most of his time with close friends and family; he has Strong ties but a low Number. Alternatively, U.S. President George W. Bush spreads himself thin across a wide number of people: high Number, low Strength.

Maintaining both high Strength and high Number is physically impossible.[23] It takes time to build Strong relationships, and time is a limited resource. Within the time you have available to spend on business relationships, how can you find the proper balance between Strength and Number?

The way to optimize the value of your network for a particular purpose is to determine the necessary level of Strength required to accomplish that goal, and then maximize Number at that level. For example, if you are selling investment banking or strategic consulting services, you need a high Strength level for someone to buy your services. These are big-ticket items that require a high level of trust in their provider. Ideally, you have a small Number of close relationships with senior executives who are in a position to buy these services.

However, if you are a movie star trying to sell the chance to see your movie, your Strength can be much lower but your Number has to be much higher. Movie stars mainly earn money by having studios sell people the chance to watch a movie for $5 to $10 per view. They try to have ties with as many fans as possible. At the same time, the movie star will want to develop Strong ties with producers and directors.

"Technology now allows social networks to make a quantum leap forward in breaking the old trade-off between quality and quantity—you can now increase both, without compromising either one," says Contact Network Corporation CEO Geoffrey Hyatt.[24] Learning to write more effective e-mails will help you increase the Strength of your ties, without spending too much time on those relationships. Building a large mailing list similarly allows you to increase the Number without spending significant additional time. Using technology to expand your number of weak ties is a theme we will return to repeatedly in this book.

How Much Time Should I Spend Building My Network?

People who know how to leverage their networks are called successful. People who just know a lot of people are called socialites. Do you want to be a successful person or a socialite?

All cocktail parties come to an end, but on the Internet there is always another person with whom you can connect. This can be both healthy and hazardous; it's very tempting to spend far too much time chatting with far too many people. We recommend focusing only on building your network to the extent that your marginal benefit equals your marginal cost. Otherwise, you will be so busy maintaining your relationships that you will have no time to leverage those you have formed.

For example, you are an entrepreneur seeking to build a new consulting company. Through strategic network building, you have accumulated a list of fifty leads (potential clients). Should you spend time in three more venues to find ten more leads, or should you start working through the list you have?

There is no simple way to determine the right amount of time to spend on building your network. Maintaining your existing relationships should be a baseline mandatory part of your daily schedule. In allocating your time, we suggest following this three-step process:

1. **Review everyone in your contact database** to create a list of hot leads (potential customers, employers, or whatever sort of person you are pursuing). This target list also includes people who are not themselves leads, but can introduce you to leads. The head of the local church knows many people; maybe it's worthwhile to ask him if he might know customers for your business?

2. **Approach all of the leads over the next few weeks.** Work on building your relationship with them. Over time, and depending on context, either try to sell to them or else ask for referrals.

3. **Focus on meeting new people only after you have pursued the majority of the existing leads.** Serving your current customers should be your highest priority, followed by pursuing your hottest leads. Let us say that you sell your consulting services successfully to 50 percent of your leads (which would be very impressive!). In a new chat room, there is only perhaps a 25 percent chance that you will meet someone with that 50 percent chance of revenues—so you only have a 12.5 percent chance of earning revenues from participating in the chat room. The bird in the hand is worth far more than the bird flitting through cyberspace.

If you find that hot leads are languishing for a month without you even calling on them, or if you are taking more than a week to respond to important messages, then now is definitely not the time to spend three hours becoming active in a brand new online community.

Holes in Your Network

There aren't too many healthy nuclear families on American TV, but we'll use one of our favorites: the Simpsons. In Figure 2-1 you can see a partial map of

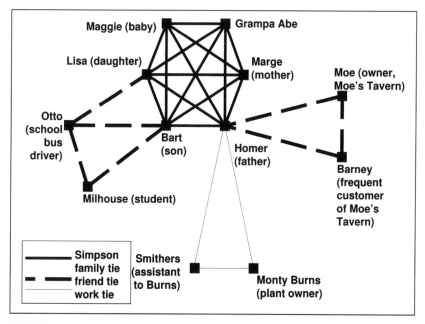

FIGURE 2-1. Relationships among characters on *The Simpsons*. (Created with Inflow Software; courtesy of Valdis Krebs)

the relationships between the major characters on the show. In other words, who has a strong tie with whom?

As in most social networks, the characters fall into several major subgroups: family, friends, and work colleagues. Ronald Burt, in *Structural Holes: The Social Structure of Competition,* defines a "structural hole" as the weak connection between two clusters of densely connected people. He argues that both people and companies benefit by sitting in a structural hole of a network, because they can serve as brokers.[25] Your Diversity is a rough measure of the number of structural holes that you fill.

In Exhibit 1, Homer is in a structural hole between Moe and the plant workers Burns and Smithers; Homer is the only access that Moe has to the plant group. Structural holes can generate two types of benefits:

1. **Control benefits:** By sitting between two groups, you have control over the flow of information between them. For example, Homer loses his job at the plant, but doesn't want Moe to find out because Moe might cut off his beer credit. Homer can prevent Moe from learning about the job loss, because Moe does not have alternative sources of Information about Homer's work.

2. **Information benefits:** You have superior Information because of your privileged position. Bart can tell Marge that Milhouse has a crush on Saman-

tha Stanky, and Marge will not have a simple way to verify this information. Marge is not directly connected to Milhouse, so she needs to go through an intermediary to find out the truth.

We recommend that you seek opportunities to place yourself in structural holes. For example, interorganizational working groups, joint ventures, and industry lobbying groups are all excellent venues for you to become a new connection between groups.

Filling a structural hole can be very lucrative, monetarily and in social capital. Executive recruiters, investment bankers, and other professional middlepeople make a healthy living bridging these holes. Even if you do not charge money for making those connections, being known as the "go-to guy" for connections to a particular group of people is highly advantageous.[26]

We should mention an inevitable difficulty you will face in positioning yourself as a "bridging tie," someone who bridges across structural holes. It is relatively easy to build Strong ties with people with whom you have redundant ties. It is much harder to build Strong bridging ties with the people with whom you have the least in common. However, your relationship with the CEO in the Philippines, whose culture is radically different than yours, is precisely the sort of bridging tie that will likely create greater value for you.

Closed Networks

If you are an aspiring politician, wouldn't it be helpful if your last name were Bush, Kennedy, or (in India) Gandhi? Members of these families benefit by being in a highly interconnected network, one in which there are virtually no structural holes. This is a closed network, "in which everyone is so connected that no one can escape the notice of the others."[27] In the chart, all of the Simpson family members constitute a closed network.

Another powerful example of a closed network is a business school "section." At many business schools, students are grouped into sections of perhaps 80 students and take many classes together. Precisely because the section is so interconnected, the members are more likely to trust and support one another.

Membership in a closed network has two benefits:

1. **Improves access to Information.** Remember the children's game "Telephone?" Information deteriorates in quality as it passes through more steps. In a closed network, you have multiple ways to access the same Information, so it is more likely that you will get accurate Information. Marge very quickly finds out what Homer has been up to because she has so many channels through which to check on him.

2. **Easier to reward and punish group members,** which in turn makes it less risky to trust other members. You are less likely to cheat another member of your business school section in a business deal, because that abuse will hurt your relationships with many of the others. Similarly, Moe, Homer, and Barney can punish outsiders to their bar group by making fun of them.

The implication for you: if possible, join a small, selective group in which you can get to know everyone. If you are not lucky enough to be born into a large and powerful family, nor fortunate enough to marry into one, creating such a high-Strength network requires a significant amount of time. However, we believe it's well worth the investment. The Value Investors Club and aSmallWorld.net are examples of such selective, interconnected networks online.

Balancing Structural Holes and Closed Networks

Elizabeth Rosenthal, a business consultant and coach, conducted a study of quality improvement teams in a U.S. Midwest manufacturing firm. These teams were small and closed; everyone knew everyone else. However, each participant had a unique social network that he or she brought to the team. These networks included people from the company, previous jobs, outside activities, family, and friends.

Rosenthal found that the more successful teams were composed of members with networks marked by structural holes. Those holes were both inside and outside of their firm. For example, an engineer might know people in marketing at his employer's and might also know end users working at another company. All of his relationships were valuable to the team as a whole.[28]

Both structural holes and closed networks can create social capital. Several studies have identified a common pattern: you can benefit by participating in a closed network whose members have strong external networks that span structural holes.[29]

In the Simpsons graph, Homer is particularly valuable to the family, because he has access to the work network, and he also has access to the bar network where he can get involved in entrepreneurial opportunities (e.g., inventing the "Flaming Homer" cocktail). Because Grandpa is not plugged into as many subnetworks, he has fewer opportunities and resources that he can share with the family.

Elite universities, investment banks, and strategy consulting firms follow this model precisely. They recruit talented people from top schools around the globe. These people are Diverse by national origin, education, and so on.

Once these people start work for McKinsey & Company (for example), McKinsey works very hard to create a closed network of Strong bonds among the coworkers. The combination of a Strong, closed network whose members are themselves very Diverse is a powerful resource for McKinsey's clients.

The Advantages of Using Social Software for Building Your Network

In the rest of the book, we will explore seven ways in which social software can dramatically increase the power of your network:

1. **You can improve your Character, and make the quality of your Character more visible.** You have the chance to serve more people, and more people have the chance to learn the content of your Character.

2. **You can become more Competent** because you have access to the collective wisdom of far more people than ever before possible. This is particularly true in network-dependent professions such as sales, in which your Competence is directly tied to the quality of your network.

3. **You can build relationships with the right, Relevant people** who can support you in achieving your goals and vice-versa . . . regardless of where in the world they are located. It is also much easier to search online networks for the most Relevant people than it is to search traditional face-to-face networks.

4. **You can Strengthen all your ties by being of greater value to people and by communicating more frequently.** We all know people whom we rarely, if ever, see face to face, but with whom we feel strongly connected because of e-mail, phone, and other remote communication technologies.[30] Also, many social software services that allow you to see who is a "friend of a friend" help facilitate transfer of trust (assuming you only link to trusted relationships, not random connections with anyone who asks you or looks interesting). You are more likely to close the deal you are trying to close, because you can be introduced by a trusted intermediary.

5. **You can gain more Information about your network.** You can learn about people by leveraging content that they have already created. While this does not eliminate the value of "small talk," researching people does allow you to move more quickly to deeper conversation.

6. **You can increase the Number of relationships you have** by increasing both the Strength of your strong ties and the Number of your weak ties. Not only can you create more latent ties, but you can also become a latent tie for many other Internet users with whom you share relevant interests.

7. **Lastly, you can build a radically more Diverse network.** When meeting people face to face, you are restricted geographically and culturally. Virtual interaction can open doors for you globally. Automatic translation technology will soon make it feasible to build relationships with people with whom you do not even share a common language.

You have probably heard of "passive income," that is, streams of income that produce money with minimal additional effort on your part. Your virtual presence opens the door to "passive networking." People around the world can find you and contact you, even while you are asleep. Both of us have benefited from lucrative business opportunities that came unsolicited because we positioned ourselves to be latent ties.[31]

3

Face-to-Face Versus Virtual Communications

On the Internet, nobody knows you're a dog.—PETER STEINER, *NEW YORKER* CARTOON[32]

A dam Robert Guha writes "Apple Archive," a popular weekly column for LowEndMac.com. He is widely considered one of the top experts on older Apple Macintosh computers. He is also only 18 years old, and began writing his column at age 14. "He got the job through online networking," says Adam's father, Richard Guha. "They never knew how young he was."

Richard Guha is a principal of the New England Consulting Group and the former President of Reliant Energy, Retail, a $6 billion company. He has a successful track record as an executive in some of the world's largest corporations, including Procter & Gamble and US West. "I am just starting to discover the power [of online networks]," he says. "I came late to the party. I discovered that each of my kids have Web sites and blogs, as well as a network of friends everywhere from online networking. They cannot conceive of a world in which people network any other way." Guha points out that despite his own business success, his son is more famous than he is, at least online. A search for "Adam Robert Guha" produces more than 6,600 results, while one on "Richard Guha" returns less than 50.[33]

By age 30, you have likely spent roughly 130,000 hours in face-to-face interaction.[34] Now consider a typical businesswoman. She has been using e-mail perhaps ten years and the Internet approximately five. The average Internet user is only online approximately 11.1 hours a week.[35] Her entire experience with virtual interaction is probably not even 5,000 hours.

The next generation is another story. Users with six or more years experience are online nearly three times as long each week as new users.[36] Children today may spend several hours a day in virtual communities, such as Neopets and Habbo Hotel, or in cooperative multiplayer games, such as Everquest or The Sims. For them, virtual interaction is an integral part of their social life.

As early as 2001, 48 percent of teenage Internet users said that their use of the Internet improved their relationships with friends; 32 percent said Internet tools helped them make new friends. Twenty percent said that instant messaging is the main way they deal with friends, including serious kinds of communications such as telling their friends unpleasant things or starting and ending relationships.[37]

This trend is not limited just to young people. As people use the Internet more, they tend to use it for more serious and emotionally sensitive purposes. "An extra year of Internet experience [resulted] in a 70 percent increase for all e-mailers in e-mailing family members for advice and a 63 percent increase in those sending e-mails to family members expressing worries."[38]

This is carrying over into the business world as well. In 2001, more than 50 percent of all business meetings were face to face; by 2004, only slightly more than 40 percent of business meetings were face to face.[39] In 2004, 24.1 million Americans worked at home during business hours at least one day per month.[40]

The ready availability of high-speed Internet access ("broadband") is a driving factor. Consider South Korea, arguably the most wired nation in the world, where 21.3 percent of citizens have broadband at home.[41] J. Bradford DeLong, professor of economics at the University of California, Berkeley, writes:

> South Korea's experience so far with broadband access and high-bandwidth applications reminds us that they are called information technologies for good reason. Koreans eliminate wasted time in acquiring information and seem to communicate more easily. . . . South Koreans . . . are discovering interesting circles of friends and conversation partners . . . And they are becoming a smarter, tighter, and more knowledgeable society.[42]

We discuss below some of the key differences between face-to-face and virtual communications.

"Do you, LovesWaterfalls, take this woman, NYCPuppyLover, as your lawfully wedded bride?"

In 1999, David Teten decided to get married. He wrote a full prospectus for himself in the style of a traditional Wall Street prospectus—essentially a detailed personal ad. It summarized his selling points (he's a hopeless romantic); plant, property, and equipment (his laptop); plans for subsidiaries (children and grandchildren); risk factors (he will probably never get paid to work as a runway model); and profiled his targeted investor. It mentioned that he was looking to sell 100 percent of his shares to an eligible, accredited retail investor.

The value of writing such a prospectus is that it made clear up front to his future wife exactly what he was seeking and what sort of person he was. In addition, he could distribute the prospectus not only to appropriate women whom he met virtually, but also to his friends who might have leads for potential investors.

After going out with 33 prospects, David Teten eventually met his wife online, at SpeedDating.com.[43]

If anything has proven that rapport, trust, and even love can be initiated via a long-distance connection, it's online matchmaking. Online dating has become a popular and often preferred way to meet a romantic partner because of its efficiency, confidentiality, and convenience. Building business relationships online will grow for the same reasons.

Online dating is the largest legal segment of the U.S. online content industry, with estimated spending of $449.5 million in 2003, or 29 percent of all paid content spending. That is more in revenues than either business/investment or entertainment/lifestyle content sites receive.[44] Twenty-seven million Europeans—nearly one in five Internet users there—use an online dating site each month.[45] Match.com has approximately 1 million paying subscribers[46] and 15 million individual listings,[47] equivalent to over 5 percent of the U.S. adult population.

Both a "push" and a "pull" are driving the dramatic growth of online dating. The "push" is the frustration with traditional methods of meeting people; the "pull" is the unique power of online dating.

THE "PUSH": WHY TRADITIONAL METHODS OF FINDING ROMANCE ARE INEFFICIENT

Traditional face-to-face methods of meeting people are extremely inefficient. This is true regardless of whether you are meeting for business or romantic purposes. When meeting people face to face:

→ **Your choices are extremely limited geographically,** because you are restricted to meeting people in the places you live or visit. A widowed Japanese grandmother living in Ohio has a very small pool of people in which she is likely to find someone compatible.

→ **You are primarily locked into meeting people connected with your immediate network.** If your goal is marriage, then you probably want to meet people with whom you have many common ties. Someone you meet through your social network is likely to have been preapproved by your mutual friends. However, let us say that your goal is a short-term transaction, whether that is buying a used car or a short-term romantic relationship (OK, that's a euphemism.). The Internet facilitates this, because you can meet someone who shares your goal but is totally disconnected from you socially. You are compatible enough to accomplish your goal, but either of you can terminate the relationship very easily and not worry about seeing the other person again.

→ **Certain superficial factors (mainly appearance) are disproportionately influential.** The best-looking woman at the bar gets a disproportionate amount of attention, even though that woman may be a very inappropriate partner. By relying heavily on her physical beauty to attract attention, that beautiful woman may have underdeveloped social and empathic skills. Similarly, more attractive and fit people consistently get offered higher salaries than their less attractive and athletic brethren.[48] Your online photo is clearly a very strong driver of the interest you attract. However, when you meet someone virtually, you also have time to learn about her interests and background before, which gives you a fuller picture of a potential mate's desirability.

THE "PULL" OF ONLINE DATING

 Meeting people virtually gives you the chance to do certain things that you simply cannot do in any other way. In particular:[49]

→ **You can meet people you would never otherwise meet.** You will meet only those people who are most compatible with you, because you can screen out the people who do not fit your target profile.

→ **Online dating is private, convenient, confidential, and (at least initially) low-commitment.** With a partner you meet online, you typically do not have many common acquaintances who help bind you together in a common network of interests and activities. This makes it easier to both enter and exit the relationship. Of course, once you date for a while, you meet one another's friends, and your networks become interlocked.

→ **Online dating is far more efficient than traditional ways of meeting people. You do not waste time with inappropriate matches.** It's hard to say to someone you just met in a bar, "I'm a Norwegian dentist with plans to move back home, and I'd like to have at least five kids. Are you interested in going out with me and potentially marrying me?" On the Web, you can ask exactly that. Whether the answer is yes or no, the other person has a clear incentive to be honest.

→ **Lastly, "it is quite possible that online dating is safer than conventional dating."**[50] Many people perceive online dating as riskier because you are meeting people without a shared social context. However, the study *Love Online: A Report on Digital Dating in Canada* found that people had as many or more "uncomfortable" or frightening experiences with traditional dating as with online dating. The first reason is that online dating gives you time to get to know a person and double-check his story before committing to a face-to-face meeting. Second, online dating makes it much easier to reveal information gradually. You can just trade e-mails for a while from a temporary e-mail address before giving away your home number. This makes it much harder for someone to harass or stalk you.

Because online dating reduces search and transaction costs, the transaction volume has increased. In other words, online dating has made it much easier to meet people. Similarly, social software makes it much easier to do business with more people.

Virtual Worlds

Another phenomenon that has driven social use of the Internet is the growing popularity of massively multiplayer online role playing games (MMORPG), such as Anarchy Online or The Sims Online. Millions of active members participate in these virtual worlds, which feature far more than just hack-and-slash or shoot-em-up style gaming, including politics, commerce, journalism, parades, and even weddings.

Terri Perkins, Online Product Manager for Funcom, the makers of Anarchy Online, explains:

> Trying to explain a virtual world to someone who has never experienced it can be like trying to explain "blue" to someone who has never had sight. For years, even one of my best friends in real life would laugh at me as I'd get caught up in the life of someone whom I'd never met face to face. It was this friend that recently dragged me to an in-game wedding.[51]

But the social connections don't stop in the game:

> A couple approached our booth at one game convention and thanked us for providing the world that allowed them to meet. The duo met in AO, the relationship blossomed, and they were to wed in real life. We hear from people who found support from people in the game while their real life was going through some very rough times. One group formed a coding company made up of all remote people that have never met.[52]

Multiplayer online games such as these forge such Strong relationships because they feature an important element not present in many communities: a sense of shared purpose. Teaming up temporarily to go deeper into the dungeon may not forge much of a relationship, but spending months or years building up a city on Rubi-Ka and defending it from rival clans, or partnering to create a successful virtual business in Alphaville, certainly will.

An Urban Legend: 93 percent

> Axel met Pablo at a holiday party for members of a city sports league. Tall, eloquent, and well-dressed, Pablo looked like the very picture of a respectable businessperson. Axel was favorably impressed. When Axel came home, he did a quick Web search on Pablo. The very first result that he turned up was an Administrative Proceeding by the Securities and Exchange Commission against Pablo for violation of the Securities Exchange Act of 1934.

Many people believe that the lack of nonverbal cues makes virtual communication inherently inferior to face-to-face communication. UCLA professor Albert Mehrabian completed research in 1967 showing the significance of nonverbal cues in communications. He concluded, in part, "The combined effect of simultaneous verbal, vocal, and facial attitude communications is a weighted sum of their independent effects—with the coefficients of .07, .38, and .55, respectively."[53] Out of context, this implies that in face-to-face conversation, 38 percent of communication is inflection and tone of voice, 55 percent is facial expression, and only 7 percent is based on what you actually say.

This study has grown into a very widely quoted and misunderstood urban legend. Many communication skills teachers misuse this data to indicate that your body language, intonation, speaking style, and other nonverbal methods of communication overpower your actual words. As a result, many people are concerned that virtual communication is much more difficult because body language, tone of voice, and facial expressions cannot today be fully conveyed over the Internet.

The idea that your words don't really matter is a gross distortion of Mehrabian's study, which only addressed the very narrow situation in which a listener is analyzing one person's general attitude towards the other (positive, negative, or neutral). Also, in his experiments the parties had no prior acquaintance; they had no context for their discussion. As Mehrabian himself has said explicitly, these statistics are not relevant except in the very narrow confines of a similar situation.[54]

In fact, most of us aren't nearly as good at reading other people's body language as we think we are. According to the *Harvard Management Communication Letter:*

> Most of the research into nonverbal communications shows that people are not very good at masking their feelings. Emotions do leak out regularly, in many ways. And yet, the research also shows that most of us are not as good at decoding those emotions as we would like to think. Young people are significantly worse at both signaling emotions and reading them. Although we do learn as we grow older, we should remain wary; in the end, body language conveys important but unreliable clues about the intent of the communicator.[55]

The Internet puts Information about people at your fingertips before and during your interaction with them. The public Information about them can give you much more useful insight into their motives than nonverbal cues. We discuss these issues in more depth in Chapter 21.

One pattern that makes it easier for you to evaluate people: Businesspeople almost always use their real name and real company online, because pseudonyms make it hard to market. By contrast, the vast majority of online daters use pseudonyms for privacy.[56]

I Haven't Met You But I Like You

Andrea Pellittiere, owner of Eleganza Meetings, Events & Conferences Services Inc., has used online networks to attract many clients and partners, including when she was a customer relationship manager for a program assisting American companies to establish business in Europe.

"Before joining Ryze and Ecademy, I did quite a bit of face-to-face networking. Although I was meeting new contacts, the expense and time involved in attending 4 to 6 events a week was taking its toll. Now, while I still attend face-to-face events, much of my networking effort takes place online.

"As an introvert, online networking has been an extremely profound experience for me. I am not necessarily shy, but do tend to show a natural reserve when I first interact with people face to face. This is because I prefer to listen and process internally what the other person is saying before I respond. As the relationship progresses, I become more effusive and my initial reserve quickly drops away.

"But in a face-to-face networking situation where you have seconds to make your first impression, this trait can be mistaken for a lack of enthusiasm and passion, when nothing could be further from the truth! At times, my focus on the other person and my emphasis on listening could actually be detrimental.

"For me, Ryze and Ecademy have allowed me to compress the relationship development process. I can showcase my personality and style through my online profile, blog, and participation in online forums. Potential business partners, clients, and anyone else visiting my profile will have a far richer and detailed impression of myself, my company, my aspirations, and how I can best serve them than a thirty second face-to-face introduction would allow."

Counterintuitively, several academic studies have found that people like each other better when they first meet virtually than when they first meet face to face. In a 2002 paper, New York University professors J. A. Bargh, K. Y. A. McKenna, and G. M. Fitzsimons explored this pattern.[57] A key explanation was that people tend to project their ideal or hoped-for qualities onto those whom they initially meet remotely. Because they have minimal data, they err on the optimistic side when evaluating the unknown person.

Let us say you believe, along with over 30 percent of Americans, that "Most people can be trusted."[58] You meet Aretha virtually, and you treat her as a trustworthy person. In response, she acts in a trustworthy way. Countless studies have shown the power of your expectations in shaping behavior of those you encounter.[59]

The NYU study describes four key differences between face-to-face and virtual interactions, which encourage greater self-expression and, in turn, greater bonding:

1. **You have greater anonymity while communicating virtually.** You are free of the expectations of your peer group, and the traditional sanctions for new behaviors are absent. For example, you are normally a quiet and reserved person. Online, you can be more aggressive in pursuing a sale than you normally would or make more jokes than you normally would.

2. **Outside of your usual social group, you have much more freedom to discuss your taboo or negative aspects (or those that may be perceived as negative).** In a job interview with a conservative investment bank, Joe Daniel

is unlikely to discuss his gay partner because of concerns about discrimination. However, he may join a Web-based group for gay businesspeople, which could be a powerful network for him.

3. **The aspects of traditional face-to-face interactions that may make you anxious are absent.** Some people are hesitant to speak because of lower status or power, or because they are distracted and anxious about their physical appearance. For example, women are less likely to be interrupted in online discussions than in face-to-face discussions.[60]

4. **You have more control over the conversational pace virtually.** Instead of the instantaneous replies needed while talking face to face, you can take your time in responding.

Social Equalizer

Tim Berners-Lee, one of the creators of the Internet, said, "The power of the Web is in its universality. Access by everyone regardless of disability is an essential aspect."[61] When you are meeting people virtually, disabilities that would hinder or prevent face-to-face social interaction can become a nonissue.

Dr. Gregor Wolbring is a biochemistry and bioethics professor at the University of Calgary and founder of the International Centre for Bioethics, Culture and Disability (BioethicsAndDisability.org). He offers information worldwide through his Web site, virtual discussion group, and online courses. He develops most of his contacts virtually.

A wheelchair user himself, he says, "I find online interaction very empowering because it allows me to reach more people and help more people than I would ever be able [to] without it. I just hope it will become more broadly available and the digital divide for disabled people becomes smaller."[62]

Wolbring sees virtual interaction as a social equalizer for disabled people in five key ways:

1. **It allows disabled people to interact with so-called nondisabled people without having to reveal their nonnormative body structure or functioning.** This allows disabled people with low self-esteem and with high fears of rejection to communicate with the world.

2. **It allows disabled people to interact with people all over the world,** even if they are not able to travel because of financial or mobility restrictions.

3. **Virtual learning allows the teaching of disabled people who otherwise have no access to education.** Less than 2 percent of disabled people in developing countries are in regular schools.

4. It allows for dissemination of knowledge that would be too expensive for disabled people to obtain otherwise.

5. It allows for more efficient advocacy.

 He notes that every Web site designer should be aware that many Web sites and Internet tools are still not disabled accessible. The World Wide Web Consortium (W3.org) provides free accessibility tips and tools.

True Lies

Clive Thompson writes that we put far too much faith in personal interaction for building trust:

> Our culture still fetishizes physical contact. . . . Executives and politicians spend hours flying across the country merely for a five-minute meeting, on the assumption that even a few seconds of face time can cut through the prevarications of letters and legal contracts. [But] as more and more of our daily life moves online, we could find ourselves living in an increasingly honest world, or at least one in which lies have ever more serious consequences. . . . In its unforgiving machine memory, the Internet might turn out to be the unlikely conscience of the world.[63]

A recent study by Professor Jeffrey Hancock at Cornell University showed that people are generally more honest in virtual communications than face-to-face or on the telephone.[64] His test sample told lies in 37 percent of telephone calls versus just 14 percent of e-mails.

Why? The key factors, Hancock says, are the immediacy of the communication and whether or not it is being recorded (see Table 3-1).

According to this research, people particularly tend to lie in face-to-face conversation in spontaneous response to an unexpected demand: "Do I look fat in this?" or, "How do you like my new haircut?" Those little white lies are every bit as common in business as in personal life. If you are trying to build Strength in business relationships, both honesty and the appearance of honesty are, of course, priorities. E-mail may actually be the best medium for that.

When someone makes a commitment to you, we recommend e-mailing them saying something like, "I write to confirm that you will finish the report by Friday 9 AM." Seeing it in writing will influence them—and you—to take the commitment more seriously and will hold everyone more accountable.

TABLE 3-1. Honesty in Communications

	Percentage with lies	Immediacy of communication	Recorded or not?
Telephone	37 percent	Immediate	(usually) not recorded
Face-to-face	27 percent	Immediate	"recorded" by the other person's observation of your face, which creates a higher risk of getting caught
Instant messaging	21 percent	Immediate	potentially recorded completely, the person may or may not save the text of the instant messaging session
E-mail	14 percent	Not immediate	recorded completely

Remote Negotiating

Carnegie-Mellon Professor Don Moore and his colleagues completed a study on how to make e-mail negotiations more successful.[65] In particular, they wanted to find out how to prevent e-mail negotiations from breaking down.

Earlier studies have found that negotiators using e-mail, as opposed to negotiators using traditional lines of communication, felt negotiations took longer, felt less satisfaction, and perceived the process to be less fair. Moore wanted to bridge this gap by helping negotiators leverage the advantages of remote negotiations without the trust-damaging disadvantages.

In the study, MBA students from Kellogg and Stanford conducted negotiations entirely through e-mail. The researchers made two discoveries about how to dramatically improve the likelihood of success:

1. **Participants who shared personal Information about themselves established better rapport and had more successful negotiations.** Even simple biographical details (photo, background, education, and personal interests) and some casual social chatter before the negotiations began made it much more likely that negotiations would be successful. Face-to-face or virtually, people like to do business with people they know. The researchers also encouraged the participants to use emoticons—symbols used to express emotion through e-mail, e.g., ";-)" for a wink and ":-I" for indifference.

2. **Participants who were members of the same business school were much less likely to hit a dead end than people who were negotiating across business schools** (Stanford versus Kellogg). The implication: when negotiating remotely, you should emphasize the groups that you have in common with your counterpart. You may have worked for the same company, lived in the same neighborhood, and so on.

Several related psychological patterns create the greater success rate for people who are in a common group. That common group is often a closed group; we discussed earlier the many advantages of functioning inside a closed group.

→ **People see people who are similar to themselves as more attractive than those who are dissimilar.** It's easier to negotiate with people about whom you feel positively.

→ **Any interaction with another group member is a repeated game, not a one-time interaction.** Membership in a common group encourages you to be more honest and pleasant with your fellow group members because you will likely have to see them again. By contrast, sometimes very polite people are inconsiderate when driving a car, largely because they believe that they are highly unlikely to interact with the other drivers ever again.

→ **Groups share information internally,** which means that your actions impact your reputation throughout the group. If you develop a reputation as an unpleasant or dishonest negotiator with a coworker, that reputation will spread fast.

Moore found that casual socializing and common group membership provided a basis for a positive relationship. That allowed the participants to express positive feelings for one another, which in turn led to a better rapport, which in turn led to more successful negotiations.

Stanford professor Michael Morris and colleagues completed another study[66] which found that negotiators took advantage of e-mail by exchanging more complex, multiple-issue offers than when they negotiated face to face. They could easily e-mail complex documents with all of their changes redlined. However, e-mail reduced rapport-building conversation about contextual issues. For example, they suggest that it's easier face to face to get a feel for how strongly management at another company is pushing its team to complete a particular deal.

 Negotiators using e-mail also asked fewer clarifying questions that could prevent misunderstandings and build rapport. E-mail negotiators compensated for this lack of communication with more explicit statements about the relationship, but these were less effective in preventing mistrust and misunderstanding.

Rich Data

Virtual communication is not inferior, just different. Virtual communication can reduce opportunities for miscommunication, precisely because the participants may avoid using nonverbal subtleties. The process of writing text down forces people to articulate themselves and think clearly.

The key disadvantage of remote communications is that it may be harder to identify nonverbal signals: sarcasm, emotion, jokes, etc. The absence of those subtleties sometimes leads to miscommunication in a way that occurs less often when people are speaking.

We believe that some people are resistant to using online networks because they incorrectly have the same expectations of them that they do of face-to-face relationships. A study by Jonathon N. Cummings, Brian Butler, and Robert Kraut found that while e-mail may not be as effective as the telephone or face-to-face interaction for maintaining the emotional aspect of relationships, it is more effective for communicating information and potentially for getting collaborative work done.[67] If you are using virtual communication for the purposes for which it is appropriate, it can be extremely valuable.

Dina Mehta, a consultant and avid blogger (a blog is an online journal, which we will discuss more in Chapter 9), writes:

My blog is my social software. It is also my social network. It has my profile and much more; it has my identity fleshed out, through my posts.

A profile with history that allows you to know so much about me. I started blogging in March 2003, and already readers have seen me add new professional interests and take my qualitative research skills into new areas. Some know I love music and Pink Floyd, others have been with me to my cottage in the hills, read about my holiday and meetings with some wonderful bloggers on my trip, seen me change homes, celebrated with me when I got a project due to my blog, and even wondered where I am when I've gone silent on my blog for a few days. . . .

A profile that changes, grows, flows—not a cold résumé or "about me" page filled with past achievements and accolades—but is touchy-feely and one that says more about me through my thoughts, interests, preoccupations, rants, rambles and angst—that makes me more than just a consultant or a qualitative researcher—or a demographic statistic, "female blogger from India."

A profile that is salient too—it gets me high up on Google in many areas of search—so I do get noticed.

A profile that is my online identity—yet one that has led me to many face-to-face meetings, some that have resulted in new friends, others that I am pursuing professional interests with. And some that are a wonderful combination of the two.[68]

Meeting someone face to face allows you to absorb very rich data: the quality of a man's suit, how he interacts with his colleagues, and so on. The virtual medium can provide a different type of rich data. Because you read much faster than you can hear, in a very short time you can read the work that someone has produced over a long period of time. Articles, blogs, and discussion forum contributions can provide deep insight, not to mention news coverage, regulatory filings, and other coverage.

The Power of Virtual Teamwork

University of Southern California Professor Ann Majchrzak; University of North Carolina Professor Arvind Malhotra; and Jeffrey Stamps and Jessica Lipnack of consulting firm NetAge recently completed a study of 54 far-flung virtual teams in 31 different companies, from Intel to Royal Dutch Shell. They report: "[W]hen a project requires a diversity of competencies and perspectives and the work can be done by means of electronic documents and tools, it's better to opt for a far-flung team than for one that works face-to-face. Such teams . . . are free of many of the psychological and practical obstacles to full and effective participation that hobble their traditional counterparts."[69]

The three best practices that guided these highly effective virtual teams:

→ **Exploit diversity.** An effective team manager should make a point of soliciting everyone's opinion. Another idea: require everyone to take a standardized personality test, so each member will have a sense of the personalities involved.

→ **Use technology to simulate reality . . or create a more effective reality.** E-mail is a relatively poor way for teams to collaborate, because of the inadequate documentation trail and unwieldiness when working with multiple e-mail recipients. Instead, use real-time synchronous tools, such as Web conferencing, instant messaging, and 24/7 chat rooms. In addition, use asynchronous workflow tools such as virtual workspaces, wikis, and blogs. Use detailed personal profiles (with hobbies, family photos, etc.) to humanize each participant.

→ **Hold the team together.** Make sure that each member's home office will not pull the team member away from the project.

Although many people believe that face-to-face meetings are required early in a virtual team's life cycle to build trust, the researchers found that the effective teams they studied built trust through regular communications, and often never met face-to-face at all. Traditionally, team members feel a social obligation to wait to make decisions until everyone is in one room. When people are working virtually, they are forced to make decisions continuously. Team leaders found it particularly helpful to create ad hoc subteams, in which members were assigned to work in pairs. The researchers also found that electronic brainstorming gave even far-flung team members more time for reflection to produce quality ideas.

Virtual communications can be far more effective and efficient than face-to-face communications:

→ **Higher Character: you are more likely to be honest, thoughtful, and reflective in your communications in a way that is difficult face to face.** You can avoid the impulsive emotional responses that often happen face to face. You are less likely to be put on the spot in a virtual communication. At the same time, people sometimes will attack one another online in a way they would not do in person.

→ **You appear more Competent because you can carefully design your responses to accommodate another person's interests.** You can simultaneously instant message your colleagues, look up facts in an online encyclopedia or search engine, and use other online resources to increase your Competence. You can't easily access all those useful resources when talking with people face to face (although even that is changing, thanks to the growth of mobile Internet access).

→ **You can focus your interactions on the higher Relevance people.** In a face-to-face event, you may spend hours talking with people who are of questionable Relevance to your goals. Online, the transition costs are lower; you can simply move on to the most immediately Relevant people.

→ **Simply because you are meeting virtually, you may be able to move more rapidly to a high-Strength relationship.** You know a great deal about the other person, so you have less of a need to spend time on small talk. You also likely selected each other based on known common interests and a good business fit. On the other hand, Robert Putnam argues that, "the richer the medium of communication, the more sociable, personal, trusting, and friendly the encounter."[70]

→ **You can provide better Information to people.** Because much of the communication is happening in writing, all parties are forced to be more clear, and they tend to be more frank.

→ **You can manage a larger Number of relationships by maintaining a basic level of communication with many people.** You can communicate simultaneously with thousands of people without having to be a skilled public speaker.

→ **Lastly, even if you sometimes feel awkward meeting people who are different than you, virtual communications allow you to build a far more Diverse network.** This is particularly true because you may not even be aware of the physical traits of people you meet virtually. However, we acknowledge that online networks may be more homogeneous than face-to-face networks in their participants' interests and values.[71]

We of course are not claiming that online communications are always superior to face-to-face. In particular, we have found that at least one face-to-face meeting is often very helpful in moving a relationship up a notch in Strength. We do argue that when used appropriately, online relationships can dramatically increase the power of your total network.

Part II

Social Software

→ Smart business people have always networked. Now, the process of finding the right people, initiating a conversation, and identifying value for both parties is more efficient, because of social software.—PETER CAPUTA IV, PRESIDENT, WHIZSPARK[72]

4

Introduction to Social Software

> Social software is the next big thing: everybody's talking about it. A lot of people are developing exciting new programs to aid social interaction.
>
> Social software is being massively overhyped. It's just a sideshow run by a few geeks with a tenuous grip on reality.
>
> Social software isn't new: we've been using it for decades. We already have e-mail, Usenet newsgroups, chatrooms, instant messaging, bulletin boards, multi-user games and more.
>
> Social software isn't a new technology at all, it just reflects changes in society.
>
> Take your pick. . . . —JACK SCHOFIELD[73]

Social software expert Stowe Boyd writes that "Social tools all focus—in one way or another—on creating, discovering, supporting, or managing interpersonal relationships."[74] More technically, he defines social software as software which has at least one of the following three features[75]:

1. **Support for conversation between people and/or groups:** This includes both real-time and "slow-time" conversation, like instant messaging and discussion forums, respectively.

2. **Support for social feedback:** Group members rate the contributions of others, leading to the creation of digital reputation.

3. **Support for social networks:** This allows users the explicit creation and management of a digital expression of people's personal relationships, and helps them build new ones.

We define social software as websites and software tools which help you to discover, extend, manage, enable communication, and/or leverage your social network. We structure social software into five large buckets, below, and have listed a few representative companies in each bucket. The primary distinguishing characteristic of what is now being called "social software" is that it is bottom up, not top down. "Social software is based on supporting the desire of individuals to affiliate, their desire to be pulled into groups to achieve their personal goals"[76] (see Table 4-1).

We will discuss the most popular and accessible varieties of social software, specifically:

→ Building a personal Web presence (Chapter 5),

→ E-mail lists (Chapter 6),

→ Real-time communication tools, such as instant messaging and Web conferencing (Chapter 7),

→ Virtual communities/social network sites (Chapter 8),

→ Blogs, or Web journals (Chapter 9),

→ Relationship capital management software and biography analysis software (Chapter 10), and

→ Some of the latest ways to use technology to accelerate traditional relationship building (Chapters 11–12).

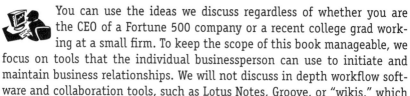 You can use the ideas we discuss regardless of whether you are the CEO of a Fortune 500 company or a recent college grad working at a small firm. To keep the scope of this book manageable, we focus on tools that the individual businessperson can use to initiate and maintain business relationships. We will not discuss in depth workflow software and collaboration tools, such as Lotus Notes, Groove, or "wikis," which also fall under the umbrella of social software, although it would be a great topic for another book. In addition, we do not discuss in detail mobile social software, photo-sharing, tagging, social television, or "folksonomics." These are extremely exciting areas of the software industry, but at least for now they do not offer you a high-impact way to open more doors and close more deals.

TABLE 4-1. Social Software Landscape[77]

	Primary Customers	
	The Public	Enterprise
General Purpose	**Realtime communications—chat, IM, VoIP, web conferencing, SMS.** AOL IM, ICQ, Gush, IRC, MSN Messenger, Net2Phone, Skype, Yahoo! Messenger **Virtual communities/social networking services.** Alumni.net, AOL, Classmates, Craigslist, ezboard, FriendsReunited, MSN Groups, MSN Spaces, Tribe.net, Yahoo! Groups, Yahoo! 360, Ziggs **Blog readers.** Amphetadesk, Bloglines, NewsGator, Pheedo **Blog software.** Blogger, Six Apart, Radio Userland, Wordpress **Face-to-face meeting facilitation sites.** Evite, Meetup **Tagging/Bookmarking.** del.icio.us, de.lirio.us, 43things	**Virtual community builders.** Affinity Engines, Aptium, IntroNetworks, Lithium, SelectMinds, vBulletin, Web Crossing **Contact data management.** Best Software, Frontrange **Biography analysis.** ZillionResumes, ZoomInfo **Blog analysis tools.** FeedBurner, Pubsub, Technorati
Primarily Business Use	**Virtual communities/social network services.** Always-On Network, COMMON.net, Ecademy, LinkedIn, OpenBC, Ryze, ZeroDegrees **Contact data synchronization.** Bebo, GoodContacts, Jigsaw, Plaxo **Job referral networks.** Accolo, H3.com, Jobster	**Workflow.** Basecamp, Groove, Lotus Notes, SilkRoad **Relationship capital management.** Contact Network, Interface Software, Leverage Software, LinkedIn, Spoke Software, Visible Path **Blogs.** Traction Software, 21Publish **Wikis.** Atlassian, JotSpot, SocialText **Social network analysis/knowledge management.** Entopia, Tacit
Primarily Personal Use	**Virtual communities/social network services.** aSmallWorld, Friendster, hi5, 20six, LiveJournal, Multiply, Myspace, Orkut, Tickle, Xanga **Dating sites.** eHarmony, lavalife, Match.com, PerfectMatch, Spark Networks, TRUE, Yahoo! Personals **Photo-sharing sites.** Flickr, Fotolog.net, WebShots **Mobile social software.** dodgeball, Plazes, nTAG, WaveMarket	

For an updated version of this table, please visit TheVirtualHandshake.com/map.

While the proliferation of and investment in social network sites, blogs, and other tools has brought these technologies into the mainstream, social software is hardly a new phenomenon (Table 4-2):[78]

TABLE 4-2. Very Brief Timeline of Social Software

1971	Ray Tomlinson invents e-mail.
1973	First group chat program.
1975	First mailing list, MsgGroup, first computer conferencing system.
1978	First Multi-User Dungeon (MUD) for multiuser gaming.
1979	USENET newsgroups created.
1984	Birth of the Fido network of Bulletin Board Systems (BBSes).
1985	Whole Earth 'Lectronic Link (WELL) community begins.
1988	Internet Relay Chat (IRC) invented.
1991	Tim Berners-Lee posts "World-Wide Web: Executive Summary" to USENET group.
	"Gopher," the first simple menu-driven client to Internet resources, launches.
1992	Tim Berners-Lee creates his "What's New?" page, arguably the first blog.
1993	Howard Rheingold publishes *The Virtual Community*.
	Mosaic Web browser released.
1994	"Christ is coming" is the first spam on USENET.
1995	Ward Cunningham launches the first wiki.
	AltaVista, the first full Web search engine, launches.
1996	ICQ: first peer-to-peer instant messaging appears.
	January: 100,000 Web servers.
1997	April: 1,000,000 Web servers.
	Slashdot, the first blog to enable reader comments, goes online.
	Jorn Barger coins the term "weblog."
	SixDegrees.com, first site based on the "six degrees of separation" concept, launches.
1998	Open Directory Project (DMOZ) begins, later acquired by Netscape.
1999	Peter Merholz coins the term "blog" as a contraction of "weblog".
	LiveJournal and Blogger launch.
	kuro5hin, a blog where users vote for what goes to the front page, launches.
	Napster launches.
2000	HotOrNot.com created with zero capital.
2001	Wikipedia, an open collaborative wiki encyclopedia project, goes live.
	Movable Type (leading blog software) initial beta release.
	Ryze social network service launches.

2002	10,000,000th Web server goes live.
	10,000,000th post on Blogger.
	Friendster launches.
2003	Venture capital investment in social network space exceeds $50 million.
	Wikipedia hits 100,000 articles.
	Howard Dean campaign uses blogs and Meetup to organize more than 100,000 supporters.
	LiveJournal and Friendster pass one million accounts.
	Skype released.
2004	Skype hits 10 million downloads.
	Social Networking Metalist (SocialSoftware.BlogsInc.com) lists more than 200 different social networking systems.
2005	Skype hits 100 million downloads.

5

Building Your Virtual Presence

→ When I took office, only high energy physicists had ever heard of what is called the World Wide Web. . . . Now even my cat has its own page."—BILL CLINTON, ANNOUNCEMENT OF NEXT GENERATION INTERNET INITIATIVE, 1996[79]

How many times have you researched a potential business or personal partner by searching for her name on the Web?

Twenty-three percent of U.S. adults have used the Internet to search for information about their customers, co-workers, potential employees, and supervisors. Almost all of us have a virtual presence, and that is often peoples' first impression of you.[80]

Why do people search for information about other people? Curiosity is the motivation for the majority of these searches. Other reasons include researching a job candidate's background, looking for specific information (e.g., address or phone number), researching to find a new job or prepare for a job interview, and checking out rumors.[81] Up to 10 percent of all online searches on most popular search engines are for proper names.[82]

Your online image is even more important than your handsome new suit and shiny smile, because your online image can help you to get that meeting so you can show off your handsome suit.

We recommend taking control of your virtual presence. For example, a simple first step is to attach your biography to the end of an article that you write for your company's Web site. People who look you up will see that bi-ography and learn more about you. A more sophisticated approach is to cre-ate a personal Webpage. Both of these approaches will at least provide you with some text to which you can point people.

Your virtual presence usually includes a brief biography, your favorite links, and anything else that you think helps to establish professional cred-ibility. One of our favorite virtual homes is that of the multiply-talented David Weinberger.[83] His page includes the three parts shown in Table 5-1.

Some people dislike a formal virtual presence for individuals. They think personal sites are too self-promotional and perhaps a sign that the owner is looking for her next job instead of focusing on her current job. We suspect this prejudice will fade in time, as more and more people create a formal Internet presence for themselves. Many leading busi-nesspeople have detailed personal Web sites as part of their corporate sites, including Bill Gates and Richard Branson.

While one might expect it from these prominent business leaders, today 13 percent of American Internet users maintain their own Web site.[84] We ex-pect this figure to increase significantly as more and more social interactions happen virtually.

Analogously, at some tipping point during the mid-1990s, an e-mail ad-dress became culturally mandatory. Today, when nearly a quarter of U.S. adults use the Internet to search for information about their customers, coworkers, potential employees, and supervisors, they are surprised if you are a businessperson with several years' experience and a search does *not* pull up a biography, a news clipping, a profile on your employer's site, or some other information about you.

Are you a real person if you do not exist online?

Where Should You Set Up Your Virtual Presence?

A simple way to create your virtual presence is to build a homepage for your-self in a virtual community. We recommend using a virtual community in which building a profile is free and the profiles are viewable by search en-gines. You can also register at an online profile service like Ziggs.com. Using one of these services as your primary virtual presence gives you limited flex-ibility and control, but is much simpler than maintaining your own site.

You may want to follow the example of Jan Hinrichs, CEO of online net-work openBC. He points the domain Hinrichs.de to his own openBC profile. This approach allows you to go ahead and set up a permanent domain, and you can change where it points whenever you choose.

TABLE 5-1. David Weinberger's Personal Webpage

Left-brain version	No-brain version	Right-brain version
Stomach-Churning, Full o' Hype Overview *The Wall Street Journal* called him a "marketing guru." He's the co-author of the *The Cluetrain Manifesto*. . . [873 more words] . . . "Dr. Weinberger lives in the Boston area with his wife and three children, where he is made uncomfortable by writing about himself in the third person."	"Him write good. Him help companies do stuff. Him smell ok."	

Many universities, real estate firms, and financial services firms encourage their employees to create a personal home page under their organizational umbrella. If you are affiliated with an institution like this, then we definitely recommend you consider taking advantage of the opportunity.

However, there is a catch. When you leave that institution, or if the institution changes its policies, you may lose control of that home page. All of the links to that page will become invalid, and you may lose the content that you have painstakingly built.

Alternatively, you can build a page that you design yourself. This gives you total control over the site.

How to Set Up Your Own Web Site

 You have the highest level of control with a Web site that you design and make hosting arrangements for yourself. In just four steps, you can maintain a functional Web site for no more than the cost of a cheap lunch every month:

1. **Register your domain name** at a low-cost domain name registrar.

2. **Design a site.** You can use Microsoft Word's built-in Web Page Wizard to design a simple Web site. The cost is zero, assuming you already have Microsoft Word. Amaya (w3.org/Amaya) and Mozilla (Mozilla.org) are two free, well-supported Web page editors.

3. **Host your site** with an inexpensive hosting service. Many domain name registrars offer reasonably priced hosting. If you are not very technically experienced, it may be worth paying a slightly higher price for the convenience of dealing with a single provider for both the domain name and the hosting.

   Do not use a page on a free service such as GeoCities or Tripod for business purposes. The ads give you a highly unprofessional appearance, and the search engines are less likely to rank your page highly if they will even include your site in their index.

4. **Hand-submit your site to the top three or four search engines** (Google, Yahoo!, MSN, etc.). The rest of the major search engines and portals will pick you up either by using the major engines as their back-end provider, or by including your Open Directory listing (below).

5. **Register with Open Directory** (DMOZ.org) in the appropriate category. The Open Directory listing is one of the most important factors in search engine results, because it will automatically create many high-quality inbound links to your site. The other search engines will eventually crawl

your site if you are listed there. However, getting listed can take weeks or months. DMOZ does not notify you of your application status, but you can track it yourself at Resource-Zone.com.

Choosing Content for Your Site

Your virtual presence is your primary face to the virtual world. To be effective, it should be clear, focused, distinctive, and useful.

→ **Define your niche.** To which public do you want to communicate?

→ **Define yourself.** What do you want people to know about you? What personal information is relevant? See Chapter 15 for more on displaying personal information online.

→ **Differentiate yourself.** What makes you exceptional?

→ **Be original.** Post original materials relevant to your industry.

→ **Be an industry resource.** Become an aggregator of news about your profession, with the added value of your personal commentary.

You will not attract the same traffic as Yahoo!, but that is fine. If you are Sofiya Kozlova, a chemist who specializes in beneficial uses of recycling material and industrial waste; cement chemistry and surface processes; and trace metals/vitamins additives, then you care most that you rank high for people who are researching those specific, narrow subjects. The better content you have on those subjects, the higher your Web site will rank.

You may be concerned about the terms under which you authorize readers to reuse the content you publish. If you are giving the content away on your site as a way to demonstrate your Competence to a large Number of people, then make it as easy as possible for your readers to help you with that.

We encourage you to make it easy for people to republish your content. Creative Commons (CreativeCommons.org) is an effort to simplify this for content creators by providing a variety of free, legally sound licenses that allow your work to be shared, while still retaining some of your rights and all of your ownership.

For example, all of the free content on TheVirtualHandshake.com is licensed under the Creative Commons Attribution License, which states:

You are free to:

→ Copy, distribute, display, and perform the work.

→ Make derivative works.

→ Make commercial use of the work.

Under the following conditions:

→ Attribution: You must give the original author credit.

→ For any reuse or distribution, you must make clear to others the license terms of this work.

→ Any of these conditions can be waived if you get permission from the copyright holder.[85]

Andrius Kulikauskas of Minciu Sodas (www.ms.lt), a think-tank for organizing knowledge workers around working openly, makes a compelling case for placing your content in the public domain.[86] "It's important to make sharing straightforward. The real value," he says, "comes from working across multiple spaces, with many different networks of people."[87] Freely sharing content helps you build valuable relationships. You want to attract the smartest readers; one of the best ways to do that is to post the most valuable content.

6

E-Mail Lists

→ There seems to be an inverse correlation between how much attention a technology receives and how impactful it is. In my circles, e-mail, instant messaging, and email lists are king, but receive only a fraction of the attention of wikis or social networks.—JIM CASHEL, CHAIRMAN, FORUM ONE COMMUNICATIONS[88]

Chris Pirillo started sending out informal e-mail messages about the latest computer downloads and utilities to his friends while still a college student. Within ten years, he grew that practice into Lockergnome (Lockergnome.com), a collection of almost two dozen free technology newsletters boasting more than a million unique subscribers. Lockergnome sells advertising in the newsletter and promotes a variety of other products through affiliate programs.

Pirillo's powerful personal network has also spawned an exclusive think tank of Internet professionals (Pirillo.com) and an annual convention, Gnomedex (Gnomedex.com). The 2004 fourth annual conference boasted 300 attendees and top industry speakers such as Apple Computer cofounder Steve Wozniak.

The success of these lists has helped create a reputation for Pirillo as one of the top e-mail publishing experts, and has opened numerous other opportunities, including a regular column in *Computer Power User;* a hosting spot on Tech TV; a book on e-mail publishing, *Poor Richard's E-mail Publishing;* and the opportunity to coauthor *Online!* with prominent computer columnist John Dvorak.

As Pirillo says in his online autobiography, "What started out as a simple gesture turned into a worldwide phenomenon before I knew it."[89]

Pirillo is not alone. Approximately 23 million U.S. Internet users exchange e-mails with other online group members several times a week. Half of those who e-mail an online group say that one of their main reasons to do so is to create or maintain personal relationships with members.[90]

An easy way of growing your network is to participate in or run your own e-mail list. An e-mail list is simply a list of names to which the list owner and/or the participants can send e-mails. You can create and manage a short list of your friends from your e-mail program. However, as soon as your list grows beyond a few dozen names, you may want to consider using a more sophisticated e-mail list manager. This can be free or very low cost, using a service such as Yahoo! Groups or ezboard.

Hosting a list is the virtual equivalent of hosting a regular meeting or event. Running your own e-mail list is much more effective than simply becoming active in a preexisting list, because you have full control of the list and the participants, and because your personal brand is on every communication within the group.

Newsletters Versus Discussion Groups

Video editor Steve Covello used a virtual community to help some colleagues land a very lucrative series of projects, and in turn to help himself advance professionally. Covello subscribes to an online mailing list community called WheresSpot, "The Internet Community for Prisoners of Advertising" (WheresSpot.com). WheresSpot is run on the free Yahoo! Group platform.

In 2000, Covello was a freelance video editor working with director team GoodGuys (Brian Jackson and Nate Crooker) on *StreetTeam,* a reality-based hour-long TV show featuring Sony Music artists. In 2001, another subscriber to WhereSpot posted an inquiry for references on directors who do reality-based production for use on an upcoming job for a major beer maker. Covello replied directly, describing the GoodGuys and his work experiences with them.

In the end, the GoodGuys beat out approximately 100 other directors to be awarded what has turned into a three-year national campaign comprised of approximately 140 TV commercials. This was one of the GoodGuys' largest-ever assignments. At the time, Covello had never met nor spoken with the person who originally posted the inquiry on WheresSpot, and to whom he made his original critical recommendation.

Covello has since started his own postproduction boutique, Double Wide Post. This is a partnership with Double Wide Media, whose members include Jackson and Crooker.

 There are two major categories of e-mail lists: newsletters (only you can send material out) and discussion groups (anyone can send an e-mail to the group).

Most lists are set up so that anyone can join without screening. The advantage is that your network can grow indefinitely. As list members publicize your list to their friends, your list will grow with little effort on your part. You do not have to take the time to filter anyone.

However, keeping the list open and not screening new members has a downside. The list loses some of its relationship-building power, precisely because anyone can join. The members do not feel privileged to be in the group, and you will never have had a real two-way interaction with most of them.

If you decide that you want your list to be an online discussion group, we strongly recommend creating some sort of screening method for new members and/or for e-mail postings. You could manually moderate the list, approving each e-mail before sending it out. Alternatively, you could create a high barrier to membership by interviewing or screening all applicants and making it clear that inappropriate behavior is cause for termination from the list.

Without some filter, online discussion lists have a tendency to degrade in quality. Less-desirable members will send out spam (inappropriate commercial messages) and flames (personal attacks). As a result, your quality members will unsubscribe and your list may disintegrate.

You may want to consider the approach of Mike Rosen, a film producer who runs an informal list of social and business events in Houston. He does not maintain a virtual presence; the only way to get on this list is to meet Mike face to face. Meeting him becomes a more worthwhile occasion, because he can offer you access to a valuable resource.

There are three major topics for most lists: ideas/conversation, events, and jobs.

"You have to read this . . . .": Ideas and Conversation Lists

The most common topic for most lists is simply sharing ideas and conversation, including pointers to useful Web sites, interesting articles, personal opinions, and so on. If you are running this kind of list, we recommend sending out links to articles as opposed to the text of the articles themselves. This will ensure that you are not in violation of copyright laws. In addition, some authors' success and even salaries are based on the amount of traffic their articles generate. Letting the author of an article know that you have sent out a link to his or her article is doing that author a favor. This is an excellent way to build relationships with writers.

Richard Taylor, a Connecticut executive recruiter, runs one notable example: the Strategic Executives Networking Group ("SENG"). SENG is a network of more than 15,000 executives who share business introductions, marketing resources, job opportunities, and career information with other members. Joining requires that you e-mail Taylor @TheSeng.org. This screening process allows Taylor to get to know, at a shallow level, every one of the people on his list.

All communications in SENG filter through Richard Taylor, that is, participants cannot e-mail everyone in the group. The disadvantage of this restriction is that it creates a far less active community. But the upside is that Taylor has full control over the tone and volume of the list.

Because he has complete control, participants feel much more connected to him when he aids them than they would in a more open community. When he accepts a person into the community; forwards a note on his/her behalf; or publicly endorses someone; that person becomes indebted to him.

For example, Taylor occasionally sends out a note with the following structure: "I have just reviewed an article co-written by fellow SENG member and friend Jon Barney for the *Harvard Business Review* entitled, "The New World Disorder." . . . It's a very worthwhile read! If you would like a copy of this excellent article, simply request a reprint directly from Jon Barney, Medley Advisors, at the coordinates below.

Mr. Barney is grateful to Taylor for the publicity, and when Barney responds to the hundreds of inquiries he receives, he has a chance to market Medley Advisors personally to everyone who writes.

This incident is also an example of how SENG members can access the entire list. They must give before getting; they give some valuable tool or information in exchange for getting the contact details of a list member. Once Barney has been in touch with another SENG member, he is free to add that other SENG member to his own network.

Taylor has found that his audience does not appreciate being sold to or "spammed," that is, receiving explicit commercial solicitations. Instead, Taylor regularly sends out e-mails like the following:

"My staff has just completed an updated version of our Leveraged Buyout/Private Equity & Venture Capital Database in Excel. It now has over 2,500 listings, most with private e-mails, phone numbers, mailing addresses, and Web sites. If you are in need of more information, simply request."

When people write in to request the database, Taylor mentions the price and offers to sell it. The advantage of this structure is threefold. First, this e-mail (without the price) is much more likely to be forwarded on to other mailing lists. Second, it creates a higher level of audience participation. Third, it makes the list look less commercial.

We do not necessarily advocate Taylor's approach in sending out e-mails in this format, which require people to e-mail in for more information. It creates more work for both the reader and the sender, and some people may find it misleading or confusing. However, Taylor reports that this approach has worked very well for him.

Taylor benefits from his mailing list in three ways:

1. **The list increases his visibility among potential clients**—employers who might request his services.

2. **The list reaches many potential candidates who might fill his searches.**

3. **He can market additional products and services to the list** because of the trust he has built.

While e-mail lists are ordinarily considered slower-paced communications, they can also be used for higher intensity events. The International Virtual Women's Chamber of Commerce (IVWCC.org) holds a monthly virtual meet-and-greet using a simple mailing list. The event typically generates five hundred to a thousand messages over three or four days. By using what is already the dominant communication tool for most participants, attendees can engage effectively with one another without traveling. The participants use their standard e-mail filters to deal effectively with the high message volume.

"What's Happening This Week?": Events Lists

Events are another common topic for mailing lists. Craig Newmark founded craigslist (craigslist.org) in 1995 as an informal event announcement list for the San Francisco Bay area. Over time, the site added job ads, résumé postings, classifieds, and personals, and expanded to cover other cities. It is now one of the most visited sites on the Web, generating over 1.9 billion page views a month.[91]

 If you create your own events list, make sure that you have permission to forward an event before doing so. Also, make sure that the event is open to the public. Otherwise, you run the risk of irritating the event organizers and/or the people who want to attend the event.

"Have I Got a Job for You!": Jobs List

An excellent way to boost your electronic exposure is to open a jobs list for your industry and/or function of expertise. This is particularly true if you are looking for a new position yourself.

Once your list reaches a large scale, you will have to start being significantly more careful about the contents. First, double-check that you have permission to forward a job. Otherwise, you may get a complaint from the potential employer about the flood of résumés that is arriving.

Second, double-check that you have full details about the job in the e-mail (particularly salary and location); otherwise you are likely to receive dozens of inquiries from confused job seekers. Partial information can be worse than no information at all.

As your list grows, you can start thinking about monetization. For example, many recruiters will share a fee with you if you refer an appropriate candidate to them. On the one hand, you are largely dependent on their integrity to get the fee. On the other hand, the marginal cost to you of forwarding the position to your list is trivial.

7

Relating in Real-Time

→ The Internet is a telephone system that's gotten uppity.—CLIFFORD STOLL, AUTHOR, *SILICON SNAKE OIL,* 9TH ANNUAL SCO FORUM, AUGUST 1995[92]

Danielle Bailey, owner of The Chayton Group, a Web hosting and design firm, uses instant messaging ("IM") to provide a very personal level of service: "My clients really appreciate the personal response and tell their friends that I 'walk them through everything step by step'—and I'm more than happy to do it. I prefer IMs over e-mail any day. I prefer it over the telephone because I can't help more than one person at a time via telephone, whereas with IMs I've helped as many as 6 clients at once. I don't get confused because the whole previous conversation is there in writing for me."[93]

E-mail, Web sites, and most of the other media we discuss allow you to talk with people at your convenience, with a lag between each time someone talks (asynchronous communication). In this chapter, we discuss the many ways in which people are communicating with one another virtually in real-time (synchronous communication).

The technology in this area is advancing extremely rapidly. As a result, we expect more and more interactions that historically would happen face to face, in real time, to happen virtually, also in real time.

Instant Messaging

As with many other social software tools, IM initially became popular among tech-savvy young people, but has since expanded into mainstream business use. The term IM encompasses any software that allows instant text communication between two or more people. A recent study from the Radicati Group found that 85 percent of all companies in North America now have employees using IM, and 362 million people use IM worldwide.[94] Forty percent of U.S. online consumers use IM.[95] The most popular providers are AOL Instant Messenger, Yahoo! Messenger, MSN Messenger, ICQ, and Internet Relay Chat (IRC).

Instant messaging allows interactive conversations in a way that e-mail cannot. "[W]hen instant messaging is rolled out in the enterprise setting, 15–25 percent of e-mail and telephone traffic disappears." Why? One major reason is that over 40 percent of business telephone calls today lead to voicemail. Telephone calls now behave like e-mail: you send a message and wait for a response from the black hole.[96] IM allows you to ping people precisely when you know they are available to talk.

In one October 2004 study, more than two-thirds of South Korean middle, high school, and college students reported, "I rarely use or don't use e-mail at all." In the world's most wired country, young people see e-mail as difficult to use because you cannot tell if the recipient got your message. They report that it is slow, and the process of using e-mail feels as if you're doing a task, as if you are doing your homework.[97]

Instant messaging offers five advantages over e-mail and the telephone:

1. INDICATION OF PRESENCE

With IM, you know exactly when the person you are targeting is available. You never have to leave a message. If the person you need to speak with is out, you can set an alert to be notified when he becomes available, avoiding the frustration of "playing tag" via e-mail or voice mail.

Of course, you may not want to let the entire world know when you are available. As one reader wrote to us: "I REALLY WISH someone would have warned me to be very careful that I only give my IM ID to people I know VERY well!!! I have needy people IMing me all day long whose feelings are very hurt if I don't spend the next HOUR or more IMing about absolutely nothing of importance. . . . I have to hide the fact that I am online, which is annoying, because there are certain people I WOULD like to know that I am available to IM!"

To address this problem, some IM services allow you to make your presence visible to some users while masking your presence status to others.

2. MULTITASKING

Instant messaging does not require your undivided attention. Many IM users simultaneously answer multiple IMs, process their e-mail, use the Web, or even talk on the phone while IMing.[98] Because of the option to multitask, IM is less disruptive to workflow than telephones.

3. WRITTEN RECORD

A transcript makes it easier to communicate your conversation to others. For example, if you develop a list of action items, all participants have it for future reference. As discussed in Chapter 3, this increases accountability and reduces the likelihood of future disagreement over what was said.

4. REDUCED EXPENSE

Instant messaging does not involve long distance phone charges.

5. SEARCHABILITY

IM is not only a way to keep in touch with people; it also makes it easy to meet new people. For example, on AOL you can search for people with similar interests to yours, and then IM them and introduce yourself.

> David Pulaski, CEO of IM-Age, a company providing security and policy compliance software for IM, says, "I see [IM] being imbedded into every single application that you can think of three to five years from now."[99]

Chat

No sooner had people started communicating via e-mail than they wanted to communicate in real time and with multiple people. To meet that need, chat was born just two years after the invention of e-mail. Chat typically means IM used by three or more people in a preorganized discussion room. Participants type in their messages, which are then repeated immediately and simultaneously on the screens of all other participants in the same room.

More than 29 million U.S. Internet users had participated in chat rooms by 2002.[100] The most effective business chat rooms typically control admission, rather than just staying open to all.

> Branding expert Rob Frankel runs a weekly public chat every Monday morning in which he donates one hour of his time to anyone who drops by. He likens it to the academic tradition of "office hours." He says that consistency is critical, as is a "give first" attitude:
> "Some days we get 20 people, some days only three. It doesn't matter how many show up. What matters is that I offer it. For two rea-

sons: First, part of my brand ethic is to never let anyone leave empty-handed. I don't want anyone to think they can't afford to get good branding help. So I scale my fees and services. The chat is free, but the information is very valuable. It shows new people how helpful a Branded Community® can be [Frankel's term for a virtual community that is used to promote your brand].

"Second, every clinic session is archived at FrankelBiz.com, easily searchable so that FrankelBees can read the transcripts at their leisure. This increases the useful content (also free) at FrankelBiz, which further delivers on the brand's promise of good, ethical people helping other good, ethical people build their businesses."[10]

Internet Telephony

Sometimes there is no substitute for the human voice. A study by the Microsoft Social Computing Group showed that it's not just the subtleties of a voice, such as pitch, tone, and pauses, but the mere fact of a voice that conveys a strong sense of "social proximity."[102]

While Internet telephony (Voice Over Internet Protocol, or VoIP) has been available since 1995, it only caught on at first among hobbyists. Setup was complicated and sound quality was poor. By 1998, commercial carriers began using VoIP as the basis for conventional phone-to-phone national and international long distance—at lower rates than previously, but with a required investment in new equipment.[103]

The impact of widespread VoIP use cannot be overestimated. As U.S. Federal Communication Chairman Michael Powell said, "I knew it was over when I downloaded Skype. When the inventors of KaZaA are distributing for free a little program that you can use to talk to anybody else, and the quality is fantastic, and it's free—it's over. The world will change now inevitably."[104]

Starting in 2003, Skype offered free computer-to-computer VoIP worldwide. It was far from the first to offer this, but Skype was easier to use and had higher quality than almost any predecessor. Skype has since added conference calling (free for small groups) and the ability to make calls to conventional phones at a fraction of previous rates. It is now practical to connect with someone anywhere in the world just for a chat, without even thinking about cost. Internationally oriented social network sites, such as Ecademy and openBC, have taken to Skype quickly, adding a dedicated field for Skype ID to user profiles. Bloggers the world over have begun adding a "Skype Me" button to their sites. Skype also offers the same "presence" feature described above for IM.

Stuart Henshall, a knowledge management and innovation consultant, says that the real disruptive nature of Skype is not the free person-to-person calling, but the possibility of "always-on" conferencing. "What would the impact be if all conferencing capability was instantaneous and free? . . . Who knows what happens when people go from seconds per month in conference calls to hours and hours?"[105]

Less than two years after launch, Skype had already attracted over 100 million downloads.[106] Many imitators, including the major telecommunications companies, will undoubtedly follow Skype's lead. It will become much easier to build Strong relationships internationally because of this new technology.

Web Conferencing

In 2002, iCohere, a provider of virtual community software, hosted a four-day online conference on collaborative learning. Attendees created personal profiles, viewed both live and prerecorded presentations, and talked (and talked and talked).

Mimicking the social interaction of face-to-face conferences, they could also send IMs to anyone whose profile caught their eye, and invite them into a Web conference room where they could talk further. The majority of attendees participated in these conference rooms throughout the event.

iCohere not only generated revenue from the 150 attendees, but prospective customers gained exposure to the company's platform. Many clients learned about and purchased iCohere's software from participating in these events, and have now begun producing similar events of their own.

In addition, attendees realized the value of participating beyond just learning; several consultants obtained clients as a result of their participation. One consultant, located in Vancouver, Canada, obtained a contract from a Director of e-Learning at a major nonprofit in Washington, DC. The first time this consultant met her client was on a trip to visit the client after the project had been sold.

Web conferencing is a broad term encompassing many technologies, including all the previous ones mentioned in this Chapter. Worldwide, conferencing service revenues (broadly defined) were $2.9 billion in 2003.[107] Essentially, it is technology that allows for multimedia remote conversation. Three elements characteristic of almost all Web conferencing are:

1. **Slideshow presentations.** A presenter controls the pace of the presentation for all participants.

2. **Cobrowsing.** All participants can look at the leader's browser.

3. **Application or desktop sharing.** The presenter can make a single application or the entire desktop viewable to all participants. (This feature alone can enable the other two, at least in a crude way.)

Most Web conferences include some integrated voice communication—frequently integrated VoIP, but sometimes a separate conventional phone conference. Conferences may also integrate online discussion forums for conversation before and after the real-time events.

When Web conferencing first became available in the 1990s, software companies, in particular, quickly adopted it to cut down on sales and marketing expenses, and companies in a variety of industries began using it for training. Today, Web conferencing, including integrated audio, is available on demand for as little as U.S. $0.01 per person per minute. You can have a dedicated Web conferencing room for just a few U.S. dollars a month. At that price, Web conferencing can be used in ways much like Rob Frankel's informal chats or Skype conference calls, but with far richer communication.

We think Web conferencing is a greatly underused channel.

Going Mobile

However attached we are to our office computers, we are even more attached to our cell phones. As of 2004, there are approximately one billion Internet users in the world,[108] but nearly 1.5 billion mobile phone users.[109] "With sales of 600 million units a year, mobile phones are simultaneously the world's most widespread communications devices, computing devices, and consumer-electronics products."[110] Dr. Edward Tenner, science historian at the Smithsonian Institution, said, "The thumb is the new power digit."[111]

It only makes sense that people want to expand the capabilities of the cell phone to provide even more social interaction. Social software for mobile phones generally falls into three categories:

1. **Text messaging** (SMS, or Short Message Service). Allows you to transmit all-text messages without disturbing the people around you or even in the midst of chaos. Messages can also be sent to a group of people, enabling broadcasting. Protesters used text messaging heavily to coordinate the 1999 anti-World Trade Organization protests in Seattle, and later to coordinate the 2001 overthrow of President Estrada in the Philippines.[112]

2. **Mobile blogging,** or "moblogging," or "photoblogging." Allows you to post to your blog from your mobile device, including pictures from a camera phone. This turns every mobile phone owner into a real-time reporter. Even small newspapers like the *Ventura County Star* (Insidevc.com) are enabling participatory journalism, offering readers the ability to post photos directly to their Web site. You can even post audio and video to the Internet from a mobile device ("podcasting").

3. **Mobile social networking.** Combines "location-based services" with profiles stored online to help you identify and connect with nearby friends, friends

of friends, or people with a common interest. While the early adopters are young people looking for dates, this technology can easily be applied in a business context. nTAG Interactive is using this technology to help businesspeople connect with like-minded people at conferences.[113]

As mobile devices become more capable, including better input and output devices, you can expect that you truly will be able to take your network with you wherever you go.

Convergence

Multiuser chat has been common in virtual communities since shortly after its development. A growing number of virtual communities are now including IM and VoIP applications to enable real-time communication between members. Friendster made a major splash in September 2004 with the announcement of its integration with Voiceglo, which enables free voice communication between Friendster members. Soon more virtual communities will offer live video chat for individuals and small groups.

With the introduction of these real-time tools, virtual communities are becoming multidimensional communication platforms. Michael Jones, president and cofounder of Userplane, a company that provides integrated real-time text, audio-, and videocommunication tools for virtual communities, explains: "Users need to be able to broadcast their presence, as they do in the real world. The idea of allowing users on one Webpage to see other users on the same Webpage and communicate with them is allowing a Web site to act as a space, providing live community. These new tools take the benefits of IM, VoIP, and Presence, and wrap them in one easy to use application, bringing the community element to everyone (and everything)."[114]

8

Social Network Sites and Virtual Communities

→ What should young people do with their lives today? Many things, obviously. But the most daring thing is to create stable communities in which the terrible disease of loneliness can be cured.—KURT VONNEGUT, JR., COMMENCEMENT ADDRESS AT HOBARTH AND WILLIAM SMITH COLLEGES, 1974[115]

The International Executives Resource Group (IERGOnline.com) is a not-for-profit organization of "C-level" senior business executives focused primarily on helping its members find new jobs. The IERG started as a support organization for executives in transition, but it is evolving to be a general-purpose networking group for senior executives. They have an active virtual community and also hold face-to-face meetings every two weeks in New York and Boston. Membership includes CEOs, COOs, presidents, and managing directors, many of whom have run companies or divisions with more than $100 million in revenue. The typical age is mid-40s. The members live all over the world, but the greatest concentration is in the U.S. Northeast.

The requirements for admission are:

→ Senior general management or line management role.

→ Five years minimum international experience.

→ Earning now or previously a minimum annual base salary of $150,000.

→ Commitment to participate in face-to-face meetings and/or share at least one personally vetted, senior-level job lead monthly.

→ Commitment to supporting fellow members of the group.

→ Payment of annual dues.

Applicants must be nominated by an existing member and pass a phone interview. The Admissions Committee particularly looks for people who proactively offer to introduce IERG members to executive recruiters and who can share qualified leads with the group. Anyone who fails those tests is unlikely to be offered entry.

One Admissions Committee member makes sure to talk briefly about her own job search when interviewing an IERG applicant. If the applicant fails to offer any advice or brainstorm any leads, that applicant will probably not be invited to join.

Both members and external executive recruiters can search through the online profiles to find appropriate people to meet. In addition, members can opt to participate in three separate mailing lists: "FYI" (for events or news items), "Leads" (job openings), and "Requests" (requests for assistance, introductions, information).

A typical e-mail sent to the "Requests" mailing list reads:

> A friend of mine has developed a consumer product that is ready for commercialization. A business associate of hers has offered to manage the private placement process to attract angel investors and would stay on during the product launch as CFO/COO. He has asked for 15 percent of equity (undiluted) for doing so (which he would vest into over time). Is this a reasonable and standard equity percentage, or is his request too rich, considering that she has invested about $100,000 of her own capital in the project and two years of her time to-date?
>
> If anyone is knowledgeable about deal structures and can provide insight on the above, please let me know.

The IERG has approximately 400 members. Many members report that they have started companies with partners they met through the IERG, or found jobs through introductions provided by IERG members. Precisely because it is a group focused on helping people going through the stressful process of a job search, it is relatively easy to build high-Strength relationships.

The Microsoft Social Computing Group defines a virtual community as "a gathering of people in an online 'space' where individuals come together to connect, interact, and get to know each other better over time."[116] Eighty-four percent of all U.S. Internet users—almost 100 million people—participate in one or more online groups on a regular basis. This includes those who joined groups they had an affiliation with offline, for example, professional or fraternal groups.[117] *More Americans have used the Internet to contact a group than have used the Internet to read news, search for health guidance, or to buy something.* The majority of those contacting online groups (56 percent) say they first became active in a group—even traditional, face-to-face organizations—after they began communicating with it online.[118]

The major categories of virtual communities are[119]:

1. **Communities of Interest:** People with a common interest. Example: SeniorNet (SeniorNet.org), a community for senior citizens that includes discussions about a broad range of topics, such as travel and finances.

2. **Communities of Purpose:** People who have gathered together for the purpose of accomplishing a specific goal. We contrast this with Communities of Interest, where discussion and knowledge exchange are purpose enough. Example: Wikipedia (Wikipedia.org), a community-created free encyclopedia.

3. **Communities of Practice (CoPs):** People in the same profession, who participate in the group both to advance the profession at large and to share knowledge with other professionals. Example: MediaBistro.com and MediaVillage.com, for media professionals.

4. **Business-to-Business Communities (B2B):** Companies and their suppliers, partners, and customers. Example: Fibre2Fashion (Fibre2Fashion.com), a marketplace and community for the garment industry.

5. **Business-to-Consumer Communities (B2C):** Businesses that want to build relationships with existing and new customers. Example: Major League Baseball (MLB.com), which has a large portfolio of active communities for fans of all the major baseball teams.

6. **Business-to-Employee Communities (B2E):** Community for the employees of a specific business. Example: FirstGov (FirstGov.gov) is the U.S. federal employee portal.

7. **Community Platforms:** People who want to create their own virtual community. This has led to explosive growth in community platforms, which are sites that allow you to create any community you want around any interest that appeals to you. Among the most popular business community platforms: Ecademy (Ecademy.com); Ryze (Ryze.com); openBC

(openBC.com); and Yahoo! Groups (Groups.Yahoo.com). The members of these sites have created an endless array of micro-communities around such subjects as: microcap stocks, Cornell alumni, libertarian economics, and almost every other interest imaginable.

Most communities do not fit neatly into just one of these categories, but represent a blend of two or more. According to Internet researcher David Reed, this ability for people to self-organize and form these groups is "the technical feature that most distinguishes the Internet's capabilities from all other communications media before it."[120]

A major subcategory of virtual communities are social network sites, a category popularized by Friendster. Traditional virtual communities allowed you to see only one degree away, that is, you might have a list of people in the community with whom you frequently talk. By contrast, "social network sites" give you the ability to see whom your friends know, and whom they know, and so on. Today, virtual communities and social network sites tend to have different sets of functionality.[121] However, we expect the line between these groups to blur over time.

To clarify the terminology: "Social software," also known as "social network software," is the general term we use for software that allows you to build, analyze, enable communication in, and leverage your social network. "Social network sites" (or "social networking sites") is the widely used umbrella term for virtual communities such as Friendster, MySpace, and hi5 which allow you to see whom your relationships know.

How to Find Your Virtual Neighborhood

To find a community that suits your interests, we suggest using some of the tools below as a starting point[122]:

→ **Any search engine.** For example, let us say that you served for several years in the navy. If you search for "military community," you will likely pull up the largest online military destination, Military.com. Try looking up the name of the function, industry, or geography that you are targeting, along with a phrase such as "mailing list," "newsgroup," "community," etc.

→ **Yahoo!** has a comprehensive, well-categorized list of association Web sites by industry.

→ **ASAE** (American Society of Association Executives, ASAEnet.org) has over 6,500 groups indexed in the United States, plus thousands of non-U.S. member associations.

You may be tempted to focus on business-focused communities such as MediaBistro.com. However, any community can have business relevance. For example, you may participate in a chat room for Chinese people because you are looking for Mandarin movies for your children. You may end up selling a consulting project to a Chinese-American. Once you get to know people within a given community, ask around to learn what other communities the members are involved in and recommend.

Freshman Year at the Firm

Everybody has heard stories about how staying in touch with former colleagues has helped someone to get a new job. However, these connections can also impact the highest level of executive decisions.

One Fortune 500 CEO, an attorney by training, was preparing for a hostile deposition in an anti-trust case. When he reviewed the deposition documents, he realized that the team coming to depose him was from the global law firm that acquired his former firm. He had practiced with that blue-chip law firm as an associate straight out of law school. He immediately logged into the alumni program of his former firm, and researched what his fellow associate class members had been up to. He was able to locate a few who were now partners, and picking up the phone, he began inquiring about any tidbits about the team. Although the former colleagues were restricted in what information they could share with him, he was able to get an insider's view on the team that was coming in for the deposition.

As a follow up, the Fortune 500 CEO sent a note to the partner in charge of the alumni program at his former law firm, thanking him for having organized such a valuable resource.

Your former colleagues are a valuable pool of relationships. When you connect with a fellow graduate of the same employer, you benefit from immediate perceived Competence because of the common corporate training and language. This is particularly true for "academy companies" with rigorous training programs and strong brand names.

You also benefit from a preexisting Strength in the relationship, because of the common bond. In particular, if someone in the community is considering a relationship with you, the shared community makes it easy to conduct due diligence. Suppose Tara and Maria both worked at McKinsey, and Tam sends Maria a résumé to apply for a job at her new firm. Even if Maria does

---

Cem Sertoglu is a contributing author to this section. Mr. Sertoglu is a cofounder, Director, and former CEO of SelectMinds, the leader in corporate alumni relations solutions. He was previously with strategy consulting firm Farmer & Company and a Corporate Knowledge Manager at Knowledge Transfer International.

not know Tara personally, the common network makes it easy for her to evaluate Tara's qualifications.

The participants in a corporate alumni network tend to be high in their Relevance to you, because they are clustered in your industry. Finally, participants in corporate alumni networks tend to be very Diverse in seniority and career level, since they are defined by having worked at the same company, not where they are in their professional lifecycle.

If you are not aware of a corporate alumni network you are qualified to join, a good place to start your search is the major search engines. Try combinations of your former employers' names and the phrases "alumni," "ex-employees," and "former employees." Visiting your former employers' Web sites is a good idea as well, because most networks have links from the corporate home pages of the owner companies. You typically have a higher chance of finding an alumni network organized by a former employer if you have worked in management consulting, accounting, technology consulting, law, or investment banking.

Corporate alumni networks fall into three categories: company-owned alumni networks, grassroots alumni networks, and antagonistic alumni networks created by disgruntled ex-employees. We ignore the last category, as these sites are more useful for complaining than for business.

COMPANY-OWNED ALUMNI NETWORKS

Progressive companies recognize the value of former employees. If managed effectively, alumni networks are private talent pools for companies seeking high-quality hires. When a company rehires a former employee (a "boomerang"), it realizes savings in recruitment, training, and retention costs, not to mention the drastically reduced chance of a mishire. In professional service firms, the potential gains also include new business development opportunities; former employees often move into decision-making roles and can become clients.

Company-owned alumni networks benefit from the company resources, and thus typically have the strongest technological capabilities. Because most such companies integrate the alumni network into their exit process, their networks also tend to have larger, more inclusive group of participants.

 Alumni networks range from a couple of hundred participants to more than 100,000 in the case of some large accounting and consulting firms. The benefits that these programs offer suggest that their proliferation will be very rapid. SelectMinds estimates there are now just over 70 company-owned online alumni networks, including 38 run by Select-Minds.[123] The remainder are run internally using in-house technology or software from providers such as Hubbard One. Out of eligible potential members, the average joining rate is approximately 35 percent. Of those registered members, 60 percent visit the network at least once a month.

GRASSROOTS CORPORATE ALUMNI NETWORKS

 More than 38 million people globally have registered for free at Classmates.com, as alumni of over 130,000 schools and 2 million companies.[124] Grassroots alumni networks typically start with one alumnus or alumna who takes the initiative to start a list using a free tool like Yahoo! Groups or Friends Reunited (FriendsReunited.com). One challenge in front of these networks is the lack of a verification mechanism to ensure that participants are bona fide former employees of the companies. In addition, grassroots networks grow mainly through word of mouth; their reach tends to be more limited than that of the company-owned networks. Yahoo! Groups is the largest host of grassroots networks, followed by the workplace alumni section of Classmates.com, and then MSN Groups (Groups.MSN.com).

The most sophisticated grassroots networks, including P&G (PGAlums.com) and Microsoft (MSAnet.org), run virtual communities on their own platforms. However, sophistication usually requires resources, so be prepared for a modest fee to join some of these grassroots networks.

University Alumni

In November 1999, Daniel Zumino, a 1969 Stanford MBA, landed $8 million via e-mail:

> Based in Paris, Zumino used the broadcast e-mail capability of the Stanford Web site to contact alumni in the technology sector. He briefly described a European start-up company in need of investors.
>
> Within 24 hours after his e-mail, Zumino received about 10 replies, including 6 from potential investors, and 4 from people offering help for developing the business in the United States. The most promising contact was a Stanford MBA working in the San Francisco Bay Area for

Andrew Shaindlin is a contributing author to this section. He is the Executive Director of the Caltech Alumni Association and was previously with the alumni organizations at the University of Michigan and Brown University. He is the founder of two online discussion groups: ALUMNI-L, the alumni professionals' discussion group with more than 1,100 members, and MINARY-L, the list server for 250 alumni education professionals. Contact: shaindlin@alumni.brown.edu.

a major venture capital organization. He referred Zumino to the firm's European office, and the investment manager there who took over the project turned out to be a Stanford MBA as well.

With these links established—all via e-mail—the group was well on its way to the regular process of meetings and due diligence, which led to an $8 million venture round in March 2000.

"What struck me," says Zumino, "was that not only did I get quite pertinent responses to the initial e-mail, but the whole process was extraordinarily effective. Literally a matter of days to establish contact in Europe. The longest part of the fundraising process was the legal piece—about six weeks."

Although the speed of the deal was probably unique to the dot-com era, the power of the e-mail medium and ability to leverage a Diverse network was not.

Most of your core networks are fairly homogeneous: they tend to be people from the same industry who live in the same region. University networks are quite different. An alumni population is a pool of educated people who spend several years together and then scatter all over the planet to radically different professional roles. This is extremely valuable to you, because no matter where you are or what you are doing, you will probably find a Relevant graduate of your school. Your university network is resilient over time, easy to evaluate, and Diverse.

There are two categories of online resources that let you leverage your school network: your university's alumni site and commercial sites with an alumni component.

YOUR UNIVERSITY'S RESOURCES

Online resources typically available from alumni associations include:

→ **Directories:** Most universities offer a password-protected "white pages" to give you a way to learn about and contact other alumni. The best ones provide searchable fields that guide you to alumni based on a variety of parameters, such as employer name, job title, and in some cases even special interests, past job experience, or other professional expertise.

Some universities have selected the "opt in" model for their directories, which gives users a much more limited capability. These directories require alumni to proactively visit the school's Web site and "opt in" to being listed in the directory. More effective for building the network's power are the ubiquitous "opt out" systems where alumni are listed with at least rudimentary contact and background information, unless they specifically request to be omitted from the directory. According to William K. Harris, Chairman and CEO of Bernard C. Harris Publishing Co., many opt-out directories will provide contact information for more than 90 percent of alumni.

→ **Campus Personnel Directories:** Most people entirely overlook the power of the campus personnel directory. You can use the faculty directories to reconnect with former professors or their peers. Your former instructors can be a valuable part of your business network. Keep in mind how they might benefit from connecting with you: research funding, student site visits, internships, or additional industry contacts.

→ **Permanent E-Mail Address:** Many colleges and universities offer e-mail forwarding for free to their alumni. This gives people a standardized way to reach you, no matter how many employer and personal e-mail addresses you go through over the course of your life. In addition, the name of your school in your e-mail address shows other alumni that you have a common bond.

→ **Class Notes:** Many institutions now offer online class notes (updates on what classmates are doing). We are used to reading the notes to find out about people we know, but you can use them to learn about people you do not know, and pinpoint fellow alumni who might prove to be highly Relevant contacts for you. Reading the class notes is like reading the transcript from a cocktail party in which only the most successful people speak.

→ **Alumni Job Posting Sites:** Many schools provide proprietary sites for employers to post jobs.

→ **Alumni Résumé Posting Sites:** Hand-in-hand with the job posting services are sites that allows alumni to post résumés for potential employers to view. Even if you are not recruiting an employee, you may want to contact some of the people listed in the site who share your professional interests.

→ **Discussion Lists and Forums:** Your school may provide the chance for people with similar interests or affiliations to interact via group e-mail or Web discussion forums.

COMMERCIAL ALUMNI NETWORK SITES

Several social network sites rely on university and even high school identification to bond members to each other. TheSquare.com, for example, only includes alumni of 39 selective universities. Multischool sites tend to have more sophisticated technology than alumni office sites, because they are commercially funded and developed. Classmates (Classmates.com) and Friends Reunited (FriendsReunited.com) are two other popular sites in this category. As mentioned above, they both have expanded to include alumni of corporations, the military, and other organizations. TheFaceBook.com focuses on serving current college students.

In addition to alumni sites, use other virtual communities to their fullest by listing all schools and colleges you attended in your profile. This will help other alumni identify you as a fellow traveler and increase your chances of making a highly Relevant connection.

9

Blogs (Web Logs)

All the social network sites are a dumbed-down version of what's going on in the blog world.—MARK PINCUS, CEO OF TRIBE NETWORKS, INC.[125]

Attorney Martin Schwimmer reports that at least 20 percent of his firm's revenues is directly related to clients who came through his blog:

Martin Schwimmer is an independent lawyer who represents owners of some of the most famous trademarks in the world. He was formerly a partner at Fross Zelnick Lehrman & Zissu. *Managing Intellectual Property* magazine selected Schwimmer as one of the best trademark lawyers in the United States.

Schwimmer started his blog (SchwimmerLegal.com/blog) in May 2002. He spends approximately 30 to 60 minutes per day maintaining it, primarily commenting on intellectual property news. He needs to keep apprised of the news just to do his job; the marginal cost of his time in maintaining the blog is low, because he is leveraging his preparation time.

His blog has created three networks for him:

1. **Search engine users.** For search terms like "trademark," he is typically on the first page and the highest-ranked lawyer. Clients have approached him solely as a result of his very high search engine placement, which is created largely by the blog.

2. **Fellow bloggers in his space.** The blog keeps him in contact with other bloggers in his sector. Some referrals have come out of that.

3. **Certain clients, colleagues, and practitioners** have become regular readers, and the blog Strengthens his bond with them.

Blogs first gained popularity in 1998, attracted an enormous amount of media attention starting in 2000, and are continuing to grow rapidly. In their simplest form, they are nothing more than an online diary or journal. 8 million people—7 percent of the 120 million U.S. adults who use the Internet— say they have created a blog or Web-based diary.[126]

A teenager's blog entry might read:

I'm still waiting for my CD player to come back to me in the mail. This week makes 4 weeks that i had to live without toonz waiting to get it returned to me after being sent to the factory to get fixed. Im chattin wit K, thats about it. Im cuttin it short cause i having nothing more to converse about. C ya when i c ya, which will probly be soon, since im so bored i have nothing more to do but to waste time typing to me kewl blawg. LMAO, bye![127]

What is so exciting about that? The basic ability to post information on the Web has been widely available since the mid-1990s. Blogs look very similar to traditional message boards.[128]

The answer is that blogs enable a networked conversation between and among people on the Web. Blogs make it extremely easy for even the most inexperienced user to publish content to the Web. Twelve percent of Internet users have posted comments or other material on blogs.[129] In addition, blogs are supported by standardized technologies that allow each blog to reference the information on other blogs. Blogs allow for all the ease of conversation of an industry conference, with all the advantages of virtual communications.

Blogs offer higher visibility and a much larger potential reach than membership-based social networks. They also give you complete flexibility to express yourself visually and verbally and reinforce your personal or company brand. A blog can become a powerful tool for building business relationships.

What Is a Blog?

A blog is a collection of Web pages made up of usually short, frequently updated entries arranged in reverse chronological order. Originally, blogs were used primarily for commenting on other Web sites: news stories, research articles, and so on. This was distinctly different from electronic journals or diaries, which were personal ideas and stories. But because the underlying technology is essentially the same, the two styles have blended, and now there is a continuous spectrum: from personal, "what's on my mind" musings, to collaborative efforts by groups of professional journalists, to the writings of leading businesspeople and politicians. They cover every topic imaginable. Blogs are also growing in popularity within companies and other organizations as a collaborative internal and external communication tool, but that is outside the scope of this book.

 Blog popularity is difficult to measure, as most do not publicly report their readership, and the process of syndication makes their reach much larger than the actual traffic to the individual site. Several sites, such as Technorati.com and Blogdex.net, measure popularity based on inbound links to the blog. This measures not only readership numbers, but also people's attention (i.e., those that people reference in their own blogs are those that people believe are most important).

 Some examples of popular blogs are:

→ **Businesspeople:**

Mark Cuban, Owner, Dallas Mavericks: BlogMaverick.com.

Anita Roddick, Founder of The Body Shop: AnitaRoddick.com.

Jacob Reider, M.D., a family doctor and medical school professor: DocNotes.net (named by Forbes as the #1 medical blog[130])

The **coauthors of this book:** TheVirtualHandshake.com/blog.

→ **Academics:**

Lawrence Lessig, Professor of Law at Stanford Law School and founder of the school's Center for Internet and Society: Lessig.org/blog.

Glenn Reynolds, University of Tennessee law professor: InstaPundit.com (one of the most popular blogs).

→ **Venture Capitalists:** Andrew Anker, David Hornik, Kevin Laws, Naval Ravikant, and Martin Tobias: VentureBlog.com.

→ **Journalist:** Dan Gillmor, columnist for San Jose Mercury News and Silicon Valley.com and author of *We the Media:* typepad.com.

Who writes and who reads blogs? Twenty-seven percent of U.S. Internet users (32 million Americans) report that they read blogs. However, we believe the actual number is much higher, as many Web sites are actually using blog technology without their visitors realizing it.

For example, About.com, the #25 most popular Web destination among

U.S. Internet users,[131] implemented blog technology in May 2003. In January 2004, more than 22 million U.S. Internet users, approximately 15 percent of the total U.S. audience, visited About.com at least once.[132] All Yahoo! Groups are accessible using RSS, a technology primarily used by blogs to publish information in a format appropriate for syndication. Those Yahoo! Groups that are one-way, rather than discussion groups, are now largely indistinguishable from a blog. More than a million Yahoo! Groups exist. Clearly only a portion of those who reported reading blogs were referring to About.com and Yahoo! Groups.

One of the reasons for the rapid growth of blogs is their versatility. You can use a blog for announcements, event calendars, knowledge exchange, or topical commentaries—the same purposes for which people use mailing lists. Readers who use e-mail as their primary form of communication prefer mailing lists for these purposes, while blogs typically provide greater Web visibility and syndication opportunities. A blog reader (discussed below) allows you to get new information from many blogs and other news sources without giving away your e-mail address to all of them and further clogging your e-mail inbox.

We expect these two forms of communication, blogs and e-mail, to merge as the technology evolves. Eventually almost all Web sites will incorporate blog-like technology, and will be used for many more purposes than just the simple "This is my opinion on the latest news" format that many blogs use today.

What's So Special About a Blog?

In the early days of the Web, many companies found that individual departments had set up Web sites without any approval or involvement from corporate management. Today, you see this same phenomenon with blogs and with instant messaging systems. "If the people will lead, the leaders will follow."[133] The fact that people are adopting these technologies without any promotion from corporate management clearly shows their usefulness.

Technologies other than blogging are readily available to make publishing on the Web easy and affordable (Chapter 5). What is it about blogs, then, that has made them so popular?

→ **Ease of use.** Blogs are optimized for the process of commenting on other Web-based content, such as articles, news stories, and other blog posts. You can read something on the Web, press one button on your browser, write your thoughts, press another button, and you are done. This is far easier than the traditional lengthy process of creating and modifying a Web site.

→ **Ease of setup.** Blogging software that allows people to collaborate and keep a shared record of their work can be set up in a matter of minutes at minimal expense, typically with little or no technology expertise.

→ **Blogs are human.** Corporate Web sites are usually so sterile and sanitized as to be totally devoid of any opinion or any real point of view. Educated, skeptical consumers find typical corporate Web sites unfriendly. Blogs, on the other hand, are approachable and encourage dialog. One of the leading companies developing social software for corporate use is Socialtext. Compare the corporate background information at SocialText.com with the company's blog, at SocialText.com/weblog. The corporate backgrounder is dry and impersonal; the blog is personal, always up to date, and reflects the unique human voice of Socialtext's CEO, Ross Mayfield, and his colleagues.

→ **Blogs carry a conversation.** Even when blogs do not carry comments on the blog page itself, bloggers talk about other bloggers and carry on a distributed conversation. There is both a depth and breadth to this "networked conversation" that is not found in traditional discussion forums.

→ **Blogs create and are created by networks.** Bloggers link to other bloggers—in their posts, in their link lists, in their comments, and in other more subtle technical ways. Blogs, therefore, help people connect with others with similar interests. Blogs are supported by a standardized and easy method to reference others' information, and to disseminate that information. Information flows much more smoothly through blogs than through almost any previous method of publishing.

→ **Search engines like blogs.** Blogs tend to produce sites that have exactly what search engines want: lots of keyword-rich pages with frequently-updated content that is heavily and appropriately linked to other content. The number of citations to a given scientific paper is typically a good measure of its authoritativeness. The number of entrepreneurs who know a given venture capitalist is a good predictor of his deal flow.[134] Similarly, the number (and nature) of inbound links is a measure of the credibility of a given Web site or blog. In traditional face-to-face networks, participants do small favors for one another all the time. Blogs allow you to do this very publicly; if you want to thank Martin Schwimmer for helping you out, just link to him. This increases his visibility and his search engine ranking.

Blogs are not a radical innovation; they are the synergy of many other technologies. The unique combination of the features above has fueled their growing popularity.

Anatomy of a Blog

Blogs vary greatly in their design, features, and layout, and few contain all the potential elements. So rather than calling this an archetypal blog, let us call Figure 9-1 a typical blog:

(A) **Header:** The title of the blog and a brief description, perhaps a logo.

(B) **Navigation:** Links to commonly accessed static pages or key blog posts. There is usually a link to a bio and contact information for the author(s).

(C) **Posts:** Blog posts are displayed in order, newest at the top. Multiple recent posts are usually listed on the blog home page.

(D) **Post title:** The topic of the individual post. This will be displayed as the headlines in syndication. It is also often a hyperlink to the individual post (a permalink, defined below).

(E) **Permalink:** This permanent link will still link to the post after it's moved off the front page and into archives. Some blogs use the word "Permalink," but it's also common to use the time of the post or the "#" symbol.

(F) **Comment:** Visitors click on this link to comment on the post and view the comments by other readers.

(G) **TrackBack:** Clicking on this shows a list of other blogs that reference this post.

(H) **Calendar:** Visitors click on a linked calendar day to view that day's posts.

(I) **Search:** Search through the blog posts for particular words.

(J) **Archives:** Posts from earlier months are automatically archived and linked to by week or month.

(K) **Categories or Tags:** Links to show only posts within the selected category.

(L) **Blogroll:** Links to other blogs that the author of the blog reads (supposedly) on a regular basis. People often blogroll blogs for political reasons, i.e., they want the person they are referencing to feel complimented.

(M) **Syndication:** These links provide a feed of the blog's content for use by newsreaders or other conduits through which the blog's information can travel.

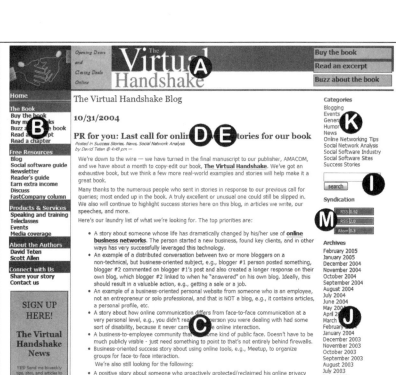

FIGURE 9-1. The Virtual Handshake Blog: Elements of a Typical Blog

Starting a Blog

 There are three ways to operate a blog:

1. **Blog hosting service.** The easiest way to get started with a blog is to use a hosting service. There is no software to install; simply set up your account, decide on a few options, pick a design template, and start writing. The most popular blog hosting services are Blogger.com, LiveJournal.com, and Xanga.com, although they are mostly oriented toward individual use. MSN Spaces and Yahoo 360° are recent entries from two industry giants. SilkBlogs.com, SocialText.com, and TypePad.com offer blog hosting suitable for corporate or professional publishing use. Over 95 percent of existing blogs use a blog hosting service.[135]

2. **Blog software on your server.** This option requires some technical expertise, but it also gives you maximum control over the look and feel of your blog. Movable Type (MovableType.org) and the open-source WordPress (WordPress.org) are particularly popular.

3. **Use blog software to publish pages to your server.** This combines many of the best features of the other two options. The software may be Web-based, like Blogger.com, or may be software running on your local computer, such as Radio UserLand (Radio.UserLand.com).

For your readers who primarily use e-mail as opposed to reading blogs, we suggest that you notify readers of new blog posts via e-mail. Some blogging tools (e.g., Blogger) allow you to e-mail automatically a special e-mail address whenever you post, which you can then direct to a Yahoo! Group or another mailing list platform. Alternatively, the approach we use with The Virtual Handshake Blog is to use summaries of our best recent blog entries as the basis for our regular e-mail newsletter.

 To keep track of the blogs that you read, we recommend that you use a news reader (also known as a RSS reader or news aggregator). It's very inconvenient to visit manually and regularly the blogs that you follow. By plugging all of your blogs into one news reader, you can centralize the information that you are receiving and review it more quickly. Five percent of U.S. Internet users use RSS readers.[136]

News readers may be a Web-based service, such as Bloglines (BlogLines .com) or NewsIsFree (NewsIsFree.com). They can also come in the form of a desktop application, such as NewsGator (NewsGator.com), AmphetaDesk (Disobey.com/amphetadesk), or Radio Userland. Desktop readers offer more features and the ability to read while offline. Web-based readers offer the convenience of access to your personalized collection of newsfeeds from anywhere.

Once you have set up your blog, the number one rule of building a successful blog is to commit to writing regularly. Some blogs consist primarily of long, thoughtful articles (e.g., Clay Shirky's blog, Shirky.com). Others consist primarily of links to other posts, articles, and Web sites, either with or without commentary (e.g., BoingBoing.net). Do not feel obligated to stick to one of these styles: the important thing is that you write.

Why Would Anyone Want to Read What I Have to Say?

Success is sticky. The current "A-list bloggers" will continue to be at the top of the list so long as they keep doing what they are doing. The popularity of blogs follows a traditional power-law distribution, i.e., a very small number of blogs get the majority of the traffic. The most popular are more visible because of their popularity, which in turn attracts more visitors.[137]

So, what is a new blogger to do? If you want your blog to be read by anyone other than a few close friends, you need to do more than just write down your random thoughts. First and foremost, define your target. What topics do you want to cover? Familiarize yourself with what other people are writing in the area you are considering. Is there a hole in the coverage? What is your unique angle? Figure this out before you start, because the blogging community ("blogosphere") does not need any more navel-gazers. John Hawkins, author of the popular conservative commentary blog Right Wing News (Right WingNews.com), wrote: "You have got to be distinctive enough so that readers can pick you out of the herd. If there are 50 other blogs out there talking about the same things you're talking about and saying roughly the same things—well to put it bluntly, why should a reader bother with reading your blog?"[138]

Work on your writing skills. The most popular blogs are well written, even if they may have an informal style. While blogging is great writing practice, please note: it is not that "practice makes perfect," but rather, "perfect practice makes perfect." If you have bad habits, and you practice them, they become even more ingrained and harder to break.

If you are unsure about your writing skills, ask a friend who is a journalist, editor, or author to give you an honest opinion. If you would like help in this area, take a class, or pick up a good book on writing, such as Rudolf Flesch's *The Classic Guide to Better Writing*.

A common question people ask: how can you find time to blog? One answer is leverage: your message board posts, replies to e-mail, and speeches become your blog, which becomes part of a group blog, which becomes your articles . . . which becomes your book.

Another approach is to link more and write less. David Teten runs his personal blog (Teten.com/blog) so that it requires very little time to write and to read. In the course of his work, he regularly comes across Web sites, articles, or tools that would interest his friends. He blogs the item and often will not bother to attach detailed commentary. The marginal cost to him is low, but the marginal benefit to his readers and him is high. Like most people, he occasionally also exchanges detailed e-mails with people about various subjects. He will sometimes convert that e-mail into a blog post, after editing out any personal or confidential information.

Make It Personal

If you are using your blog as a tool to build your network, remember that people relate to people, not to companies. Write in the first person, write in a natural style, and have a genuine opinion. People are tired of corporate-speak, as well explained in *The Cluetrain Manifesto*[139]:

> Conversations among human beings sound human. They are conducted in a human voice. Whether delivering information, opinions, perspectives, dissenting arguments or humorous asides, the human voice is typically open, natural, uncontrived. People recognize each other as such from the sound of this voice. . . .
>
> Corporations do not speak in the same voice as these new networked conversations. To their intended online audiences, companies sound hollow, flat, literally inhuman. In just a few more years, the current homogenized voice of business—the sound of mission statements and brochures—will seem as contrived and artificial as the language of the 18th century French court.

If your blog is professionally oriented, you probably do not want to treat it like a diary and write about everything going on in your personal life. But do not be afraid to talk about yourself and to have a genuine point of view. This is what allows your readers to relate to you as a real person, not some abstraction.

> Fred Wilson, a venture capitalist with Flatiron Partners and Union Square Ventures, runs a blog at AVC.Blogs.com. He primarily writes about business-related issues in the New York area. At the same time, he periodically discusses his three children, music that he likes, and his vacations. Precisely because he discusses those personal aspects of his life, the blog becomes more human and draws more traffic.

The advantage of educating people about you through a blog is that it's a very efficient use of everyone's time. Because we read much faster than we speak, your reader can learn about you in-depth in a fraction of the time it would take in a telephone or face-to-face conversation. While it may take some time for you as the blogger to write your blog, you only have to do it once. You leverage your work with every person who reads you online and whom you meet face to face.

Connecting with Readers and Other Bloggers

The same techniques that help you build a powerful personal network will help you build a large and loyal blog readership. Much of what makes blogs so distinctive are the many ways in which they allow people to connect:

→ **Enable comments.** Blogs are most effective as a relationship-building tool when you invite feedback. While you can simply provide a link to your e-mail, a comments feature built in to the blog is simpler to use and creates a public dialogue.

→ **Blogroll the blogs that you read** by creating a public list of links to them on your blog. Doc Searls coined the term as a reference to "logrolling," defined as the exchange of favors or praise. Blogrolls are a way of publicly connecting with and doing a favor for other bloggers.

→ **Leave comments on others' blogs.** Link back to your own blog (most comment systems allow this in some way), where perhaps you may expand on your comment with a lengthier post.

→ **Reference other bloggers in your posts.** This is perhaps the most important way to connect with other bloggers. In addition to the social value, there is a great deal that goes on behind the scenes technologically when you link to other bloggers' writings.

TrackBack[140] is a technology that sends a notification back to the referenced blog post from the referencing post. If TrackBack is enabled, the receiving blog can automatically build a list of other blogs that reference it, and the author of that blog will generally receive a notification.

Blog search engines also monitor these cross-references in nearly real time. If you have TrackBack enabled, every time a blog post is made, a notice is sent to a centralized notification service. When the blog search engines index your post, they also record which other blog posts you have referenced.

→ **Connect with those who connect with you.** On a regular basis, check the blog search engines to see who is referencing your blog. See what they wrote, and leave a comment. Your Web site traffic statistics and incoming Track-Back notifications are other possible sources for seeing who is reading you.

While the basic concept of blogging is quite simple, the addition of these other technologies adds a significant benefit to blogging as a relationship-building tool by automating much of the process of making connections. Most of these technologies are very easy to set up and use once you are aware of them and how they work.

Promoting Your Blog

The most important way to promote your blog is to connect with other blog-gers, using the techniques and technologies described above. Lee LeFever, an online communications consultant, offers his advice:

> Find the most popular bloggers in your niche—the A-listers—and build relationships with them. If you make the connection and a good impression, they may become a reader and frequent linker (which is what you want). This is an excellent way to build visibility. I have been linked from Scoble and Many-to-Many [two popular blogs in his area of expertise] multiple times and each time my audience grows.[141]

 Three other other ways to promote your blog are more formal:

1. **Syndication.** Syndication allows others to display headlines and excerpts from your blog on their Web site. There are several directories of sites that provide this kind of syndication, and you will want to list your blog in these directories.

   You can also syndicate your posts yourself to a number of sites that offer topical organization of links to articles and posts. These sites are or-ganized by topic, so you will need to select which topic is most appropri-ate for each individual posting. Topic Exchange (TopicExchange.com) and K-Collector (w4.Evectors.it) are popular examples.

2. **Blogging groups within the virtual communities.** Most of the general-purpose virtual communities have at least one group for bloggers. These are good places to make other bloggers aware of your new blog, to discuss blogging in a more direct conversational format, and to request construc-tive feedback on your blog. About.com also has a very popular discussion forum (ironically) for bloggers at Weblogs.About.com/mpboards.htm.

3. **Search engines.** If you follow our recommendations throughout this book, your site will automatically get indexed by most of the major search en-gines. We also recommend manually submitting your site to the major spe-cialized blog search engines.[142]

   These will help you to reach hundreds or even thousands of people with whom you do not yet have a personal, one-on-one connection . . . but may in the future if they become a regular reader of your blog.

Blogs are a tremendous tool for building your network. We are not saying that you should blog instead of participating in targeted virtual networks. We are saying that if you are not blogging, you are missing out on one of the most effective ways to build visibility and Competence online.

10

Relationship Capital Management Software

> each of us is at the center of the universe.
> so is everyone else.—ee cummings

For more than a year, Michael Perrone, 45 years old, tried everything to get a job. With over 10 years in large-scale Unix & Microsoft Systems Administration, he was looking for a position that leveraged his technology background. He had asked all of his near and distant relatives for job. He had sent out literally hundreds of résumés, and had attended huge numbers of networking events.

Perrone saw on craigslist.org that Rainmaker Systems, which provides outsourced sales and marketing services, had a job opening that looked perfect for him. He sent a résumé, but only received an automated response confirming that Rainmaker had received his e-mail.

He started exploring other options to get into Rainmaker (and circumvent the Human Resources screening). He saw Susan Smith, the hiring manager, listed on relationship capital management service LinkedIn. She was a friend of a friend. Perrone sent a cover letter to his friend, who in turn passed it on to Smith.

Rainmaker interviewed two dozen people, and Perrone ended up receiving the offer. "I spent all this effort physically going out and meeting people for job leads, and ended up landing this one by the click of a mouse," says Perrone.[143]

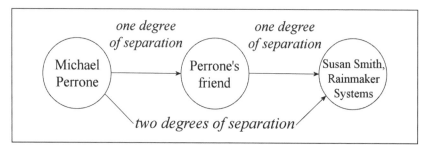

Figure 10-1. Two degrees of separation.

Historically, you knew the people that you knew, that is, you had visibility into your network of only one degree. You usually had only a faint idea of whom your contacts knew.

However, the power of your network multiplies enormously if you can tap the network of your second-degree contacts—your friend's friends. The challenge is visibility. It's difficult enough to track our own relationships. How do we track the relationships of other people?

Relationship capital management software helps you to get better data about the people that you know; to see which people your immediate relationships know; and to learn more about all of those people. Andrew Weinreich, CEO of I Stand For, Inc., and former CEO of Six Degrees and Joltage, said, "You are no more than two degrees from anyone you [realistically would] want to meet. The problem is finding the right two people. The reason for an infrastructure or ecosystem that defines every relationship between people is to ensure that you are always pursuing the shortest and most meaningful path to the target person. The only reason that you may believe that you are further away is lack of Information."[144]

In this chapter, we'll discuss this rapidly-growing area, along with biography analysis software. In Chapter 21, we also discuss how to take full advantage of contact management software.

Your Colleagues Are a Natural Social Network

Relationship capital management software companies, such as Contact Network (ContactNetworkCorp.com), Leverage Software (LeverageSoftware.com), Spoke Software (Spoke.com), and Visible Path (VisiblePath.com), allow you to analyze and leverage the combined professional network of all your coworkers. They help you calculate a path—ideally the shortest path—to the company or person you are targeting. In that way, you can reach almost anyone through a trusted introduction.

These services usually work by indexing your address book, your e-mails, your IMs, and other digital information to analyze whom you know and the

Strength of each relationship. They can aggregate this information across everyone in your company and calculate relationship paths from you, through your colleagues, to many other people. All of these firms view corporate sales teams as the primary purchasers of this technology, but the software has many uses beyond simply sales.

For example, David Teten may have traded many e-mails with Randolph Altschuler, co-CEO of outsourced professional support firm OfficeTiger. However, perhaps David never entered Altschuler's contact Information in his contact manager software. Relationship capital management tools will note that David traded those e-mails and knows Altschuler. Contact Network has found that 92 percent of its customers' searches reveal previously unknown connections to target companies or people, and more than 50 percent of requests to colleagues for an introduction to generate a useful contact.

All of these products have a variety of settings for people to maintain privacy and control of their contacts. In most cases, the software can even be set so that all requests and responses are anonymous, until each coworker chooses to reveal his or her identity.

Enterprise social networks are particularly powerful because they can be enormous; theoretically, a GE employee can reach out to any of her more than 300,000 colleagues for assistance. Fellow employees also have a natural incentive to help one another.

The drawback of proprietary corporate networks is that they are, logically, proprietary. Only employees of a particular firm can join and leverage that tool. If your firm does not have one of these tools you can lobby for it, but you cannot benefit until it is installed.

The Whole World Can Be Your Network

Relationship capital management Web sites such as LinkedIn allow anyone to join and to "link" (publicly indicate a trusted relationship) to other people whom they already know. To join, just register and then invite your trusted professional colleagues to "opt-in" and join as well. Compared with the "opt-out" structure of Contact Network, Leverage, Spoke, and Visible Path, the benefit of this approach is that each relationship between two people is explicitly validated from both sides. The disadvantage is that it requires both parties to join, so the chances of any one particular connection being in the database are significantly lower.

If the person you are trying to meet is in the system, LinkedIn can be invaluable for opening the door. Recipients of requests via LinkedIn communicate directly with *83 percent* of the people who are introduced to them via a gatekeeper relationship.[145] By contrast, any salesperson or job-seeker knows that unreferred e-mails typically have a much lower success rate.

The reason for this high success rate is that recipients receive only requests that their trusted relationships consider worthwhile. Users have total control over which requests to forward to their relationships, and will not forward a request that they think is not worthwhile.

Biography Analysis Software

The Boy Scout Motto, "Be Prepared," applies to business as much as it does to campfires. Before any meeting, we suggest you do some investigation to learn about the history, character, and personality of the person whom you are going to see. There is a tremendous amount of Information about people available online, mostly free.

Let's say the person used to have his biography on the website of Net2Phone, but he has since left the firm and his bio has been taken down. No problem. The Internet Archive (Archive.org) periodically creates a full copy of much of the public web. You can use it to read the website of a firm as it appeared on a date from some time in the past.

Many companies collect and sell biographical Information, which can be very helpful for this sort of due diligence. Among the best known are Dun & Bradstreet and Who's Who. A very useful new service is Zoom Information (ZoomInfo.com), which has compiled records on 24 million professionals in 2 million companies.[146] ZoomInfo continually scans millions of corporate Web sites, press releases, electronic news services, SEC filings, and other sources. From this material, it extracts biographical data on business professionals, and summarizes the Information into an automatically created profile of each person. Users can search for people and companies using job title and education, as well as the size, nature, and location of the firms for which they have worked.

The Expert You Need Is Right Down the Hall

Aventis, a major pharmaceutical company with more than 70,000 employees worldwide, faces continual pressure to discover new drugs and bring them to market more quickly. In particular, Aventis wanted to increase research collaboration within its globally dispersed Drug Innovation and Approval organization. Researchers tended to become siloed in their work. Interviews with scientists also revealed frustrations in being able to find appropriate knowledge that they were sure existed somewhere in the company—for example, being able to find the internal research history of a compound or previous learnings around a particular enzyme.

As part of a corporate initiative to become a more networked enterprise, Aventis saw an opportunity in better connecting people for knowledge transfer and resource sharing, and chose Tacit Software as their solution. In the three-month pilot, Tacit helped Aventis save 7.8

person months in research time. One scientist was trying to develop a macrophage assay by culturing macrophages and using cell sorting. Normally, he would have spent up to two weeks searching through literature to find examples of different protocols on various methods for culturing, and an additional two weeks to identify appropriate cell sorting technology. Instead, he used Tacit software to find other scientists who were able to provide the information and relevant experience he was looking for. This information was not published in any public repository, but Tacit's technology was able to make the connection between these scientists and reduced the research effort by an estimated four weeks.[147]

Companies such as Autonomy (Autonomy.com), Entopia (Entopia.com), and Tacit (Tacit.com) sell software which automates the analysis of unstructured information. Their tools scan employees' data to learn about who knows what and who knows whom. We will not discuss this functionality in depth; our main interest in this family of software is that these companies all include useful tools to analyze corporate social networks.

For example, Entopia advertises these benefits from their social network mapping technology[148]:

→ **Accurately portray the flow of critical information** across the company by leveraging the actual day-to-day employee activity around content.

→ **Ensure that knowledge is reaching all parts of the organization that need it** by gaining insight into—and continuously monitoring—employee interaction and collaboration.

→ **Actively prevent the loss of critical skills from the company** by analyzing the effects an employee departure will have on the remainder of the organization.

→ **Create successful teams, groups, and divisions** through the discovery of individuals with expertise related to a topic and natural communities of practice around certain subject areas.

→ **Understand the dynamic relationships across an organization** without requiring additional action on the part of employees.

This software gives you a picture of the knowledge in your company based not on title, but on actual activity. Unlike traditional manual social network analysis, employees do not need to fill out lengthy surveys or change the way they work with one another.

You cannot use what you don't know. All of these tools in this Chapter help make visible the invisible social networks.

11

Software to Help You Meet Face to Face

I am prepared to meet anyone, but whether anyone is prepared for the great ordeal of meeting me is another matter. —MARK TWAIN[149]

When Sandra Yancey first conceived of eWomenNetwork, an online network for women, she did what any smart entrepreneur would do: market research. The focus groups and studies indicated that women wanted to connect online. In fact, they did not want to meet face to face, because there were already too many meetings to attend.

"You can't always get what you want, but if you try sometimes you might find you get what you need."[150] When the question was hypothetical, the women said they wanted only interaction online. In practice, initiating the relationships online was fine, but many also wanted face-to-face meetings. Within four years after eWomenNetwork launched, the group was holding monthly face-to-face events in over eighty North American cities.

Ecademy and Ryze, two online business networks, both started as face-to-face event organizing companies. They expanded online to help sustain the interaction between meetings, but still offer monthly events at dozens of cities around the world. Even though many of the members only participate virtually, the face-to-face interaction among even a fraction of the members

Strengthens the entire network. As Carolyn Haythornthwaite's research has shown, you can build stronger relationships when you use multiple ways to connect with people (see Chapter 3).[151]

Meetup

The service that practically defined this category was and is Meetup .com. Meetup is a tool for organizing face-to-face meetings for local interest groups. It is based on the simple premise that people with common interests want to meet face to face, not just online. Meetup provides tools for meeting organizers, suggested locations, monthly dates, and times for the meetings, and the easy ability for members to RSVP to indicate if they are planning to attend. Local Meetup Groups are connected globally. There are over 5,000 topics, most all of which have been suggested by members. Organizations and companies can also create branded Meetups with enhanced functionality for a fee. Since its founding in 2002, Meetup has already attracted over 2 million members and 185,000 Meetup groups.[152]

Meetup has been most popular for political and social cause organizing. Meetup attracted attention across the United States in the 2004 presidential campaign, when supporters of the major candidates all used it to organize grassroots support. Howard Dean (most prominently), John Kerry, and Wesley Clark each attracted more than 100,000 members to their respective Meetup groups. Meetup is also popular for connecting members of several virtual communities, including BookCrossing, Slashdot, and LiveJournal. Members of these communities clearly have a desire to meet face to face, but did not have a mechanism for that before Meetup. Meetup is particularly popular in the entertainment industry (filmmakers, screenwriters), and among style and design professionals (graphic designers, interior designers, and fashion designers).

"The biggest surprise for us is that the meetings are turning into longlasting sustainable groups that meet month after month," says Scott Heiferman, CEO of Meetup. "Whether a knitting Meetup, political Meetup, dog Meetup, etc., these people treat their groups like local institutions."[153]

Signing up and showing up for a Meetup may seem like a bit of a stretch outside your comfort zone, but keep in mind that it is for the other attendees, as well. The other people you meet, besides being interested in the topic, are also interested in meeting people, somewhat technologically savvy, and willing to take some chances themselves. That makes for an attractive combination.

Software for Face-to-Face Events

There are several ways in which online tools can augment face-to-face events:

→ **Inviting attendees.** Using an invitation service allows the event organizer to contact invitees without the complexity of an e-mail merge. Simple invitation services, such as Evite, Sendomatic, and rsvpBOOK, allow you to easily send an event invitation to a large number of people and then automatically tabulate their RSVPs.

→ **Handling RSVPs or registration.** Attendee self-registration lightens the work load on the organizer. If you can make the attendee list available to other attendees, that is even better. Cvent offers sophisticated total event management services for professional event planners.

→ **Displaying and discussing the agenda.** Most registration systems allow attendees to provide some sort of comments to the organizer.

→ **Learn more about attendees and connect before the meeting.** This is one of the most important and effective ways in which online tools can enhance face-to-face meetings. By reviewing the profiles of other attendees, you can determine in advance particular people you want to connect with and learn more about them before you meet face to face. Powermingle.com offers online pre-meeting forums for conferences and exhibitions. When social network sites such as Ryze host an event, they allow users to print out beforehand an attendee list with basic profile Information, allowing attendees to research beforehand those people whom they most want to meet.

→ **Sustain dialogue and collaboration after the meeting.** If the follow-up discussion between a few people can be publicly online, other people can contribute their ideas, volunteer their services, and help make connections, even if they were not involved in the particular conversation during the event. This creates a more powerful dialogue than what could otherwise happen: people breaking off into small, private e-mail discussions. The event organizer can facilitate this by highlighting some of the topics of conversation from the event in the group mailing list.

At zero or a trivial cost, any event can become more productive by using some of the tools we discuss in this chapter.

12

The Future of Social Software

→ The future lies in designing and selling computers that people don't realize are computers at all.—ADAM OSBORNE[154]

We see the social software space growing explosively in the coming years. Social networks are the context in which we are born, mature, work, live, and die; more and more technology will inevitably be used to support and extend our networks.

 For more information on current social software technologies, please see TheVirtualHandshake.com. We briefly list below some of the major trends we see in the near future:

Identity Management

One of the challenges in participating in multiple communities is maintaining a consistent identity across all of them. At the same time, many people like the ability to create a different public image on a business site as opposed to a more socially-oriented site. In the future, you will possibly have a single digital identity, which you own and manage independently from the various networks in which you participate. Microsoft's Passport service and the Liberty Alliance (ProjectLiberty.org) are two major initiatives in this area. To allay the very real privacy concerns, we expect the technology to offer an opt-out mechanism.

Interoperability Between Communities

Ken Jordan, Jan Hauser, and Steven Foster paint a vision of this future[155]:

> Today, your online profile and activity on Utne.com has no way of affecting your online profile and activity on iVillage.com. Because each virtual community is conceived and built as a "walled castle," no opportunity is provided for you to have a consistent experience as you go from one community to another. . . . With the coming of federated network identity, this is likely to change; some form of interoperability between online social networks will probably emerge. . . . For instance, once this new functionality is in place, after you review a Grateful Dead album on Amazon.com, you may find yourself greeted with a link to a Grateful Dead discussion page when you enter AOL.

Integration of Collaboration and Social Network Functionality

As more and more people do business with others they meet virtually, a natural evolution will be for them to have their collaboration tools immediately available within the community in which they meet, rather than having to turn to a second system. Peter Quintas, CTO of SilkRoad technology, explains[156]:

> The next logical step of today's social network services is that as you build and grow your network of trusted contacts, you also use it as your daily entry point into communicating with them. You will be able to publish to secure blogs that are only visible to your network. Your network will become your buddy list for instant messaging and group chat, with presence information also available to them. You will be able to communicate through any channel on any device, and that communication will initiate with the address book of your social or business network.

> Once a person is established as a trusted contact in your network, your converged communication tools can be intelligent about delivering messages to multiple channels and devices based on presence (i.e., you receive the message anywhere). You also have the ability to hide bits of personal contact information (like your home phone number), yet still be able to deliver messages to it through the trust relationship.

Integration into Desktop Productivity Tools

Microsoft's Social Computing Group page (Research.Microsoft.com/SCG) lists some of the projects that will likely end up in future versions of their operating systems and desktop applications, including Personal Map, a tool that models a user's social network based upon communication activity such as e-mail and IM.

We also see continued development in some of the newer technologies we've already discussed, particularly mobile applications and peer-to-peer applications. Mobile applications will allow us to take our social network with us wherever we go, and peer-to-peer applications will provide the technological scalability needed as use of these tools becomes commonplace.

Whatever technologies may emerge, it's clear that the overall trend is toward more and better electronic tools to help us build and maintain our relationships.

Part **III**

You Are the Virtual You

→ An image . . . is not simply a trademark, a design, a slogan or an easily remembered picture. It is a studiously crafted personality profile of an individual, institution, corporation, product or service.—DANIEL J. BOORSTIN, *THE IMAGE: A GUIDE TO PSEUDO-EVENTS IN AMERICA*[157]

13

Netiquette

Think before engaging the keyboard.
—INTRODUCTION TO NETIQUETTE FOR THE
RADIO CONTROL SOARING EXCHANGE[158]

From: SexySam2398@AOL.COM
Subject: Experienced Executive Job Applicnt

"Dear Mr,

I honestly do not know if I'd like to work as a researcher or rather be be placed by your company at one of your customer firms. Therefore I have decided to mail you my with resume. I have worked on a few short projects since I lost my full-time gig—I was fired by a crazy boss that no one got along with. But I didn't include those in the resume because these were really short-time assinments. . . . that's why there's a blank space recently. I also completed my Master's degree in Dec of 2003 (please refer to my attached.) Also, I'm also doing some dog-walking now. I am seeking $100 thou plus bonus plus I'm looking for an office where I could bring my pups each day."

— Job applicant to Nitron Advisors

It is painful to count all of the bullets that this candidate has shot in his own foot: grammar errors, spelling, meaning, politeness, and strategy. Unfortunately, any hiring executive can share horror stories of candidates who make these errors and more.

Etiquette matters even more virtually than face to face. People can see how well you observe the local etiquette remotely, but they cannot see how eloquently you speak or how well you are dressed. So they use your level of observance of the rules of etiquette as a proxy for your general professionalism. Our goal in this chapter is to update Miss Manners and Emily Post for your online relationships.

E-Mail Etiquette

Writing is a required skill for entering the ranks of professional employees; half of all companies take writing into account when making promotion decisions. And yet, a third of employees in the nation's blue-chip companies write poorly, and businesses are spending as much as $3.1 billion annually on remedial training. The explosive growth in use of e-mail has particularly increased the need for writing skills.[159] We summarize below some basic ideas which will help you to be a more effective communicator online.

Choose your content

→ **Write only what's worth reading.** George Bernard Shaw said, "Do not do unto others as you would that they should do unto you. Their tastes may not be the same."[160] The litmus tests you can use in evaluating whether to send a message:

- **Is it true,** and have I verified it with a reliable source?

- **Will it add real value** to every person I am sending it to?

- **"What would happen if everyone did this?"** (the Golden Rule of Communication)[161]

→ **Proofread and think "AAAA."** Your message should contain a correct Address, correct Attached files, suitable Attitude, and a clear request for the reader to perform a certain Action.[162] It is important to specify your intentions very clearly when writing an e-mail, particularly a public one. Don't say, "I wanted to get together to talk." Say, "I have been doing a lot of research on [hot issue in the industry], and I would be happy to share with you what I have learned. I am now looking for a new position, and also wanted to see if we could meet to discuss ideas you might have."

→ **Respect privacy.** Never forward or post the contents of someone's private message to you without their consent.

→ **Play nice.** When conversation becomes highly emotional or opinionated, it's easy to forget this simple concept. Of course, we recommend never using curse words or any other language that reasonable people could find offensive.

→ **Include context.** Rather than write just "yes," write "Yes, I think we should hire Nguyen." It's very easy for readers to forget what was being discussed when they wrote you their original email.

→ **Keep it brief.** When David Teten interned at Procter & Gamble, one of the first rules he learned was that all memos should be one page. The same principle applies in e-mail. To prove that we practice what we preach, we have condensed this entire book to just ten bullet points (Chapter 24).

→ **Never ever forward hoaxes, chain letters, virus alerts, or petitions.** The e-mail about Microsoft's alleged "e-mail tracking" is false, as is the e-mail about the rat found in the Coca-Cola bottle. Just delete it. If it looks suspicious, it is. If you feel the urge to investigate, visit Snopes.com, HoaxBusters.CIAC.org, or UrbanLegends.About.com. Inform the sender that he's promulgating silliness, to cure the problem at the root.

→ **Let them know if it is truly urgent.** Trina Hoefling, author of *Working Virtually*, recommends using the phrase, "Please reply by Oct. 4," or something similar, in the subject line.

Write the right subject line

→ **Be as specific as possible in your subject line.** John Caples, author of *Tested Advertising Techniques,* argues that a headline represents 80 percent of the value of an ad. Career strategist William S. Frank argues that the same principle applies to your e-mails.[163] Recruiters are much more likely to read an e-mail with the subject "MBA/CPA/CFO for job A2398" than "Résumé Attached."

→ **Write as much of the e-mail's body as possible in your subject line.** "Confirming lunch Monday noon at Ponderosa" is a great subject line—there is no need to even open the e-mail. However, keep your subject headings to less than 40 characters. Some e-mail programs do not allow recipients to read more than approximately 40 characters in the entire subject line.

→ **When replying to a message, double check that the subject line is accurate.** If you just hit reply, you will merely insert a "Re:" in front of the original subject. Let us say you are looking for Lee's e-mail address. You search for and find a month-old e-mail from her, hit reply, and write a new note. If you do not review the subject line, then the subject line will have no connection at all with the content in your new e-mail.

→ **If a third party refers you, always use that person's name in the subject line.** "Let's meet," is weak. "Ed Reilly referral: meet re: widget sale" is effective.

Format appropriately

→ **Avoid fancy formatting.** Many people have e-mail readers that do not support sophisticated formatting (italics, bold, etc.).

→ **Be polite.** Do not write in ALL CAPITALS; many people perceive it to be the text equivalent of shouting. We also discourage you from using exclamation marks! . . . they make you seem very emotional and heated.

→ **Configure your e-mail client properly, particularly the "From" field.** Sixty-three percent of e-mail users cite the "From" line as the most important factor motivating them to open e-mails.[164] And yet we frequently get e-mails with gibberish like lkasd23498@verizon.net as the sender. We strongly recommend configure your e-mail program so that both your name and your organization show up as the sender. Send a friend a test message to make sure that you have configured your program appropriately.

Respect your reader

→ **Choose the right recipients.** Do not send an invitation to your house-warming party to your entire contact list, including your friend who just moved to Chile last week.

→ **Always use either mail merge or blind carbon copy (BCC) if sending the same e-mail to many people.** This will prevent replies from recipients going to all the original recipients. In addition, it preserves the privacy of the e-mail addresses of your correspondents. Many e-mail spam filters reject or flag e-mails where the recipient is in the BCC field. For that reason, an e-mail merge is preferable, although it may take more effort. We strongly recommend investing ten minutes to learn how to use e-mail merge in your word processor. This is an invaluable tool for keeping in touch with a large Number of people.

→ **Do not hit "Reply All" unless absolutely necessary.** Much of the time, you are simply clogging others' inboxes with unnecessary carbon copies.

If you are not confident in your e-mail communication skills, we suggest that you BCC a close, perceptive friend on important, non-confidential e-mails. Your friend can give you advice on how to make your communication more effective.

Etiquette for Virtual Communities

Reaching out to a virtual community without thinking is an excellent way to damage your public image.

Johnson is a member of a virtual community for senior executives. One day, he received an e-mail that encouraged people to delete a Windows file that allegedly was created by a certain virus. Trying to be helpful, he forwarded that e-mail to the entire list. A number of people deleted that file (which was actually an important system file) before a technically knowledgeable person on the list sent out an e-mail correcting Johnson.

Johnson demonstrated bad judgment in front of several hundred colleagues and wasted their time. He also potentially damaged their computer systems.

A virtual presence can be powerful for rapidly building your perceived Competence. A higher Number cuts both ways: more people can see your contribution, but more people see you when you make a foolish error.

If you observe the simple rules below, you will avoid stepping on virtual toes:

→ **Follow the house rules.** Any sophisticated virtual community will have an "About Us" or "Policies" section in which you can learn the local etiquette. For example, some have one (and only one) day a week on which promotional messages are allowed. It's the responsibility of the group moderator to make that information clearly and easily available, and the responsibility of all participants to know and follow the rules.

→ **Lurk before you leap.** Observe the conversational content and style of the group and be sure it's aligned with your purpose and principles before posting. Follow the conversational style of the group (i.e., formal and academic versus informal and chatty).

→ **A good posting may address multiple points, but only one major topic.** Addressing unrelated topics is confusing and makes it difficult to connect your post to the conversation. However, addressing multiple points from the same conversation in a single post is preferable to responding to each person's point individually, as it would cause the number of messages to grow out of control if everyone responded individually to everyone else's posts.

→ **Each post should be relevant to the entire community and make a point that other people have not made.** Do not send e-mails to the whole group consisting only of brief lines, like "Congratulations" or "Thank you"; better that you send those e-mails directly and privately to the recipient.

→ **Cross-post with care.** "Cross-posting" is the act of posting the same message to more than one group or list. If people receive from you more than two or three copies of the same message via different lists, it will likely be perceived as spamming. That said, there are certainly circumstances in which cross-posting makes sense.

→ **Keep your quotations of earlier contributions short.** Many online postings draw on earlier dialogue. If you simply reply and automatically include the earlier e-mails, you will create an unnecessarily long contribution, which will annoy other people. Use ellipses (". . .") or summarize.

→ **Do not send abusive, obsessive, or blatantly self-promotional e-mails.** Also, do not share confidential membership lists with anyone.

→ **Make connections when there is a good reason, not randomly.** In many small virtual communities, announcing that you have joined the group and mentioning your background and interests is standard etiquette. However, make sure you know the posting guidelines of the specific group before blasting out an e-mail announcing your arrival.

→ **Be professional in all your interactions.** Maintain appropriate boundaries between your professional and personal life virtually, just as you would face to face.

→ **When in doubt, don't post.** You're much better off only writing when you have something substantive to say. Never write anything that you're not prepared to see printed in the newspaper or given to your boss . . . ten years from now.

Greetings and Closings

Just as with traditional paper letters, use greetings and closings with your e-mails. Your e-mails will look both more polite and more thoughtful. The greeting can simply be your correspondent's name.

Rob,
How are you? Are you free for lunch on Friday?

Writing "Dear Rob" usually looks strangely formal and is not appropriate for many e-mails. There is one major exception: e-mails which are explicitly formal and introductory business letters. For example, cover letters for résumés or proposals for a business project should use the standard "Dear Mr. Labatt" introduction.

The closing can be your name. It may also include a closing line, such as "regards" or "sincerely." We do not recommend "sincerely yours" or other classic closings typical of printed business letters. Part of the power of e-mail is its informality; you can weaken the bond between you and your recipient if your language makes the e-mail seem more formal.

Please use a signature file, which we cover in detail in Chapter 14.

"Hello, My Name Is. . . .": Introducing Yourself

"SUBJECT: A crazy twist of fate for an introvert. . . .

"Hello everyone. . . . Happy to be a new member. And a new entrepreneur.

"I had been in sales for about 10 years but always wanted to own my own business. While competing at the Salt Lake City Winter Olympics, a friend in Houston asked if I would consider speaking at his son's school. I spoke to them about chasing your dream in life and what I had done to make my Olympic Dream a reality, and it went so well that I've been a Professional Keynote speaker ever since.

"I now speak at conventions, corporate events, schools, and churches everywhere. Lots of sales groups.

"The funny thing is I never thought about becoming a speaker. I'm actually an introvert. But put me in front of a crowd and ask me to speak about the Olympics and how to make your Dream come true, and the Passion comes out!

"Feel free to visit www.TheLugeMan.com and please pass the word about my services if you know anybody who's having an event.

"Looking forward to getting to know you all.

"Ruben Gonzales"[165]

Does this sound like someone you would like to meet? In just a few short sentences, you know that Ruben is articulate and passionate and has an interesting story to tell. While it is self-promotional, it does not come across as a canned sales pitch—it is natural and appropriate to the context (the Entrepreneurs Network on Ryze).

When a small group meets face to face and many of the participants do not know each other, it's customary for everyone in the group to introduce themselves. In a larger group (above perhaps 25 people), it becomes impractical, as it would simply take too much time and be impossible to remember.

The same is true virtually, although the size threshold may be a little higher. Just as in face-to-face meetings, the culture that the participants want in the group determines whether or not introductions are appropriate. Introductions, and the inevitable "welcome" messages that follow, tend to create a friendly and chatty environment. Be sure to post the policy clearly if you are the moderator, and know the policy if you are a participant.

In those communities where introductions are acceptable, we recommend it contain most or all of the following elements:

→ **A smile:** Be upbeat and friendly.

→ **Your expectations:** Why are you joining? What are you hoping to learn? How can the group be of service to you?

→ **Short, relevant history:** History creates context; context creates meaning. This will help people better frame your comments.

→ **What you do now that relates to the group's interests:** Create a mental picture.

→ **Share something personal to break down barriers:** This is one of the quickest ways to gain trust and develop a sense of camaraderie. By giving trust to the members of the group, even with a seemingly small issue, they are inclined to reciprocate. For example, talk about your pets.

→ **Invite people to connect with you:** You are not trying to sell people on your product or service, but you are trying to "sell" people on the idea of connecting with you. This is your "call to action."

→ **Affirm your commitment to participate:** Close with an affirmation that you are in the group to give, not just receive.

This will make a memorable first impression, especially if the majority of other messages consist essentially of "Hi, my name is Mary and I'm looking forward to making new friends and customers. Please visit my Web site."

In those groups in which introductory messages are prohibited, you can still introduce yourself, but in the context of participating in the conversation. The safest way to join in is with your thoughts on a current conversation, especially if you have relevant experience. Alternatively, you can start a new conversation with a question. For example:

> Hi everybody! My partner and I are starting an import/export business in Australia (we live there), and we almost have our first deal stitched up. However, if anyone out there has ideas/comments on setting up distribution channels, ANY advice would be welcome—what works, what doesn't, etc.
> Thanks (in anticipation!)
> Fred Whitson[166]

"I'd Like to Introduce You to. . . .": Introducing Your Colleagues

When you are introducing two people in the same room, just saying "Ziad, I'd like you to meet Sanjay" is usually sufficient. Ziad and Sanjay will feel obliged to have some brief discussion to find out common interests. Adding an extra sentence explaining why you think the two people will meet is helpful but not mandatory. For example: "I should mention that Sanjay is a biotechnology professor, and Ziad's fund does a lot of work in that area." At that point, they are under a certain social obligation to talk to each other.

Online, the situation is very different. Many people are so overloaded with e-mail that they simply cannot (or do not) reply to much of their e-mail. If you feel the introduction is worth the time and effort to make, it's worth the time and effort to do it right by providing context and giving both parties a convincing reason to follow up. The following outline will help you make an effective introduction:

→ **Who you are:** If the person you are contacting may not recognize you immediately by name, you should start with a brief reminder as to who you are and how they know you.

→ **Your reason for writing:** "I wanted to introduce two people who I think would really enjoy one another's company."

→ **Who you are introducing:** "I'd like you to meet my friend Jamie McLaughlin."

→ **Background on the person being introduced:** You do not have to go into great detail. It's best to give a link to their Web site or their profile page.

→ **How the person being introduced can benefit the recipient:** Why is this worth the recipient's time and effort to follow up?

→ **Encouragement to the parties to connect:** While this may seem obvious, the encouragement clearly shifts the responsibility for follow-up to the other parties and helps create a stronger sense of social obligation. If you are making an unrequested introduction, simply repeat for both parties.

Making these introductions is one of the most important aspects of growing your social network virtually. The following story from software developer Ron Lichty about an introduction made via LinkedIn, illustrates this well:

One of the things that's cool about this LinkedIn thing that's totally a side effect is that you get to be part of your friends' connections.

The sequence that drove this particular realization to surface was that Aaron Ludtke wanted to contact Ted Goldstein. The relationship chain looked like this:

Aaron Ludtke -> Ron Lichty (me) -> Tom Chavez -> Ted Goldstein

Aaron and I worked together at Apple, and are now co-chairs of the Software Architecture and Modeling Special Interest Group (SAM-SIG) of SDForum [a Silicon Valley networking group]. Tom was my first employee (both ever and at Apple—though Aaron and Tom probably ran across each other there 15 years ago).

Ted, as a senior architect and a VP at Sun, presented a technology he was responsible for to my team at Schwab in 1997–98 in some pretty intensive meetings. However, it was too long ago for me to count on his remembering me, and it was peripheral enough that we wouldn't just up and reconnect our networks.

Being part of your friends' connections is interesting for several reasons. Aaron sent me a request to meet with Ted. As Aaron's request went through me, I passed it on with this introductory note to Tom:

> Did you know Aaron at Apple? He was on the CPU software team for the high-end Power Macs. Since then he's been at Sony where he's been awarded over two dozen patents and counting, and was on the Firewire team, which he knows a LOT about. Aaron last month was my co-founder of the Software Architecture and Modeling SIG of SDForum. Getting to know him in that capacity (very well!), I'm enormously impressed with his innovative skills—I think Ted would find Aaron to be a good addition to his personal network—if nothing else! Please also say 'hi' to Ted for me—he and his Sun team presented their technology to my team in '97–'98.

This note had the following effects:

→ **Benefits to Sender**

- **I got to shine lights on Aaron he might not be able to shine on himself—he's much better off for having used LinkedIn instead of a direct e-mail.** Ted is much likelier to want to meet with Aaron for the addition of my comments about him.

- **Those additional lights add flavor and character that increase discussion opportunities.**

- **My asking Tom to send my own greetings to Ted should also benefit Aaron.** It reminds Ted that he knows me, and so Ted is hearing not just from Tom but also from me that he should connect with Aaron.

→ **Benefits to Intermediaries**

- **I just evangelized the SAM-SIG to two more people.** In fact, Ted referred to it in his response back to Aaron—he'd been to the SAM-SIG Web site, looked at the upcoming program on Model Driven Architecture, and asked Aaron to send his own greetings on to our two speakers.

- **I just re-connected to Ted myself**—it's still a weak relationship, but now it's a recent weak relationship, not just a long-ago one.

- **I may have just re-connected Aaron and Tom,** if they ever knew each other. Either way, I've provided them opportunity to network at some future time.

My first point above seems to be lost on some users of the LinkedIn system. I regularly get queries from people who want me to give them the e-mail address of the person I'm linked to, instead of using the LinkedIn process. People aren't getting the subtle benefit of having the intermediary people stamp their imprimatur onto their résumés. Being part of a query strengthens everyone's network!

How Not to Be Confused with Spam

The rising tide of commercial e-mail spam is so great that e-mail is becoming less and less effective as a communications tool. One estimate is that an absurd 90 percent of all e-mail traffic today is spam.[167] To write Competent e-mails, it is critical to avoid letting a spam filter or your reader mistakenly process your e-mail as spam.

Because of the anti-spam backlash, the United States Congress passed the CAN-SPAM Act effective January 1, 2004. The European Union and other countries have passed or are considering similar legislation. For the most part, all you really need to do to observe these laws is observe basic e-mail etiquette.

We generally recommend customizing each e-mail. For example, one prominent activist investor has two assistants who work full-time on managing his network. When he sends out an e-mail to selected people on his list with some material (e.g., a news article about a mutual friend), he and his assistants first use an e-mail merge program. They then make sure to add personalized comments to each e-mail (e.g., "Has the baby said his first words yet?"). They will typically add those custom comments to 1,000 out of 1,200 e-mails sent, making the e-mails far more effective as a vehicle for keeping in touch with people.

If you are sending out bulk e-mails to thousands of people you have no prior connection with, you are probably sending spam, and we vehemently discourage the practice. We summarize below some questions to ask yourself before sending the same e-mail to more than a dozen people.

→ **Is your subject line accurate, honestly self-descriptive, and concise?** Forty characters, or five to seven words, is a reasonable limit.

→ **Do you have permission to e-mail?** You should have either a preexisting relationship with the recipient, explicit permission to include the person on one of your e-mail lists (he has "opted in") or be sending one personal e-mail that is clearly personalized.

An e-mail that starts, "Dear Mr. Kumar, I write because I would like to offer my Web design services," will probably be perceived as spam, precisely because you could send the same e-mail to almost every business in America. However, if you mention who referred you, or say that you admire the blue and white color scheme on Mr. Kumar's home page, then it will be clear that this is a customized e-mail written by a human. Your response rate will be much, much higher.

There is one conventional exception to the "opt-in" rule that a person must explicitly choose to be on one of your mailing lists: any time you have a major career change, you're permitted to send a "professional update." For example, when you switch jobs, move to a new city or publish a book, we recommend notifying almost everyone in your contact database, even though they did not explicitly opt in to a formal mailing list. Keith Ferrazzi, author of *Never Eat Alone: And Other Secrets to Success, One Relationship at a Time*, sent out an e-mail to most of his contact list upon the recent publication of his book. While it was certainly promoting the book, the opening sentence clearly set the tone: "I wanted to reach out to you because it's a really great moment in my life."

→ **If you sent a person an e-mail based on your mailing list, is it clear how people can unsubscribe from that mailing list?** Even if they explicitly subscribed a month ago, they may change their mind. Ideally, they should be able to unsubscribe with just one click. All requests to unsubscribe must be processed within ten days.

→ **Is your physical address included in your e-mail?** Including your address is a good general practice. In addition, the CAN-SPAM act explicitly requires that you include this information when sending commercial mass mailings.

If you want to double-check that your own e-mails will bypass spam filters, run your message through a program that analyzes e-mails for potential problems, such as ContentChecker (www.lyris.com/contentchecker). See SpamLaws.com for the actual laws, plus articles and cases in the United States, European Union, and other countries.

Flame On

People are much more prone to e-mail deliberately hostile and insulting messages virtually than they would be to say hostile and insulting statements face to face. This is called "flaming." A few reasons for this very consistent phenomenon: your counterpart is not sitting in front of you and so does not seem "real"; the medium contains less little emotional content than a face-to-face meeting; and it seems easy to extricate yourself and never have to interact with the other person again.

Some ways to prevent escalation around emotionally charged conversations:

→ **Remember the human.** Remind yourself: a real human is sitting on the other end of the message you received. Correspond with her with respect.

→ **Assume good intent.** If something you read upsets you, reread it, thinking what the best possible intention could have been when they wrote what they wrote. This is a major advantage of virtual communication, as this would be difficult to do in person. "Excuse me, could you please repeat that? What you said really ticked me off, and I want to hear it again and see if I can not get so ticked off."

→ **You are never backed into a corner online.** Face to face, you can end up stumped for an answer, feeling like you have to fill an awkward pause. This frequently causes people to say misleading things to get out of an awkward spot. How many times in the real world have you wished you could take back what you said? There is no Backspace key in the real world; take advantage of that magic button in the virtual.

→ **You do not have to answer immediately.** Give yourself a "buffer zone"— time to reflect on what you wrote before it goes out. Whenever you write a potentially volatile, sensitive, or just lengthy message, compose it off-line and review it closely before sending.

→ **E-mail is forever.** Do not write anything publicly that could potentially come back to haunt you, even in private. What happens if a potential employer searches on your name and uncovers a scathing flame that you wrote in a newsgroup?

→ **Provide context.** All too often, we just write short little bursts without framing them. Make no assumptions about what the other person knows about your perspective. The context does not have to be extremely short—this is a dialog, not an executive report. Providing context ("Growing up in Belarus, I didn't know . . .", and so on) will help people not only understand what you are thinking, but why. We are all more empathetic and compassionate when we understand the other person's motivation.

Personal Publishing Standards

Blogs and other self-publishing vehicles may have an informal style, but they are a form of publishing and should hold by certain standards. As Rebecca Blood, author of *The Weblog Handbook,* says in her discussion of blog ethics:

> Journalistic codes of ethics seek to ensure fairness and accuracy in news reporting. By comparison, each of these suggestions attempts to bring transparency—one of the blog's distinguishing characteristics and greatest strengths—into every aspect of the practice of blogging. It is unrealistic to expect every blogger to present an even-handed picture of the world, but it is very reasonable to expect them to be forthcoming about their sources, biases, and behavior.[168]

Blood proposes a set of core ethical rules, which we've adapted and expanded here[169]:

→ **Keep your readers in mind.** Do not carry on a private conversation in public. In general, when responding to posts by others (particularly bloggers), it's best to address them in the third person, not second person. Speak to your readers, not one other person. Avoid inside jokes and specialized jargon.

→ **Clearly distinguish fact from opinion or speculation.** You are not expected to adhere to journalistic standards of fact checking. However, if you do not have an authoritative source for your information, make that known.

→ **Link to referenced material if it's available online.** By providing a link to the original source, your readers can see the information in its original context and decide for themselves if they agree with your perspective. You also help the creator of the content, both by driving some traffic directly to them and by increasing their link ranking.

→ **Credit your sources back to the original source.** If you read about a story on another blog or an e-mail list, credit that source, not just the original story. If your source learned about it second-hand, credit the entire chain. For example:

via <u>Jason Calacanis</u> via <u>Nick Denton</u> via <u>Marc Canter</u>

Each name in the sample above is a link to the entry by that person regarding the topic. This serves three purposes. First, it gives credit where credit is due. Second, by linking to their posts on a blog, the various back-end technologies described in Chapter 9 will associate your post with theirs. Depending on how their blog is configured, it will likely make them aware of your posting, letting them know that you have joined the distributed conversation on this topic. Third, this will also increase your visibility to anyone searching for discussion of the topic.

If you find yourself frequently basing your writing on others' research, you should probably start reading more original sources. The greatest influence in the blogosphere goes to people who write original material and/or who are the first in the community to call attention to interesting or valuable new information.

→ **On blogs, add to, but do not rewrite or delete, any entry.** This maintains the integrity of the larger network. Consider if another blogger had linked to your story based on your original information. If you correct your post without clearly noting the correction, if someone reads their post and clicks through to yours, it will make it look as if the other blogger is in error . . . when in fact it is you who was in error.

If you have a correction or addition, note it clearly. For small corrections, strike through the original wording and then put the corrected wording. For example, "I met Jenny Meadows back in January. ~~An expatriate South African living in Austin~~ A native Texan with a love of South Africa, where she visits as often as the law will allow, Jenny is a copy editor, and has been very successful in growing her business through Ryze."[170]

For more extensive corrections, clearly note the addition with an initial word, such as "CORRECTION:" or "UPDATE:."

→ **Disclose any potential conflicts of interest.** The risk you run in doing this is that people may question your motives. On the other hand, if you do not disclose a possible conflict of interest yourself, and it ever becomes exposed, what you have written will immediately become suspect, as will your Character. The easiest way to do this: in the "About me" portion of your blog or online profile, point out the major conflicts of interest you may have.

→ **Note questionable or biased sources.** If your source has a strong bias, letting your readers know that up front will help them better understand the referenced material.

Following these guidelines will help make it clear to your online audience that you are a person of high Character and serious Competence.

14

Manage the
E-Mail Deluge

> I believe in opening mail once a month,
> whether it needs it or not. —BOB CONSIDINE[171]

Sharon Drew Morgen is a busy author, consultant, and trainer who could easily have an assistant respond to her e-mail, or even handle many of them
with automated responses. But she does not. She explains:

"I have several contact points with subscribers—e-mail newsletters and subscription for same, ebook purchase data, tape purchase
data, etc. I use every single contact I get as a reason to make a new
connection, even if it's quick. If I get subscribers the week after the
last newsletter, I send them my copy of the one they missed with a
note. If it's just before the next one is coming out, I send a note telling
them to be patient. Folks in the middle of the month get a note telling
them what they missed and sending them to the archives. I have a system that could automate this for me, but it wouldn't be ME doing it;
the personal touch is important.

"Every single note I get, every question, every problem, is an excuse to touch someone personally. I only get about a 20 percent response rate, but from these responses I've gotten clients, business partners, and speaking engagements world wide—last one in Hong Kong,
from when I got a "Dear Sirs" note asking if a group in Hong Kong could
read one of my white papers at their conference. Why weren't they having me do it in person? They couldn't afford my fee . . . but they ended

up paying my expenses to Hong Kong, and I spoke for 'free' and met a huge number of potential clients, some of which I've already done business with.

"I also read voraciously in my field, and contact each author of each article that I believe I can add to—or at least start a conversation.

"I send out approximately 100 e-mails a day, and receive and read double that. I put 2–4 hours a day into this—every day, often at night when the rest of my day is done. Then, when I come in in the morning, I have responses."

A large network leads inexorably to a large volume of e-mail. According to one survey, 65 percent of white-collar workers spend more than three hours per day on e-mail.[172] If you cannot handle that flow, then you will feel out of control and stressed. If you are slow in responding to e-mail, people will also perceive you as being poorly organized.

As a general rule, we recommend you choose the time when you get interrupted by e-mail. Most people configure their e-mail reader to interrupt them every time an e-mail comes in. This means that you are being interrupted throughout the day. Instead, we suggest keep your e-mail reader closed most of the day. Only check e-mail once a day. That way, you avoid the unhealthy pattern of working 10 minutes; dealing with a new e-mail; working for another 10 minutes; being interrupted again. E-mail is rarely *that* urgent, and if it is, the sender should be using the telephone or instant messaging.

Manage Your Inbox

According to another study, the average North American white-collar worker receives more than 54 e-mails per day.[173] If you are feeling deluged by the endless amount of e-mail, you will find it difficult to manage a large Number of relationships.

How exactly you manage your e-mail is a very personal decision. Rather than lay out a very specific e-mail organizational system, we list here the rules that we've found in common across all of the effective systems we've seen, including our own.

→ **Keep your inbox empty.** This is the overriding principle of effective e-mail management. Mark Hurst, President of CreativeGood consultancy, draws an analogy to the video game Tapper. In that game, you play a bartender who has to serve beer to incoming customers as they stride towards the bartender. Whenever the bartender fails to serve a customer, that customer reaches the bartender's work area and is, well, very dissatisfied. Similarly, if you do not quickly respond appropriately to every e-mail you get, you will rapidly lose control of your entire workflow.[174]

David Allen, in *Getting Things Done: The Art of Stress-Free Productivity*, suggests a simple system for handling all of the many tasks—including e-mails—that cross your desk. First, he says, "If there's something that needs to be done about the item in 'IN', then you need to decide what exactly that next action is. 'Next action' . . . means the next physical, visible activity that would be required to move the situation toward closure."[175] You then have three choices with each item (including e-mails):[176]

- **Do it:** If the "next action" can be done in two minutes or less, do it when you first pick the item up. Two minutes is roughly the break-even point when it takes longer to store and track an item than to deal with it the first time.

- **Delegate it:** If you are not the most appropriate person to do the next action, forward it immediately to the person who is.

- **Defer it:** Place into your organization system as an option to do later.

→ **Organize around action, not data.** One simple way to organize your e-mail might be to create a folder for each project you are working on. However, this would make it impossible for you to quickly look at your e-mail and answer the questions, "What do I need to do next?" or "Who do I absolutely have to respond to this week?" Instead, organize around your required action. We recommend the following high-level organization:

- **Inbox:** This should be only a temporary holding bin until you decide what the next action is and place it in an appropriate bucket.

- **Deadline-driven:** Create a separate folder for each of your upcoming deadlines (by week, project, and so on). Place the messages in the folder appropriate for the deadline driving each one.

- **As soon as possible (ASAP):** Many people think this means "super-urgent," but in reality, it usually means "anytime in the next month." If it has a deadline, place it in the deadline-driven folders. You should organize these by priority, to distinguish between the "must dos," the "should dos," and the "nice to dos."

- **Delegated:** This is for items that you have delegated to other people and are awaiting a response. David Teten uses his "Sent Items" for this purpose, because so many of his e-mails are requests to employees/partners to do various tasks. He periodically reviews his "Sent Items" folder, and if someone did not respond to a request, then he can ping the person and remind him to take care of that task.

- **Archive:** Everything that no longer requires any action by you goes here. You may choose to organize this by project, customer, date, or whatever works for you. It may be simplest just to use your "Deleted Items" folder as a temporary archive.

→ **Save everything.** You never know when you will need to look up an old acquaintance or confirm an agreement. Disk space is cheap. The only things you should really delete are spam, e-zines you have finished reading and do not want to save, and notifications of new messages elsewhere (such as a discussion forum).

→ **Organize just enough.** Use a combination of organization and search to find the e-mails you need. Even though new search technologies are making high-speed searches of your e-mail practical, a few high-level categories will still help you narrow your searches. However, a complex, multilayer folder structure is burdensome to maintain and can actually make it more difficult to find what you seek. As a rule of thumb, you want to have no more folders than you can see on one screen. This allows you to properly file any message with a single mouse motion.

→ **Review regularly.** Perhaps the most difficult part of mastering your e-mail, yet one of the most important, is developing regular processing and maintenance habits. We recommend these review cycles:

- **Daily:** Once a day, clean out your inbox completely. Do it, delegate it, defer it, or file it as done. Process your Sent Items folder, archiving all of the e-mails other than those which require you to follow up.

- **Weekly:** Review your ASAP folders for tasks to do and tasks that can be archived. Whenever you plan your week, review your deadline-driven items and your delegated items for actions to schedule.

- **Monthly:** Update your folders. Move completed projects into the archive area. Delete folders for deadlines that have passed. Trim down so that your active folders do not fill more than a screen.

- **Yearly:** It's rare that you will need to refer back to e-mails more than a few months old, particularly from completed projects. At least once a year, go through your archive and move obsolete folders into a separate archive file.

→ **Keep your file sizes manageable.** Your folders can easily grow gargantuan with a year's worth of e-mail. Many backup programs have difficulty processing large files, and searches of a large archive may become painfully slow. To avoid this problem, we suggest creating a series of folders for your old e-mails, sorted by date. For example, "Archive 2005-January," "Archive 2005-February," and so on.

→ **Filter spam.** You can automatically filter the e-mails with the markings of spam in a "Suspected Spam" folder. Review that folder once a week. Just

```
Inbox
    1-Deadlines
        2005-02-10 Publisher's deadline
        2005-03-09 The Virtual Handshake course [about online networks]
        2005-06-01 BookExpo [include travel info and other details]
        [etc.]
    2-ASAP
        A-Must do! [includes the very few actions that don't have a
            deadline]
        B-Should do
            Bulk mail [mailing lists and discussion forum message
                notifications]
            Events [that he might like to attend or recommend]
            Job leads [for Scott or friends]
            Reading [newsletters, news alerts, and articles]
        C-To Do Eventually
    3-Delegated/Requests
        A-Jayne
        B-Assistant
        C-David Teten
        D-Clients
    4-Archive
        A-Projects
            Book - The Virtual Handshake
            Entrepreneurs.About.com
            FastCompany.com column
            LinkedIn classes
            [etc.]
        B-Reference
            Accounts [login info, statements, etc., from e-commerce sites,
                banks, etc.]
            Articles/research
                Entrepreneurship
                Social networks
                Social software
                Writing/book industry
                [etc.]
            Links
            Résumés
Outbox
Sent Items
Suspected Spam
Deleted Items
```

FIGURE 14-1. Scott Allen's Folder Structure

by looking at the subject headings and sources of those e-mails, you should be able to determine if your filter has accidentally kept you from seeing some e-mails that you wanted to see. Once you have reviewed the Suspected Spam folder, simply delete all of the remaining e-mails there.

As a template, we have included Scott Allen's folder structure below. He uses the numbers and letters at the beginning of the folder names in order to make his e-mail program (which sorts alphabetically) show the folders in the preferred order (see Figure 14-1).

Managing Your Bulk E-Mail

E-mail discussion lists and Web-based discussion forums can be great for learning, but they can also clog your inbox. We combine them here for purposes of discussing how to manage bulk e-mail from lists and forums.

→ **Separate your discussion list messages and Web forum notifications from your regular correspondence.** Otherwise, you will be tempted to handle messages as they come in, which is very inefficient. These messages are almost never both urgent and important, so they do not belong in your main inbox. Set up e-mail rules to route all of them into one or more folders.

→ **Set aside time to work in a batch.** Handle your e-mail when you choose to rather than when it happens. Being known for jumping right on top of every question asked is probably not the reputation you want to have. You hog the conversation and make it appear that you have nothing better to do with your time. Instead, set aside time once or twice a day to read and respond to your discussion lists. This is also more time efficient.

→ **Scan (and delete) by subject.** In many Web forums, conversations will already be organized by topic or discussion thread. For your mailing lists or for message notifications from a Web-based forum, sort the messages by subject in your e-mail program. Scan the subjects and delete (or skip in a Web forum) those that do not immediately interest you. This may be a very high percentage of them. Be ruthless. Yes, you might potentially miss one valuable message, but consider that you miss millions of other potentially valuable messages every day that you are never even seeing in the first place.

→ **Read the first, the last, and the rest . . . in that order.** If the first message interests you, go to the end of the messages you have on the topic, and pick out someone whose opinion you respect. Read what they have to say, and then decide if the rest of the conversation is worth reviewing.

→ **Read all, reply once.** Do not try to reply to every single person who has posted on a topic. Read all the replies, and craft a single response that addresses everyone. You help maintain a reasonable volume of messages, plus

you have the opportunity to be more reflective and thoughtful in your reply, thus being more likely to add value to the community. You also avoid
repeating what someone else has said or answering a question that has
already been answered.

You position yourself better as an expert by being very circumspect in
what you say, and by considering the different perspectives that have
been presented. If you are there primarily to learn, this technique is the
virtual equivalent of being a good listener.

Following these techniques, you can easily participate effectively in
dozens of discussions and even handle several hundred messages a day in just
a few minutes daily. You do not have to have a high level of activity in these
discussions to create value both for the community and for yourself.

Lifetime E-Mail Address

A lifetime e-mail address gives you the security of knowing that people
will always be able to reach you on e-mail. All you have to do is set the
email to forward to your current preferred e-mail account. For example,
Lawrence_Summers@post.harvard.edu is a sample lifetime e-mail which Harvard University could provide to graduate Larry Summers. He could set it to
auto-forward to a Hotmail account where he could review his mail at his leisure.

According to market research firm NFO WorldGroup, more than 33 million
e-mail addresses change each year, roughly double the rate at which people
change their physical addresses.[177] Rather than lose touch with your contacts
every time you move, it's much safer to provide people and companies with a
permanent e-mail address.

We strongly discourage relying on an Internet service provider ("ISP") address (Russell.Rothstein@AOL.com), or a work e-mail address as your "lifetime" contact. An ISP address locks you into that ISP. If ever you decide to
switch ISPs, then you would have to notify everyone of your new e-mail address. In addition, why should you advertise for your ISP if your ISP is not
paying you?

Relying on a work e-mail address (e.g., Jim.Conley@BigBank.com) is also
dangerous, as you will lose touch with people as soon as you switch jobs. In
addition, your employer will be in a position to read all of your personal mail
if you rely on a work e-mail address.

Recently, Simon wanted to contact a fellow member of the International Executives Resource Group who was formerly the Chief Technology Officer of a major company. Simon found the CTO's résumé on
the IERG's private Web site, and sent a note to the e-mail address on the
résumé.

However, the CTO had an e-mail address with Verizon (a major ISP). Simon's e-mail bounced because the CTO had moved and switched to a different ISP. Simon tried calling the CTO, but the CTO had switched telephone numbers when he had moved.

Imagine if Simon were a potential client or employer: would he bother calling directory information to track the person down? Of course not; he would just contact the next résumé in the pile. With a permanent e-mail address, the CTO would have avoided the problem of being unreachable.

Free Web-based mail services (e.g., Hotmail or Yahoo!) are an option, but we recommend using them only for services like newsletter subscriptions and online shopping, not professional correspondence. For one thing, you run the risk that the mail provider will cease to exist. Many people thought that their @Home.com e-mail addresses were stable, but that company died and so did all of those @Home.com e-mail addresses.

More importantly, these free services do not carry the distinctiveness, memorability, and professionalism of your own domain. The e-mail tagline ("Do you Yahoo!?") is perhaps acceptable for students, but it does not look very professional. If you use these services, it's worth the small premium to get an ad-free e-mail account.

 So where can you get a lifetime address? Many universities offer their graduates a free lifetime e-mail address. This is a great option if you have a strong affinity with your school. The best option, though, is your own domain, which is very cheap insurance to guarantee that you can stay in touch. To establish a personalized e-mail address with your domain name:

→ **Register your name** or a logical variant at a domain name registrar. If your last name (Frank.com) is unavailable, try StephanieFrank.com, FrankFamily.com, TheFranks.com, FrankMail.com, or other reasonable variants.

→ **Find a hosting company** that will provide e-mail services for that domain name. Many domain name registrars will provide free e-mail forwarding with your domain name registration, or full e-mail services for a small fee.

→ **Set up forwarding e-mail addresses** for yourself and your family. Most e-mail address providers have a catch-all option; any address @Architectural Designs.com goes to the specified address. This catchall option is extremely useful because it allows you to have an infinity of e-mail addresses. For example, if you are a small business, you might put on your Web site Webmaster@ArchitecturalDesigns.com, info@Architectural Designs.com, and Prez@ArchitecturalDesigns.com. This will make your business look more professional. In addition, you can use the filter in your e-mail program to sort these e-mails into appropriate boxes by their "Mailto" address.

Another useful way to exploit the catch-all feature is use a special e-mail address for each site you visit. For example, when applying for a credit card, tell the SuperCreditCard Company that your e-mail is SuperCreditCard@Your Family.com. This makes it much easier to filter e-mails from SuperCreditCard. If you ever receive spam to SuperCreditCard@YourFamily.com, you will know that the SuperCreditCard Company sold your e-mail address to the highest bidder. You can now route those e-mails into your spam folder.

Once you set up your permanent e-mail account, be sure to manage it closely. When you change ISPs, change the routing of your e-mail forwarding immediately. Take care of your permanent e-mail address as if it were your good name (because it is), and it will keep you connected for life.

Separate Personal and Business E-Mail Accounts

You can save yourself much time and aggravation, and potentially even protect your job, by keeping your personal and business e-mail accounts segregated.

Under U.S. law, your employer is entitled to read your corporate e-mail. Some employers have automatic filters set up, seeking key phrases such as sexual terms, vulgarities, "I hate my job," and "Enclosed please find my résumé." If you are writing e-mails with those sentiments from your corporate address, you are leaving yourself very vulnerable. You perhaps also write or receive other e-mails that you would not want an employer to read: party logistics, flirtatious e-mails to your partner, potentially offensive jokes about corporate life, and so on.

If an e-mail has any potential whatsoever to be offensive or to hurt you, don't write it at all, on either your personal or business account. You run too much danger of the wrong person reading it. Alternatively, it can be forwarded or saved and then return years later to somehow hurt you. For example, never write, "We can't promote Herbert; he's way too old." This can and probably will be used against you in an age discrimination lawsuit.

For those e-mails which you do not want your employer to see (e.g., applications for a new job), use your personal account. Encourage your friends to e-mail you there, and send personal correspondence from there. First, this protects your privacy. Second, it keeps you accessible when you leave your employer . . . as all mortals do eventually.

The Simplest Solution

The simplest solution for receiving less e-mail is to simply use e-mail less! Ross Mayfield writes, "When people ask how I find time to blog, the answer is simple—less e-mail." He recommends replacing e-mail with communication tools better suited to the task[178]:

→ **Collaborative workspaces** for critical processes and productive groups.

→ **Chat and IM** for on-demand coordination and in lieu of calls.

→ **Public blogs** for keeping up with your personal network and what used to be mailing lists.

15

The Virtual You

> Each of us will create a mirror image of ourselves on the Net, the virtual you. Your mirror image may know more about you than you do.—DON TAPSCOTT[179]

Ajit Jaokar, CEO of FutureText, a publishing and research company working with community-based mobile applications, describes his approach to managing his virtual presence:

"How can people take you seriously when your profile includes 'Tom and Jerry' [the cat and mouse cartoon characters]?"

"This was a very real question posed to me by a relatively new member of Ecademy [virtual community]. He pointed out that my profile includes Tintin, Asterix, Tom and Jerry, and also Snoopy. The implication was . . . my profile sounds like a joke.

"I then pointed out that I have been very successful on Ecademy—in terms of networking, clubs and also getting business on Ecademy (finding customers on Ecademy)—even though I do not actively seek them.

"This got his interest (finding customers).

"He then said . . . tell me how and why. . . .

"I then pointed out it's because of 'Tom and Jerry'."

"This made him say again . . . it sounds like a joke (surely I cannot be serious).

"My point is . . . putting a personal preference on Ecademy (such as cartoons and animation) which I genuinely like . . . makes me be a real person. It's simple, genuine and truthful. . . .

"But . . . he continued . . . you were going to tell me 'how you got customers.'

"I then added that his profile read like his CV [résumé].

"This, he did not take as a joke.

"He believed 'How else can I sell if people don't know what I do?'

"I pointed out that there were many people having a similar skill set to him on Ecademy.

"Why would I buy from him?

"I then pointed out some of the contacts I have made globally through my clubs . . . who are CEOs/CTOs of large companies. This impressed him especially when I pointed out that some of them were now customers.

"BUT. . . .

"He continued. . . .

"'How do I find these customers?'

"I replied . . .

"'Do you have a favourite cartoon character? Put it on your profile. Let people see who you are as a 'person'.

"There was a looong silence. . . .

"Sadly the person never got the point.

"I am happy to have got many customers on Ecademy . . . but many traditional sales people would never understand it."[180]

The core principle of netiquette is: "Adhere to the same standards of behavior online that you follow in real life."[181] The more effectively you manage your virtual appearance, the higher your perceived credibility. Your virtual "appearance" includes your photo, choice of words, Web presence, and even the sites and communities to which you link and which link to you.

An effective virtual presence is credible, consistent, and visible:

→ **Credible:** Just as you would make an effort to be as attractive as possible in an online dating service, so too should you do your best to be attractive to people seeking business relationships. In this case, "attractive" means high Character and high Competence.

→ **Consistent:** "A confused mind says 'no'."[182] If people do not get a clear, consistent, memorable perception of your identity, they will not have you in mind when looking for someone who sells what you sell. The Information you put out should be consistent and current.

→ **Visible:** Once you have created a consistent, attractive personal virtual presence, you will want to be as visible as possible—not necessarily to the entire world, but certainly to the kind of people you want to attract.

These principles are equally true on a professional home page, a profile in a virtual community, an introduction on a mailing list, or an "About Me" page.

Many people are uncomfortable talking about themselves. They think that it is an egotistical thing to do. Consider, though, that most people want to understand other people, and providing people Information about your history, personality, and interests allows them to understand you better. You do not force it on people; you offer it to them via a link. If they want to build a relationship with you, they will appreciate this Information.

If you do not control your virtual presence, it will be controlled by what others have to say about you. Of course, that is not necessarily a bad thing, so long as they have nice things to say. Consider author Lawrence Otis Graham. Search for his name, and you will see that he does not have a personal site, but his book publisher, his speaking agency, and various news organizations have all profiled him.[183]

Even before you reach his level of success, there are other ways to position yourself similarly. Once your professional life goes online, your virtual persona can very quickly take on a life of its own. It may know more about you than you do. It remembers conversations, publications, purchases, and even relationships that you may not. Most people are surprised to learn just how much Information about them there is out on the Web, and even more surprised at what that Information is.

Balancing the Professional Versus the Personal You

Many people believe that the presentation of any more than the most minimal personal Information online is inappropriate. You will also find work-at-home moms who post pictures of their naked babies in their profiles, and Silicon Valley CEOs who unabashedly list "sex" as one of their interests.[184]

No matter where on the spectrum you decide to place yourself, "you can't please all of the people all of the time."[185] Offer too much personal Information, and some will see you as unprofessional. Offer no personal Information, and many will simply choose not to connect with you because you have offered no basis for a relationship if they are not immediately interested in your products or services.

On your business Web site, we recommend you err on the side of greater professionalism and less personal disclosure. In profiles on virtual communities, particularly those that have open discussion areas, include some personal Information if you want to attract new connections. An acid test: never put up any Information that would embarrass you if your business colleague who is furthest from you in values and politics knew about it. If you do business with even one person who is very politically conservative, you put that at risk by mentioning your belief in open marriages. Many people may ignore it as simply a personal choice, but why take the risk of alienating someone unnecessarily?

In addition, you make yourself more vulnerable to identify theft, stalkers, and other undesirables by posting extensive personal Information. If you do want to post pictures of your baby, you can always put them in a password-protected area of the site.

On The Virtual Handshake Network on Ryze (TheVirtualHandshake-Network.Ryze.com), members publicly review and critique other member's pages. Out of hundreds of reviews that have been posted, consistently the most common critique is, "I'd like to see more about you in your profile."

This varies, however, from one site to another. Sites such as LinkedIn are not oriented towards business socializing, so personal Information is generally unnecessary or even out of place.

Familiarize yourself with what others on the site are doing and generally match the style of others on the site. Choosing how much personal information to display is like choosing your wardrobe for a business event: it's fine to stand out, but only to a reasonable limit.

The Recyclable Document

One of the greatest merits of virtual communications is that you can easily recycle your own words. We recommend you create a Recyclable Document with all of the information that you reuse when communicating with people virtually. Simply cutting and pasting from the Recyclable Document will save you a great deal of time and make it easier to communicate in a consistent way.

Some of the items to include in your Recyclable Document:

→ **Useful links**

- **Web addresses of your profiles:** This will allow you to quickly pull up your profiles for editing when any of your Information changes. You may also want to refer other people to them.

- **Photos:** Link to a location where you stored your photos.

- **Articles:** Primarily articles written by you or about you, but may also include articles by others that you refer people to frequently.

- **Invitation or affiliate links:** You may want to be able to refer people in ways other than the site's mechanism.

→ **Reusable text**

- **E-mail signatures:** Include all the contact information that you would have on a business card.

- **Web signatures:** For use in discussion forums. They should be between two and four lines long, and usually include a link to your corporate site. Web signatures are much shorter and less detailed than e-mail signatures.

- **Memory hook and benefit statement:** One-to-two sentences to describe what you do professionally and how it benefits your customers, most commonly used as a brief self-introduction.

- **Biography—short and long versions:** For introducing yourself, for profiles in online communities, and as a byline.

- **Haves:** What you have to offer (other than your product or service) that might be of value to others.

- **Wants:** What you are looking for (preferably other than just "leads") that is specific and timely.

- **Professional interests:** A list of 25–50 words and short phrases describing your professional interests. These are important for helping people to find you when they search for people with certain interests in an online community.

- **Personal interests:** A list of 25–50 words and short phrases describing your personal interests.

In addition, we recommend that you compile all of the e-mails that you find yourself frequently writing. The exact text will depend on your profession. For example, the following are a few samples of text to include in your "Standard E-mails" file:

→ "I am happy to help you in your job search. A few ideas for you:"

→ "Thank you very much for requesting a meeting; I'm flattered. I suggest the Sheraton restaurant for Tuesday or Thursday lunch at 1 pm."

When you receive poorly worded requests via a social software system which allows forwarding of requests from one person to another:

→ "I don't think the recipient will respond to this request." A good request should include the following elements:

- a brief summary of who you are
- a brief summary of why you're approaching the given person
- some "customized" ideas on how you can benefit the recipient
- lastly, what you're seeking from the recipient.

We explore below some of these personal items in greater detail.

Photos

Online dating sites report that profiles with photos get anywhere from seven to fifteen times as many replies as those without.[186] While some business-oriented communities do not use photos, many more do. As publisher and venture capitalist Esther Dyson says, "Photos are what make those sites feel like real communities, and they are an endlessly compelling medium, even when they depict people you don't know and will never meet face to face."[187]

Quality matters. In a recent survey by LookBetterOnline.com, a company that provides professional digital portrait photography, 74 percent of their customers reported having "some success" or "more success" with their new photo. Of those, 32 percent reported receiving greater than five times more responses.[188] While the survey did not distinguish between business and dating sites, it illustrates that the quality of the photo, not merely its presence or absence, is important.

E-Mail Signatures

E-mail signatures are a powerful tool for making your contact Information handy for others, and more generally for promoting your site(s). When participating in a discussion forum for writers you might want to list yourself as the author of a book, with a link to a page with Information about it. But in an industry-related discussion forum, you might choose just to link to your company's Web site, not your book.

We are constantly surprised at how many business e-mails we receive without a signature. You would never write a paper letter without a signature. Similarly, every e-mail message should have a signature.

Many readers prefer simple text signatures, either because of download speed or because they use text-based e-mail. Following is a simple example from knowledge management and technology consultant Judith Meskill:

Judith Meskill
Principal
Meskill.net
judith@meskill.net
Y!: [Yahoo! instant messaging ID]
t. +1.908.XXX.XXXX
f. +1.908.XXX.XXXX
company: http://www.meskill.net
Weblog: http://www.meskill.net/Weblogs/
Weblogs, inc.: http://socialsoftware.Weblogsinc.com/

this e-mail is: [ ] bloggable [x] ask first [ ] private

In addition to her contact information, she provides guidance as to whether the contents of the message may be posted publicly by the recipient. She uses the lengthy "http://www.meskill.net" format, instead of the more concise "Meskill.net," because even primitive e-mail readers can usually determine that http://www.meskill.net is a hyperlink.

Carolyn Burke uses a more extensive signature file with numerous hyperlinks to relevant Information, full contact data, a legal disclaimer, and a commitment to make a timely response:

Sincerely,
Carolyn
—

Integrity Incorporated
Click here to Subscribe to: Compass - The Compliance Newsletter

Carolyn L Burke, MA, CISSP, CISM
CEO
clburke@integrityincorporated.com
155 Dalhousie Street, Ste. 701
Toronto, Ontario, M5B 2P7 Canada
Tel 416-893-4280, Fax 416-369-0148

www.IntegrityIncorporated.com

This message may contain confidential and/or proprietary information, and is intended only for the person/entity to whom it was originally addressed. The content of this message may contain private views and opinions which do not constitute a formal disclosure or commitment unless specifically stated.

If you do not receive a response within 2 business days, please resend.

—

River Street Bridge family of values-focused companies

www.IntegrityIncorporated.com	Integrity in Security and Privacy
www.DetecttheTruth.com	Investigations
www.RiverStreetBridge.com	Advisor

Web Signature

A Web signature is the signature you use when participating in a virtual community. Most of the discussion above also applies to a Web signature. Be sure to check the guidelines for each community in which you participate, as some may have a "no signatures" policy. In general, a signature of two to four lines is acceptable.

The purpose of a Web signature is different than that of an e-mail signature. In most online social networks, a link to your profile will be displayed next to your post. If people want to learn more about you, they can and will click through to your profile page. So, in this context, the Web signature serves four purposes:

1. Shows your name.

2. Provides a shortcut to your external business site for those who are interested.

3. Makes you memorable.

4. Optionally highlights something timely you are involved in.

The basic format should look like this:

Your name.
Your business name (linked to your Web site).
An optional tag line or a brief announcement of a particular project or promotion.

For example[189]:

H. Dean Hua
H. Dean | . . . a financial planning practice.™
"Life Needs Planning."™

Memory Hook and Benefit Statement

Many people have developed a "pitch" to introduce themselves. Pitches can work well in a group setting in which people are listening to a series of introductions. However, if you start a conversation with a sales pitch, you will likely alienate everyone except the tiny number of people who are immediately in need of your services (and probably even most of them).

Dr. Ivan Misner, Founder & CEO, Business Network International, suggests creating a "memory hook": a short, relevant, and memorable description of what you do. It's intended to arouse curiosity and set the context for the conversation. It should generally be ten words or less, and the shorter the better. Use plain language that anybody can understand. Avoid buzzwords and superlatives; keep it simple and natural, but provocative.

For example, instead of saying, "I'm in commercial construction," try "I build skyscrapers!" Instead of "I'm an exterminator," use "I kill bugs professionally." Misner's book, *Seven Second Marketing,* provides hundreds of real-world examples and additional tips for creating yours.

The benefit statement shows how what you do creates value for your customers. "Some people make people smile. I make people feel good about smiling; I'm a dentist." Show how you help somebody do something.

The benefit statement may be part of the memory hook—"I build skyscrapers on time and under budget"—but you also may want to keep it separate and save it for a more appropriate time later in the relationship. As Bob Burg says in *Endless Referrals,* "Keep in mind that no matter how good a rapport is established during your initial conversation with [prospects], it's only after you have earned their loyalty that you can legitimately expect your benefit statement . . . to carry any weight with them."[190]

Being too slick can actually hurt you. You are a human being talking to another human being. Communicate in a simple conversational style, not "marketese."

Biographies

We recommend keeping your biography up to date with current Information about you, in addition to a brief professional history and some personal Information. Christopher Hurtado, owner of Linguistic Solutions, has a well-thought-out profile on openBC:

> "I'm a self-taught entrepreneur with a passion for technology, languages, learning, and teaching. I have more than 16 years of experience in translation, foreign language instruction, and cross-cultural training. I've taught English as a second language (ESL) and Spanish for English speakers. I recently co-authored *Vacation Spanish: A Survival Guide for Mexico, the Caribbean, Central & South America* (including a Brazilian Portuguese chapter).
>
> "Since founding Linguistic Solutions in 1991, I've been using high tech/high touch methodologies to manage customer relationships,

translation projects, and a worldwide network of freelance translators while serving an international clientele including both Fortune 500 companies and high-tech startups. Linguistic Solutions breaks down language and cultural barriers through translation, interpretation, foreign language instruction, and cross-cultural training.

"I was born in Baltimore, Maryland. I grew up in Venezuela, my father's native country. I'm a childhood bilingual (English and Spanish) and also speak Brazilian Portuguese. I'm married to children's book author Alysia Gonzalez. We have six children and are very active in our church and community.

"How about you? What do we have in common? Let's connect!"[191]

In your Recyclable Document, it's better to err on the side of being too long rather than too short. It's very easy to delete a sentence or two when needed.

Haves and Wants

Jeffrey Meshel, Co-CEO of Mercury Capital Corporation, writes in his Classmates profile (Classmates.com):

> What I have: access to capital, a new book (*One Phone Call Away*), a database of 4,500 individuals who I know are typically at high levels in the business community.

> What I am seeking: investment opportunities as a bridge lender in real estate; investment opportunities in P.I.P.E. transactions; to meet with hedge fund managers who invest in microcaps, real estate transactions, and/or special situations.

Many virtual communities ask you to write down explicitly your "Haves" and your "Wants": what you have to offer, and what you are looking for. You can also incorporate this information into your introductions, particularly in a group setting.

People want to help—they love to help, especially if they can do so in a way that is low-risk for them. But they cannot help unless you guide them in how to help you. "I have a great product and I want prospective customers to share it with" is not the approach to take. Every salesperson, marketer, or business owner would say the same thing. Be specific and timely, if possible, when filling in the "Haves" and "Wants" fields in an online profile.

For your Haves, consider what it is that you have to offer that is not directly related to what you typically sell. Do you have contacts in a particular industry? Or expertise on a particular topic, business-related or otherwise?

For your Wants, steer away from demands that are too directly related to selling your product. Being specific invites a connection, whereas a broad, vague request for referrals fails every time. Perhaps you're looking for expert help? To learn more about a certain industry or company? To meet a certain category of people?

Professional and Personal Interests

Your professional and personal interests are among the most important fields that people use to search for you online. When creating your list of interests, think about searchers, not just viewers. For example, if you are in the knowledge management industry, list both "knowledge management" and "KM." It's important to put not only variant words, but variant phrases. Instead of writing "product management and marketing," write "product management, product marketing." Otherwise, people looking for "product marketing" will not find you.

Ecademy offers the intriguing ability to search for people "most like you." Ecademy does this by searching through the "50 Words" entries in which each member has written his/her interests, and shows you those with the highest number of matches. This makes it easy to connect with like-minded people.

16

Privacy, Safety, and Other Concerns

→ There is no privacy on the Internet. Get over it.—SCOTT MCNEALY, CEO, SUN MICROSYSTEMS[192]

Scott McNealy's words may be a bit harsh, and have drawn criticism from online privacy advocates.[193] It's very reasonable to be concerned about identity theft, spam, stalking, and government monitoring. However, McNealy's words are also true. A great deal of Information about you is available online. If you are trying to build new business relationships online, you will probably make even more Information publicly available.

The simple truth is that more publicity equals less privacy. The challenge for those trying to create new business relationships virtually is to find a sensible balance between professional visibility and personal privacy.

The "Right" to Privacy

In the United States, privacy is not specifically protected in the federal Constitution. Some state constitutions protect the right, and numerous federal and state laws have been created to protect privacy, but as Jeffrey Rosen, law professor and author of *The Unwanted Gaze,* a book about privacy in the digital age, puts it, "Privacy is always one of the hardest values to define philosophically, and that's why it's hard to protect politically."[194]

Even if you believe that you have a "right" to privacy, you give up some of those rights when you communicate with people one on one. This is true both legally and socially. For example, when you give Nina your e-mail address and telephone number, traditional etiquette is that Nina is free to give that Information to a third person if there is some logical reason for doing so. Two significant exceptions: if you specifically asked Nina to keep this Information confidential, then Nina is committing a faux pas by passing on this Information. Also, passing on a home phone or a cell phone is usually inappropriate. It may be common courtesy for Nina not to do so without your consent, but it's neither illegal nor a breach of mainstream etiquette unless an explicit contract has been made.

Kevin Bankston, an attorney for the Electronic Frontier Foundation (EFF.org), a research and advocacy group for digital rights, including free speech, copyright, and privacy, explains:

> Information can only be "owned" in limited cases that have more to do with intellectual property than with privacy—that is, copyrighted material and trade secrets. You don't have a copyright in your personal information (although companies may be able to copyright databases that include your personal information), nor is it a trade secret. In some cases, the sharing of your personal information is regulated—there are strict rules about information handling by financial and medical institutions, for example, while the government has to get a court order if they want to get e-mails that your ISP stores. But in the vast majority of cases, the only interest that you have in your personal information—if any—is contractual. If you, as an individual, give someone else your unlisted phone number or e-mail address, and they give it to another individual without your consent, it's just bad manners, unless there's a contract specifying otherwise."[195]

When you interact with people in a public or semipublic setting, you can expect that the Information exchanged will not necessarily remain private. While we believe in the right to privacy online, we also recognize that when you choose to seek out connections and to make yourself open to receiving them, you sacrifice some of your privacy in the process.

We look at privacy from the perspective of two people who are willing to make their professional Information widely available; after all, we want clients and employees to be able to reach us. At the same time, we want to safeguard personal Information for safety and to limit unwanted communications. We recommend keeping private most Information that is not directly relevant to your professional life: your marital status, family members' names, home address, birthday, and so on. There is usually no advantage in publicizing that Information, except insofar as some background about yourself can expedite bonding.

The Illusion of Privacy

We've found that most people believe they have far more privacy online than they actually do. Following up after one of Scott Allen's recent speeches, an attendee wrote to Scott that he was worried that legitimate Information exchanged between people online could fall into the wrong hands. He was very concerned about privacy and particularly about identity theft.

Scott argued that if you become very visible online, that does not necessarily reduce the amount of privacy that you already have. Scott is neither a private detective nor a hacker, but he is reasonably knowledgeable about the Internet. Within five minutes, he learned the man's home address and telephone number, approximate age, income bracket, two former employers, the positions he held there, and his bosses' names there.

When he sent all this Information back, the man was shocked.

Have you typed your phone number into a search engine lately? Odds are it produces a map to your house. Or your name and city? Unless you are unlisted (and have been for some time), it probably produces your phone number, address, and a map. You can request that this Information be removed from a search engine, but that same Information is still available on dozens and dozens of other sites, each of which has to be contacted individually if you want to opt out. Once a researcher has your address, he can also find out who owns the property you live in, and often even the physical layout of your house, since many local property tax authorities have all their records online.

This data is available for many, many people. If you have been prominent in your field, your name is additionally probably scattered across dozens, or even hundreds of Web sites.

→ News sites may have archived stories that mentioned you or your children.

→ Your university may have posted the alumni notes in which you talk about your marriage and new baby.

→ Domain name registries may include your alternative addresses.

→ Anything you wrote in a public discussion forum may be viewable.

→ A former employer may post some press releases or white papers that include your name.

Each reference may not contain a great deal of personal Information, but in the aggregate they are a treasure trove. Unless you have been a hermit, or have been very diligent about keeping yourself invisible, your life is probably already more public than you realize.

Stalking and identity theft can, in rare cases, be truly dangerous:

"On July 29, 1999, Liam Youens contacted Docusearch, an Internet-based investigation and information service, and requested the date of birth of Amy Lynn Boyer, a woman Youens had been obsessed with since the two attended high school together. Youens later contacted Docusearch to request Boyer's social security number and employment information. Docusearch was unable to provide Boyer's date of birth, but obtained her [social security number] from a credit reporting agency as part of a credit header and provided it to Youens for $45. . . . Docusearch charged Youens $109 for [Boyer's work address].

"On October 15, 1999, Youens drove to Boyer's workplace and fatally shot her as she left work. He then committed suicide. A subsequent police investigation revealed that Youens kept firearms and ammunition in his bedroom, and maintained a Web site containing references to stalking and killing Boyer, as well as detailing plans to murder her entire family."[196]

While this tragic case is an extreme example of stalking, it highlights dramatically the ease with which a criminal can obtain private Information. Amy Boyer's murder did not have anything to do with any personal presence on the Internet she might have had—the information was obtained with simple deception and $154.

Don't Sweat the Small Stuff
(But It's Not All Small Stuff)

Given what we've described, you have three possible choices:

1. **"Get over it."** Do not worry about your privacy at all.

2. **Do everything you possibly can to stay anonymous and protect your privacy.** To do this, you would have to write to every company that stores data about you and ask to opt out.

3. **Strike some sort of sensible balance** in which you take reasonable, low-effort precautions and learn to live with the few remaining risks as part of modern life.

We recommend the third option, a sensible balance. Most of this Information was really never private in the first place—it just took a great deal more work to get. Reverse telephone books (in which you can look up someone's name given their phone numbers) existed for years before that Information became available online. Other records have been available at the courthouse or the public library for anyone so inclined to go find it.

Security expert Russ Cooper thinks privacy advocates sometimes create unnecessary fear about the Internet[197]:

> There's far less Information available about people on the Net than there is about anybody who uses a credit card. The guy with the database has the same access to your Information whether the data is sent through Amazon online or Barnes & Noble in the physical world.

What are we afraid of when we do the same kind of stuff in the real world? We give away an awful lot of privacy in the real world on a regular basis, why is this hyped up when we talk about the Net?

As easy as the Web makes it to find out personal Information about you, it's just as easy for criminals to find it out about someone else. We do not recommend going online and bragging about your new Ferrari or beautiful daughter. However, simply increasing your visibility on the Web in and of itself does not increase your chances of being a target.

It's just as easy, if not easier, for criminals to target you in the physical world as the virtual. If they want to know when you are home and when you are not, they will case your house, not try to learn online what meetings you attend. While it's certainly possible for hackers to obtain confidential information online, most cases of identity theft are actually due to a physical theft, a corrupt insider, or even an acquaintance of the victim.[198]

Sensible Steps to Protect Your Privacy and Safety

Once you have come to terms with these limitations on privacy, here are some simple steps you can take to increase your privacy without compromising your visibility.

Don't Tell, Don't Ask

→ **Protect your Social Security Number, driver's license number, birthday, passport number, and other official identifiers.** There is rarely a valid reason to give them out online. A few exceptions are official government Web sites, such as the Social Security Administration or Department of Public Safety, and the major credit reporting agencies. Make sure to double-check the domain name, since it is possible for a criminal to create a site that pretends to be a legitimate site but is really just designed to suck up personal Information ("phishing"). Never disclose this Information unless you initiated the transaction, that is, do not give it out on an inbound phone call or in response to an inbound e-mail. Many companies ask you for your "mother's maiden name" as an identifying technique, but never give them the real name. Instead, give each company a different fake name.

→ **Do not feel obliged to fill out official forms.** For example, when applying for a mobile phone or a new apartment, you may be asked for very detailed personal Information. Double-check if the company really needs your birthday and social security number. If no credit check is necessary, you can usually just omit the data.

→ **Make sure your home phone is unlisted with your local phone company, or use a pseudonym with them.** Nowadays, almost anyone who really wants to meet you can e-mail you, so we encourage you to choose the highest level of anonymity for your phone number.

→ **Do not list your permanent e-mail address, home address, home phone number, or cell number in an online résumé or other publicly viewable Web sites.** If necessary, use a disposable spam-catcher e-mail address.

→ **If you run your business from a home office, you may want to rent a private mail box** and use it for your business correspondence, domain name registration, and in any mailing lists you run. We recommend using a private mailbox service so that you have a street address, not just a box number. Also, set up a separate phone line for your business. You may also want to get a combination voice-mail/fax number from a firm like J2.com or OneBox.com. Alternatively, many people use their cell phone as their business number and voice mail.

The Value of Discretion

→ **Do not reveal personal details to strangers or just-met "friends."** Be sensibly cautious about face-to-face meetings. If you and your new friend wish to meet face to face, do it in a public place during daylight. You need not be paranoid, but you should not be an easy mark, either. Beware "fast-met friends." A common "social engineering" form of industrial espionage is to befriend someone online just long enough to get them to reveal insider Information.[199]

→ **Protect your children's and spouse's identities.** In general, you should not mention your spouse or children by name in a public forum. If you choose to maintain a personal Web site, we recommend making it password-protected. You can do this easily with specialized services such as MyFamily .com. Ross Mayfield reports:

> Perhaps the only perk my 7-year old daughter gets from being the CEO's daughter (aside from being dragged to conferences while being told it's a vacation), is her own workspace to blog privately. Of course, if I'm sitting around with my laptop, her first question is 'Daddy, can I post to my Weblog?' She is pretty excited about it, maybe thinks she has more than one reader and her posts may be a treasure for her one day. I would open it up, but I also get Google traffic for disturbing queries like 'pictures of my daughter.'"[200]

File and Password Management

→ **Use a different user ID and password for all of the important sites you visit.** If a thief knows your password on one site, it's too easy for him to then use that password on many other sites. A good way to keep unique passwords for every site is to develop a standard method for creating a password from the name of the site. This keeps you from having to refer to your master password file. For example, to create a password for Tribe.net:

1. Pick a standard word for use with all your sites—we'll use "jade."

2. Split it in half. In the middle, insert the number of letters in the domain name. "Tribe" has 5 letters, so we write "ja5de."

3. Add a letter at the beginning that is the first letter of the domain name. "Tribe" = "T," giving us "Tja5de."

Although this allows you to easily calculate the password, a hacker cannot readily deduce a pattern because each site has its own unique password. Of course, you need to create your own algorithm; do not use this one! To avoid confusion from an excessive number of passwords, it's okay to use the same password on all Web sites for which security is not critical, e.g., newspaper sites. Or visit BuyMeNot.com for a library of passwords for public sites.

→ **Always choose a difficult password.** Never ever use an easy-to-guess password, like a birthday, a single common word ("octopus"), pet's name, or wedding anniversary. Christopher Faulkner, CEO of C I Host, suggests picking a line from a song or popular phrase and use then the first letter of each word. For example, "Four Score and Seven Years Ago" becomes "4s&7YA."

→ **Keep data out of your browser.** Only use the "let browser remember this password" feature on your browser for low-sensitivity Web sites.

→ **Keep a master password file.** Keep a file on your computer, password-protected, with a list of all the credit cards, Web sites, and other venues where you need a password of any kind. Use an innocuous name for this file (e.g., "Trash notes"), so that people cannot guess what it is. Better yet, protect your passwords with a utility like Norton Password Manager or Steganos Security Suite.

→ **When you dispose of your computer, or even just the hard drive, be sure to wipe the hard disk entirely using a utility designed for that purpose.** In a recent study, MIT students purchased 158 used hard drives on eBay for less than $1,000. They found more than 5,000 credit card numbers, detailed personal and corporate financial records, numerous medical records, and gigabytes of personal e-mail. Only 12 machines were cleaned properly.[201]

→ **Consider using a hardware solution to strengthen your privacy.** For example, AuthenTec makes a fingerprint sensor, and Pass2Go and Aladdin's eToken Pro are password systems that run on removable USB keys.

Protect Your Online Presence

→ **Choose the right community for your interests.** Online communities run the gamut from business-focused to personal-interest focused sites. On business-focused sites like LinkedIn and OpenBC, there is no way to indicate your marital status or musical tastes, because those sites want to create a professional-focused culture. By contrast, sites such as MySpace.com and Tribe.net allow you to upload not only your professional biography but also whether you are "swinger, in a relationship, single, divorced, or married" (MySpace's categories). On personal-focused sites such as Match.com, there is no easy way to upload your résumé and other professional contact information. If your main interest is business, then you'll be more successful by using sites in the first two categories. In any case, make sure that your behavior on a site is consistent with the culture of that site.

→ **Configure your account to minimize social network spam ("snam").** Some users of social software services have complained about being forced to deal with too many inquiries from strangers. If you are in this situation, just check the settings for your account. On all of the major social software services, you have the option to prevent strangers from e-mailing you. You have to determine for yourself if the benefit of higher walls offsets the cost of less sunlight from new relationships.

→ **Use private messaging within a virtual community, rather than giving out your personal e-mail.** This offers you two forms of protection. First, in most virtual communities, you can easily block or ignore messages from a particular user. Secondly, if someone does start to harass you, send you spam, or otherwise behave inappropriately, they are under the terms of service for the site. The site administrators can check the content of the messages and take appropriate action, usually deleting that user's account. Should legal action ever be required, you will also have a better archive of evidence.

→ **Use a different e-mail address for public postings than you use for private, trusted correspondence.** Your public e-mail address is commonly known as a "spam-catcher" or "spam-killer." You may want to use a free Web-based e-mail service such as Hotmail or Yahoo! for this, so that you do not clutter your e-mail software with spam messages.

→ **Use forms on your Web sites for visitors to e-mail you, rather than direct links to your e-mail address.** Spammers use automated tools ("spambots") that automatically read Web sites and search for e-mail addresses to be added to their mailing lists. Also, someone you meet virtually might use your e-mail to bypass the safeguards provided by the community and contact you directly against your wishes. Create a form on your Web site that asks visitors for their name, e-mail address, and a brief message, and they can contact you without ever seeing your e-mail address.

Due Diligence

→ **Before doing business with anyone, perform an extensive search on both their name and their business name on a search engine, as well as running a literature search on them** (e.g., with LexisNexis). If the list of search results is too large to review them all, be sure not to just start on the first page of results and work your way forward—start at the back and check some random pages in the middle. Be careful, though, not to believe everything you read. The Information may refer to a different person with the same name, or may simply be inaccurate. Corroborate before taking actions based on what you find.

→ **If you suspect someone of misrepresentation, check alternative sources of Information.** If you are interested in meeting someone face-to-face, we recommend doing so in that person's office. When you meet with someone in his or her own office, you get a better feel for that person from the decorations, photographs, relationships with coworkers, and overall environment. In addition, meeting in the person's office makes it much easier for the person to introduce you to co-workers, expanding your Number.

→ **A subtle verification method is to double-check the domain name registration of the person's company.** Go to Network Solutions' Web site (NetSol.com), click "WhoIs," and type the domain name of the firm's Web site. For example, for the Trium Group consultancy, type in "TriumGroup.com." The address and phone number listed as the owner of the firm's domain name are an alternative way of verifying that a business really exists and where that business is really located.

Job Search and Privacy

No résumé posted online should include your full home address or any other Information that you would not want the entire world to know. References also should never be on the résumé; it makes it far too easy for potential employers to annoy your references with excessive calls.

Peter Weddle, one of the leading experts on Internet job search, strongly discourages people from posting their résumé in any online resume database that does not provide a confidentiality feature. Typically, such features enable people to protect their privacy by controlling which employers may access their name and contact information. In addition to the privacy issue, Weddle knows of instances in which people have lost their jobs because their boss found their resume online. The boss thought that her employee was seeking a new job, even though the employee posted that résumé years prior. Weddle suggest that an easy way to avoid this problem is to put a date on your résumé. We also recommend deleting your résumé from the job boards once you succeed in your job search.[202]

If you are going to post your résumé online, we recommend using niche job boards, such as StreetJobs.com. The advantage of these sites:

→ **They focus on a particular industry or profession.** A criminal interested in identity theft is unlikely to target these small sites.

→ **They usually have a strict policy prohibiting reposting of your résumé, so that it does not end up on other Web sites without your knowledge.** That said, they cannot have full control over how people use the data that is posted.

Privacy Policies: Caveat Emptor

Privacy policies vary greatly from one Web site to another. If you are concerned about what a Web site may do, do not make any assumptions about their respect for your privacy. The privacy policies of many sites allow them to take actions that you may find objectionable. For example, the terms of service often allow a site to make contact Information available to third parties or to republish member-created content.

Australian privacy expert Roger Clarke, in an analysis of the privacy policies of Plaxo and other services, concludes: "In general, people would be well-advised firstly to stay well clear of all address-book and 'social networking systems,' and secondly to prevail upon their friends, colleagues, and acquaintances that they should avoid making any data about them available to service-operators like Plaxo."[203]

On the matter of content ownership, one disgruntled member, when he discovered the terms of one site's privacy policy, publicly posted his opinion in an online discussion, accusing the founder of the site of being, "a vampire looking to suck intellectual property from his users so he can live."[204]

Most users, though, take a more moderate point of view. In response to the above criticism, here is what other members had to say: "People don't really post valuable [intellectual property] on there. If you really have intellectual property, it's got to be valuable to somebody other than yourself."[205] "If you put something up there that makes you look good, why the heck are you getting upset if [they] give you promotion by saying: 'Look what so-and-so put on our site'?"[206]

We certainly advocate the more moderate point of view. The key, though, is awareness. Regarding intellectual property, be aware that anything you post in a public or semipublic venue may be reused without your knowledge or express consent. Even with a strong privacy policy, some people will simply forward, recycle, and even resell your content without your knowledge or permission. Unless you are planning to monitor the entire Internet for misuse of your work, you will have no control over what happens to your content once you post it.

Be thoughtful about what you make available in these communities. For photographs, you may want to use a low-resolution version, or embed a watermark or copyright notice in the photo. For written work, do not write anything in a public forum that you would not want the whole world to read. In addition, for valuable intellectual property, you may want to use PDF format or some other format that is difficult to alter. It's too easy for a criminal to take a text file, insert his or her name as the author, and then forward the article. You can find a variety of free and inexpensive PDF creation and conversion tools at PDFzone.com. We use and recommend activePDF Composer (ActivePDF.com).

Regarding personal data, we believe that your professional Information, including your e-mail address, is not really very private to begin with. Given that there is some threat, real or perceived, to privacy in the adoption of social network services, many services are building strong privacy protections into the architecture of their products. Chris Kelly, Chief Privacy Officer and General Counsel of Spoke Software, says, "By giving users control over their data in the software, and having strong policies and procedures to assure that control is real, enterprise-class social networking companies can effectively address most users' privacy concerns."[207]

There are many people who feel differently. In particular, we do not recommend inviting your friends into these services indiscriminately. You may do yourself more harm than good if you invite someone with a hardline view about privacy, and he gets upset with you for giving personal Information to a third party. If you do not know someone well enough to know whether or not this is an issue to them, then err on the side of caution. Either speak to them about it first, or invite them using a personal e-mail from you, rather than through the site.

With a little effort and thought, you can protect your personal privacy while still maintaining a highly public personal online presence.

Part **IV**

The Seven Keys to a World-Class Network

> If a novel reveals true and vivid relationships, it is a moral work, no matter what the relationships consist in. If the novelist honors the relationship in itself, it will be a great novel.—D.H. LAWRENCE[208]

17

Improve Your Character

> Character is like a tree and reputation like its shadow. The shadow is what we think it is; the tree is the real thing.
> —ABRAHAM LINCOLN, *LINCOLN'S OWN STORIES*[209]

Richard Linhart, CEO of investment fund Opus Capital, LLC, recently raised about $70,000 for charity—with one e-mail to 258 friends:

Dear Friends,

A little over two years ago, Warren Spector of Bear Stearns sponsored a major drive to increase the number of people in the data bank for bone marrow transplants. Warren's younger sister Ruthie, a wife and a mother of three children, was battling leukemia, and no good match could be found in the existing data bank or among her immediate family. Through Warren's efforts and his personal contribution of more than $3 million, more than 30,000 people had their genetic information added to the data bank. Among the 30,000 new additions to the data bank, another 50 matches have already been made which resulted in bone marrow transplants. Ruthie did end up receiving a transplant and is now doing fine.

A close friend of ours is currently mounting a campaign to raise $5 million so that 50,000+ people can be added to the data bank. His nine-year old son is fighting leukemia. He has had leukemia since age of five, and after some period of remission, suffered a relapse in January. He is currently going through an intensive regimen of chemotherapy, but a matched bone marrow transplant is his best recommended treatment option.

. . . . For a cost of approximately $100 per person, we can grow the databank and improve the chances of anyone in our community winning a battle against leukemia. This is not just about one family. Any of us could be faced with this in our own families, and people added to the database today should be there in the future to help others. To me, the idea that a child in our community could lose a battle with leukemia, while there may be a match somewhere out there for them, is tragic beyond words.

I have two requests. First, there will be several drives in the coming weeks and months asking people to become part of the data bank. All it takes is a few minutes and a Q-Tip type of swab inside your mouth. If you are not already in the data bank, please join, and ask anyone else appropriate to do so as well. Second, please consider giving generously to finance this campaign. Based on the results from Warren's campaign (projecting forward at least 100 transplants will have been done with Warren's $3 million contribution), each $30,000 raised can save one life. Leora and I have just pledged $20,000, and we hope you can make a gift as well. We don't know of a more important use of charitable dollars.

To make a gift or join the registry, please go to the Web site GiftOfLife.org.

Thanks in advance for your help.

One investor replied to all the people on the e-mail list: "We can do this like a card-calling exercise. I will give $10,000."

Another friend replied to the list: "A voice from the south: We're in for $10,000."

Approximately 15 people wrote in to Richard directly to pledge different amounts, adding up to over $70,000. In addition, many people registered in the data bank. A friend in Houston organized a registry drive, inspired by this e-mail.

At least two people wrote in to say that they thought that the "Reply all" to Richard's initial e-mail was obnoxious. Perhaps it was, but it was also effective.

Character is defined as "Your integrity, clarity of motives, consistency of behavior, openness, discretion, and trustworthiness." "Card-calling" is a highly effective fundraising technique because it allows people to publicly display that they are generous—have a good Character—and also to demonstrate their financial success.

In the next seven chapters, we will discuss all Seven Keys to a powerful Network: how to improve Your Character, increase Your Competence, raise your Relevance, build Strength, increase the Quality and Quantity of Information, multiply the Number, and double the Diversity of your network. We start with the most important of all the keys, your Character.

Before discussing Character, we have to acknowledge the tension between managing your network *strategically*, and managing your network *successfully*. For example, if people perceive that you give to charity primarily to demonstrate your Character, you reduce the impact of your charitable donation.

Let us say you meet someone at a conference:

Fran: "Hi! I'm Fran Smithers with SFA Software. How are you?"

Wai: "I'm fine. I'm Wai Ching, with ENC Corp."

Fran: "I sell sales force analysis software. I noticed that you're a salesperson. Are you in a position at ENC to make buying decisions about software?"

Wai: "I need to refill my drink. Bye!"

A common problem with self-described "networking functions" is that most attendees are explicitly focused on meeting new people to achieve immediate professional goals: a sales lead, a new job, an executive to hire, and so on. When people are primarily focused on "What's in it for me?" and "How can you help me?," they are usually so self-centered that it's difficult to build a strong relationship with them. They are so busy listening to radio station WII-FM ("What's in It for Me?")[210] that they cannot hear you.

This is why the best relationship building does not take place at "networking" functions; it happens at meetings, conferences, virtual communities, and other venues where the people are united by a common goal *other* than meeting one another. For example, Renaissance Weekend hosts a series of nonpartisan, family retreats "to build bridges among innovative leaders from diverse fields." Prominent leaders from business, media, academe, and all other fields of endeavor attend these events. Renaissance is an extremely effective opportunity to build new relationships, because the attendees are relaxed and in a family setting.

At a business conference, most attendees are focused on "How can I make money from you?" At Renaissance, the culture is, "The person I just met has been screened as someone worth meeting. What can I learn from this person?" That is an ideal mindset for meeting new people.

We recommend participating when possible in events or virtual venues that bring together people with an altruistic goal and a common interest *other* than themselves. Conversations tend to focus initially on the common charitable endeavor, rather than "What do you do for a living?" Once you make the bond—you both care about raising money for bone marrow donor regis-tration—the conversation will naturally evolve towards other topics that are of business interest.

How can you resolve this tension between strategically managing your network and not being perceived as exploitive? We think that the resolution is first, being a sincerely empathic person, and second, ensuring that your actions are correctly understood.

If you are a sincerely empathic person, then you are the lucky possessor of a very admirable Character trait. But let us say you are not; instead, you are a self-centered person who aspires to be a better person. Figuring out how to improve your Character is a lengthy, arduous process beyond our scope. The best counsel is from Aristotle, who wrote: "We are what we repeatedly do." If you lack the Character trait of loving kindness—the sincere desire to be of service to others—then the best way to overcome it is simply to do it. Be kinder to people, and you will be a kinder person.

Stephen Covey observed that much of modern success literature is focused on the superficial: how to appear considerate. You will do better to focus on building your Character and *being* considerate.[211]

We think that the best way to make sure your actions are correctly under-stood is to be up-front. If you are a real estate broker, say, "I think this is an excellent house for you. It's slightly more expensive than the other house I showed you, and I admit that I have a financial incentive to sell a more ex-pensive house. But it's a better deal for you, for several reasons. . . ." The fact that you're being direct will increase your credibility. For more on this point, we suggest *The Trusted Advisor,* by David Maister, Charles H. Green, and Rob Galford.

The second step toward resolution is ensuring that your actions are cor-rectly understood. Monitor closely how people interact with you, because if they think that you are manipulating them they will likely show it. You want them to see you as a professional, with a legitimate business interest in sell-ing a quality house, who also has the person's best interests at heart. If you sense that they are worried or tense about you, then raise it: "You seem a lit-tle concerned. Do you have any questions that I could help you with?"

High Character, Face to Face and Virtually

Table 17-1 offers a few ideas on how to build and demonstrate your Charac-ter, face to face and virtually.[212]

Lead Your Peers

Andy Sernovitz, CEO of GasPedal and founder of the Word of Mouth Market-ing Association observes, "I believe in creating activities that let me relate to

TABLE 17-1. Building and Demonstrating Your Character

Face to Face	Virtually	Character Trait You Are Both Building and Demonstrating
Play host. Even if you are not an organizer, think of yourself as the host for an event.	**Host a virtual discussion or blog.** You can also offer to be a guest host (e.g., many blogs schedule "guest bloggers").	**Responsibility.** A leadership role pushes you to focus on ensuring the event's success.
Take the initiative. Walk up to someone you do not know, shake hands, and find out who they are.	**Meet Relevant people.** Search the virtual community and send e-mails to the people who share interests with you.	**A bias for action.** As journalist Wes "Scoop" Nisker says, "If you don't like the news . . . go out and make some of your own."[213]
Be a connector. Introduce people who would mutually benefit by meeting.	**Be a connector.** Comment on someone's blog post: "I suggest you read my friend Arash Farin's very relevant blog post."	**Consideration.** This creates a triple win: the two people have a productive discussion, and you have Strengthened your tie to them.
Be present. Talk and pay attention to the people right around you. People notice when you are ignoring them while scanning the room looking to talk with someone more important. Do not assume you understand what you hear; repeat back to verify you understand.	**Pay attention to the context.** Do not just send e-mails randomly; skim others' postings first.	**Emotional intelligence.**[214] Perceptiveness of verbal and non-verbal signals.
Ask open-ended questions that make it easy for people to relax and respond.	**Create dialogue** that is interesting and helpful.	**Communications skills.** Henry Kissinger said, "The nice thing about being a celebrity is that when you bore people, they think it's their

(continued)

TABLE 17-1. *Continued*

Face to Face	Virtually	Character Trait You Are Both Building and Demonstrating
		fault."[215] You are helping people to discover the most interesting aspects of themselves.
Acknowledge people publicly and privately. Thank people for the opportunity to meet or talk. Best, thank people in front of others.	**Acknowledge people publicly and privately.** Thank people for responding quickly to your e-mails, or perhaps for joining the community.	**Gratitude.** A desire to make others feel positive about themselves.
Find people to talk with that you do not already know, and who come from different backgrounds than you.	**Join and become active in a virtual community that gives you access to a new, foreign group of people.**	**Tolerance. Multiculturalism.**

lots of people more efficiently than I can one-on-one." Being in a leadership position builds and demonstrates your Character to all of the members in that organization.

Scott Stratten, a marketing consultant, is one of more than 1,000 network leaders on the Ryze virtual community. His "Un-Marketing Network" is one of the largest on Ryze, with over 2,500 members after just one year in existence. He is also in charge of marketing for the local Ryze group in Toronto.

In the first year of his participation on Ryze, Stratten attributes more than U.S. $20,000 in revenue directly to people he met through Ryze. He has also added over 1,000 subscribers to his newsletter, received publicity in *USA Today* and *Fast Company,* hired a creative director and a virtual assistant, and developed multiple strategic partnerships.

"Networking online is no different than networking offline," he says. "Become a known leader in the field, offer your expertise, help people out, and business will happen."[216]

A key skill for being a leader face to face and virtually is public speaking. Public speaking gives you excellent exposure to a large group of people in a format designed to give you instant credibility. If you do not have many opportunities to speak, you may want to join your local chapter of ToastMasters (ToastMasters.org), a not-for-profit designed to improve people's public speaking skills. Online, this can range from giving free teleclasses (conference calls), using a service such as FreeConference.com or FreeConferenceCall.com, on up to fully interactive online meetings using a Web conferencing service.

The most important thing a leader does with her group is to offer a space where people can get things done. Jerrilynn Thomas, founder of the International Virtual Women's Chamber of Commerce, has created a unique format for the group's monthly virtual meet and greets. She poses a series of topics to the discussion list which get people to talk about their business, but not (for the most part) in sales-pitch format.

Sample questions:

→ "Share your three top business tips with everyone to show them you are a leader in your field."

→ "Complete the sentence: I want to form alliances with the following types of companies. . . ."

→ "Lay down on our virtual couch and tell us what is ailing your business."

→ "Tell everyone about your current newsletter. Let them know how to subscribe to it."

→ "Tell everyone what makes your company unique."

Giving people explicit permission to talk about their business helps keep participants from being self-conscious that they may be perceived as spamming. The nature of the topics encourages participants to exchange knowledge and build alliances, rather than focusing just on direct sales.

It seems to work. Scott Allen attended the October 2004 event and witnessed several strategic alliances and even a couple of direct deals being made publicly on the list, in addition to whatever off-list activity occurred.

Show, Don't Tell (Walk the Talk)

It is far more powerful to show people who you are by your actions, rather than tell people who you are with mere words. Prominent science fiction writer Robert J. Sawyer writes:

Every writing student has heard the rule that you should show, not tell, but this principle seems to be among the hardest for beginners to master.

First, what's the difference between the two? Well, "telling" is the reliance on simple exposition: Mary was an old woman. "Showing," on the other hand, is the use of evocative description: Mary moved slowly across the room, her hunched form supported by a polished wooden cane gripped in a gnarled, swollen-jointed hand that was covered by translucent, liver-spotted skin.

Both showing and telling convey the same information—Mary is old—but the former simply states it flat-out, and the latter—well, read the example over again and you'll see it never actually states that fact at all, and yet nonetheless leaves no doubt about it in the reader's mind.

Why is showing better? Two reasons. First, it creates mental pictures for the reader. When reviewers use terms like "vivid," "evocative," or "cinematic" to describe a piece of prose, they really mean the writer has succeeded at showing, rather than merely telling.

Second, showing is interactive and participatory: it forces the reader to become involved in the story, deducing facts (such as Mary's age) for himself or herself, rather than just taking information in passively.[217]

We would add a third point to Sawyer's two points: showing creates perceived Character and Competence that telling cannot. For example, if you say, "I am a real people person," but you come across as arrogant, what you say about yourself will carry far less credibility than what people observe about you. One of the advantages of building business relationships online is that many more people have the chance to see how you act, and draw their own conclusions about the sort of person you are.

In a résumé or an e-mail, we always recommend that you give people specific Information about your accomplishments. "For my last job, I was the executive assistant to the CEO. Some days, I would work closely with the CEO to build financial models for analyses of potential deals. On other days, I worked with the head of the mechanics' union to discuss how we could tighten our relationship with them." Your listener will deduce that you must have a broad set of people skills to work with such a range of people. Because your listener completed the deduction himself, the insight will carry far more weight. You have provided a proof for your otherwise unsupported statement.

This principle applies not only to major accomplishments, but to smaller commitments, even those outside of the business context. Ann Baber and Lynne Waymon observe: "If you do a great job, people will assume that you are great at your profession. Conversely, if you promise to do something, but do not come through, people will assume that you are not competent. That is the "All or Nothing" Principle: If you do one thing well, people will assume you do everything well. If you do one thing poorly, people will assume you do nothing well."[218]

One of the advantages (or disadvantages) of meeting people virtually is that it is harder to segment different parts of your life. For example, you may not publicize to your coworkers that you are an active member of the International Flat Earth Research Society. However, if someone meets you online, they are likely to search for your name and uncover that you are the President of the Society.

This principle can actually encourage you to be more self-consistent. We are not saying that you should not engage in unconventional personal activities, but rather that increased visibility will help you stick to activities of which you can be proud. When your words and actions in your professional and personal life are congruent, this generates a confidence—a lack of fear of exposure—that increases your Character.

Safeguarding Your Reputation

We suggest searching for your name and your organization on the major search engines at least once a quarter for two reasons: first, to ensure that you hold a top position; and second, to monitor for negative publicity. Do not just go through the first three pages—look through everything. You might want to put your name in quotes: "Reid Hoffman" (2,000 results) vs. Reid Hoffman (145,000 results)[219].

Rob Key, President and CEO at communications agency Converseon, warns about negative PR tactics:

> Reputation attacks are characterized by organized people or groups publishing damaging fact and fiction about an organization or individual, which is then distributed globally through mechanisms such as blogs, chat rooms, e-mail, newsgroups, and Web sites. All of which are available through search engines. . . .
>
> Companies have a vast amount of content they underoptimize [in search engines]: articles, press releases, investor information, white papers, and third party content. If you fully optimize compelling relevant content, you accomplish two goals: (1) articulate your key messages to your target audience, and (2) push down the negative, irresponsible rankings down . . . out of the top rankings.[220]

So what do you do if you find some dirt on yourself? If it is inaccurate or libelous, you can contact the site and request they remove it. You can also do some damage control. Like Michael Milken, you may want to have an answer on your site to explain your point of view about negative PR you have received.[221] Or you may want to provide an ample supply of good Information about you well positioned in the search engines and on multiple Web sites, so the negative Information languishes in obscurity.[222]

Smile Like a Dolphin

Virtually every self-help book ever written discusses "the power of positive thinking." No one wants to work with someone who radiates negative energy.

In communicating virtually, your positive or negative interactions can leave a highly visible trail and consequently have much more of a long-term impact. For example, if a potential employer searches for your name and sees you complaining in a newsgroup, your future boss will think less of your Character.

Jack, a Stanford MBA, had been looking for a job for almost 18 months. An accountant by training, he dutifully set a goal for himself of meeting at least 12 people per week. By leveraging the Stanford alumni community, he was usually successful in meeting that goal. As a result, he had a "network" of literally hundreds of well-placed executives working for quality firms. He also used e-mail merge (built into Microsoft Word) to send his résumé to many, many people.

Why was he unemployed for so long? Moreover, why is "network" in quotation marks?

In addition to the culprit of a bad economy, Jack was significantly depressed by his unemployment, and this was quite visible. As a result, most people he met thought of him most prominently as an unsuccessful MBA—just because his negative attitude made him come across as unprofessional and unsuccessful. His "networking" in part prolonged his job search, because he was violating the "First Rule of Holes: If you are in one, stop digging."[223]

Some of the mistakes that he made:

→ **Sending out overly frequent update e-mails** that carried text along the lines of, "Just to update you, I am still working as an independent consultant and looking for a full-time opportunity." These had a tone of desperation, because they did not have any good news embedded in them. We advise sending out update e-mails only when you have real news, even if it's as simple as changing your phone number.

→ **Sending out résumés to multiple recruiters simultaneously using blind carbon copy ("BCC"),** which made it clear to recruiters that he was desperate and spreading his résumé everywhere.

→ **Making silly mistakes in his e-mails.** For example, sending out résumés which showed revision-tracking; people could see the changes that he made in the résumé from a prior version. Or, sending cover letters addressed to Nokia that were mailed to Ericsson. Another error: addressing letters to "Dear Sir," when so many businesspeople are genetically limited from being a "Sir."[224]

Over time, each interaction was hurting him further, because more and more people began to think of Jack as depressed and having trouble finding a job. At this point, he was less likely to be hired by someone who had met him, than by someone who merely had looked at his reasonably impressive résumé. His "networking" was actually producing negative results, even though his goals for meeting people and his activities were impressive.

The Internet worsened his problem, because dramatically more people were exposed to his unsuccessful approach than would otherwise have been the case. More and more people thought less and less of his Character.

Even if you are looking for a job—which for many people is depressing—maintain a sense of adventure about the whole process of meeting people. Reframe the job hunt as a chance to make new friends, and to meet new people who may be good partners for you over all of the coming decades.

You can "smile" virtually as well as face to face:

→ **Use upbeat, positive language.** Convey that you love your work, your career, and/or what you are selling. "I really enjoy working with the people in my group."

→ **Share the successes and positive things that are happening in your life.** "I just ran a marathon this weekend, and I can barely walk."

→ **Far more valuable, share the successes and positive things that are happening in *others'* lives in a group.** Let's say that you are a member of a mailing list for people in your section in business school. You learn that one of your section mates was in the *New York Times* because she sold her firm. You send out an e-mail saying, "Congratulations to Anne on the great news!" and attaching the article.

Using these techniques will prompt people to think of you as a more positive person, will make you a more positive person, and will together help to make you a higher-Character person.

An Attitude of Gratitude

There is little that brightens someone's day more than a sincere, heart-felt "thank you." While handwritten notes are a nice touch, you can create even more impact with a well-written guestbook entry, forum posting, or e-mail.

The great advantage of electronic "thank yous" is that they can be public, and therefore other people can see how much value the person who helped you has provided.

The key is to be very specific. A final reply to someone simply saying "Thanks!" is a nice gesture—a common courtesy—but will have little emotional impact. Instead, let the person or group know specifically how what they did impacted you positively.

For example, a Web designer sent a thank-you message to someone she met on OpenBC who had sent her a referral. She included this:

> You are a constant source for calm, practical insights here at OpenBC. I've come to value your opinion in a wide variety of situations, from heated discussions to technical inquiries. You add tremendous value to this space, and I'm very grateful!
>
> Warmest regards from a loyal fan

What could have been a mere polite acknowledgment instead became a relationship-building experience. The fact that she took the time for more than a one-liner shows the importance to her of both what was done and of developing the relationship further.

Who can you thank today?

18

Increase Your Competence

→ When you produce results you gain
credibility. When you have credibility,
you will have an easier time producing
results.—BRIAN KOSLOW, AUTHOR, *365 WAYS
TO BECOME A MILLIONAIRE (WITHOUT BEING
BORN ONE)*[225]

Yali Friedman, Ph.D., the Biotechnology Guide for About.com, explains how
he leveraged his position as a part-time online journalist into a lucrative
career by demonstrating his Competence and building powerful relationships
within his industry:

"In the second year of my biochemistry doctoral studies, I found myself unfulfilled and yearning to be better connected with the business
side of my research. I was fortunate to find an opening at About.com
to create and manage a Web site on the biotechnology industry, and
was accepted following a competitive process. I decided to position the
site as a resource for business professionals seeking to understand the
unique commercial aspects of the biotechnology industry and entrepreneurial scientists seeking to commercialize their inventions and
discoveries.

"My site became quite popular with my target audience. At industry conferences, readers from as far away as Hungary immediately recognized me from the photograph on my Web pages, making it much

easier for me to build relationships with new people. I was also named to Forbes' 'Best of the Web.'

"I quickly began to realize significant fringe benefits from my broad new international network. Corresponding with industry insiders has given me a privileged view of the issues that are driving the industry at any given time, and has led me to some valuable spinoffs. I picked up over half a dozen consulting clients while still a student. I recently published a book on biotechnology business development, *Building Biotechnology*, that is based largely on the same editorial strategy as my Web site.

"Repeated requests for information on drug patent expirations made me aware of an unmet market need for this information. This led me to develop thinkPharm.com, a competitive intelligence service which now generates thousands of dollars a month in revenue.

"I could not have become involved with these multiple ventures without my About.com role and the network that it opened to me. Now that I have finished my Ph.D., these ventures furnish me with a challenging professional career and a salary far beyond the expectations of a Ph.D. biochemist (or bench scientist), with a lesser workload."

Your Competence is your ability to "walk the talk" and to do well the job that you claim to be able to do. Your Competence is different for every person in your network, because different people have different opinions about you.

The best way to build your Competence is to do a good job. You may be an active contributor to a virtual community, but if you position yourself as a marketing consultant and your posts are full of spelling and grammatical errors, then you have weak perceived Competence.

Reputation currency is also known as "whuffie" (from Cory Doctorow's novel, *Down and Out in the Magic Kingdom*) or "karma" (from Slashdot.org's reputation system). Your reputation is a currency; if you have high whuffie, you should be able to exchange that for a higher salary or a better job. "Enterprise whuffie" is the reputation that employees can acquire by becoming known as experts in a given area.[226]

Your Outboard Brain

Hedge fund manager Michael Margolis observes that successful people "do the mundane in a sublime way." If you invest the energy to learn how to speed read, how to touch type, and how to use standard office productivity software comfortably, you will become far more productive. You will make the mundane sublime.

One example of this phenomenon is how well you manage the information that helps you do what you need to do. Author Cory Doctorow calls his blog his "outboard brain": the place where he archives information that he needs.[227] Your files, and better yet your blog, are a powerful way to organize your own accumulated learning.

Whenever David Teten has to work on a process, he collects information on how to do that process. As a result, he has accumulated documentation of best practices for every major process he has been part of: working on an acquisition of a company, raising venture capital, getting into business school, running a company, interviewing employees, finding a spouse, organizing a wedding, writing a book, and so on. Because these files are all conveniently organized, they are easy for him to share.

For example, whenever a friend of his starts a new job, he sends that person his files on how to shine in your new job. At no marginal cost, he can be a very useful resource for his friend.

The typical computer user has knowledge filed in many places: e-mail attachments, notes in a contact manager, browser bookmarks, local file folders, and so on. One option for organizing all this information is a desktop search tool, such as Google Desktop Search. This tool allows you to search the Internet, local file folders, e-mail messages, and even e-mail attachments, all in a single unified interface.

Another way to stay organized is to save documents that you review to your local hard drive. This makes it much easier to distinguish the files that you have already identified as useful from the infinite amount of information in the world. Also, Web sites change all the time; there is no guarantee that the document that you thought was useful will continue to be available at the location where you first found it, or in its current form.

We recommend saving all of your information by category (e.g., Clients, Family, Finances, Reference, and Reading). The Reading folder is a temporary area, an inbox for documents you want to read soon. As you read each document, first forward it to people in your network who would find it of interest, and then either discard it or file it under Reference.

Knowledge workers spend as much as 35 percent of their time searching for information, and are successful in finding what they seek less than 50 percent of the time.[228] By keeping your electronic files well-organized and setting up the tools to search them quickly and effectively, you will not only become a better resource to your network, you will dramatically increase your overall productivity.

Let Your Light Shine Bright

Your Competence is of little value in building new relationships if other people cannot readily learn about it. Online, it's easy to show external validation:

advanced degrees, professional certifications, awards you have received, and other publicly verifiable accomplishments. List them anywhere you include biographical information—social network profiles, article bylines, your personal Web page. Of course, do not fabricate, exaggerate, or over-glorify your qualifications. Also, be context sensitive. On business-focused sites such as LinkedIn, it is normative to upload your entire résumé with (hopefully) all of your many honors. On some other more informal sites, that can be perceived as showing off.

Even if you do not have a long list of such accomplishments, you can get public validation of your Competence through public endorsements from people with whom you have worked. These do have a very significant impact. LinkedIn reports that a profile with endorsements is four times more likely to be picked for a contact request than one without. LinkedIn contact requests are 25 percent more likely to be accepted by the recipient if the requester has even one endorsement.

If an online business network does not have a formal endorsement mechanism, they are commonly left in users' guestbooks. In this situation, it may be awkward to explicitly ask someone you have worked with for an endorsement. Instead, take the initiative and leave an endorsement for the person you would like an endorsement from. You Strengthen your relationship with that person, and the recipient will likely reciprocate.

By documenting and continuously improving every process you work on, you can become a dramatically more Competent person.

19

Raise the Relevance of Your Network

→ Problems can become opportunities when the right people come together.—ROBERT SOUTH, ENGLISH THEOLOGIAN (1634–1716)

Sean Jacobsohn made a targeted appeal to his alumni network to close a seven-figure deal for his company:

Jacobsohn is a Harvard MBA and Senior Sales Director for Wage-Works, which administers employee benefit programs. He looked in the Harvard alumni directory to identify a Senior Vice President at a bank he saw as a future client. His target firm was one of the few large financial services companies WageWorks had not yet secured as a client. He told the fellow Harvard graduate, via e-mail, whom he wanted to speak with inside the company. He specified exactly why he wanted to approach that person, and how he could be of service to the Company.

This led to an introduction to the Senior Vice President of Human Resources—the decision maker. "This was the biggest deal I ever closed, seven figures," says Sean. "And it was possible to get this started entirely online. I never met the other Harvard alumnus face to face."

Relevance is a person's value to you, defined as her ability to contribute to your specific goals. Relevance is typically driven by the value of the other person's own network: her Character, Competence, Relevance of the people she herself knows, the Strength of her relationships with them, and the Information, Number, and Diversity of her network.

As an example of why Relevance matters, one study found that the higher the prestige of a person who introduces you to a new job, the higher-prestige that job is likely to be.[229] "Them that has, gets."[230] The more powerful your network (in the broad sense of that word), the more attractive other people will find you. People who are highly Relevant are only likely to be interested in you if you are also seen as highly Relevant.

What Is Relevance?

Relevance can only be meaningfully defined as what constitutes high value to you. If you work in the aerospace industry, then you are likely to be particularly interested in relationships with aerospace executives.

"Relevance" is not a judgment of moral worthiness, intelligence, wealth, or power. It's a shorthand way of indicating that some people in your personal network are of greater potential aid for your purposes than others.

Every company is surrounded by a working group constellation: investors, lawyers, accountants, and so on. If you want to sell to that company, these are the most Relevant people to reach. They must know who you are, respect you, and like you.

Consider Carlos, a first-time novelist. The CEO of a major computer company is probably not of very high Relevance for Carlos. By contrast, the moderator of a small mailing list for authors and publishers is a much higher Relevance person who could be of immediate assistance to Carlos. That said, the CEO probably knows other senior people who could be of high Relevance to Carlos.

Target by Industry and by Company

The Internet is ideal for identifying companies and industries that would be highly Relevant for you. You can find companies in your target space by looking them up with Standard Industrial Classification (SIC) codes, through industry directories, through membership in trade groups, through virtual communities, and of course by asking people. The SIC codes are a standard way of categorizing all companies by industry. You can download an exhaustive list of SIC codes at the U.S. Securities and Exchange Commission Web site (sec.gov/info/edgar/siccodes.htm).

To develop a target company list via SIC code, a good first stop is Price waterhouseCoopers' EdgarScan (EdgarScan.PWCGlobal.com/EdgarScan/sic_list.html). From this site, you can download a free list of leading companies in all the major SIC codes.

Pick approximately a dozen SIC codes of interest. In addition, make a list of a dozen companies with characteristics of interest to you and compare their SIC codes to your initial list. Refine the list using those two techniques to create a master list of the SIC codes that are most relevant to your interests. Further refine it by geography (zip codes) and annual sales. Your target list of companies, using these selection criteria, can then be readily compiled by an information service provider such as Dun & Bradstreet (DNB.com).

What if you are interested in selling to or getting a job with a young company, which is not likely to show up in the public databases? Although the online directories do not usually include the newest companies, you can learn about relevant young companies by talking with venture capitalists and/or by monitoring such sources as VentureWire (VentureWire.com). Newly funded companies are very likely to be purchasing and/or hiring, and so may be good targets for you.

Connect "Up" Virtually

Many people have an impression that the business elites are not accessible virtually, but instead are best reached on the golf course, the board of a Fortune 500 company, or perhaps at an industry conference. In reality, many senior executives are quite accessible by e-mail, which is much less likely to be filtered by a secretary than is a phone call. In addition, senior executives are sometimes active in exclusive virtual forums unique to their particular interests. Businesspeople at all levels of seniority are using all of the tools that we discuss in this book.

Following are some tips for building relationships above you in the corporate/social hierarchy:

→ **Look for intermediate links.** Social software can help you figure out the best path to a particular person. Ask a strong tie to send an e-mail introducing you to the person you want to meet, with you listed as a carbon copy ("CC") on the e-mail. The CC makes it easy for the target to reply to you promptly.

→ **Participate in selective virtual communities geared to your target population.** For example, a senior marketing executive may participate in marketing forums such as the Marketing Executive Networking Group (MENGOnline.com) or MarketingProfs.com.

→ **Search for press releases** regarding any of the people and/or companies where you want to make connections, and use the news in the press release as a reason for contacting them.

→ **Meet the nodes.** Some virtual communities, such as Ecademy, make public lists of the "top" most connected people, based on reputation, activity, or some combination of those attributes. Connecting with these people is an excellent way to expand your network's quality and size with low marginal effort. These people usually have a high Number of relationships and are happy to meet new people. However, as we have discussed earlier, the person with the biggest Number of relationships is usually *not* the person with the most truly valuable network.

→ **Sometimes the direct approach works.** Auren Hoffman, Chairman of the Stonebrick Group, reports: "A friend of mine attended an inspiring speech by a CEO at a hot technology company. That night, my friend sent an e-mail to the CEO with his résumé saying how much he'd like to work for the company. But my friend did not know the CEO's e-mail address. So what did he do? He sent five e-mails to five different addresses—firstname.last name@company.com, firstname@company.com, lastname@company.com, flastname@company.com, firstnamel@company.com—hoping that one would get through. The next morning my friend received an e-mail from the CEO: "Heh, I got all five of your e-mails. You must really want to work here. Let's schedule an interview for tomorrow. Sure enough, two weeks later, my friend was working for the new company."[231] Another trick: search the Web for the phrase "mailto ibm.com," which will pull up samples of the e-mail format that IBM employees use. Alternatively, try using Yahoo!'s Advanced People Search.

Collecting Names (as Well as Gift Bags) at Events

The attendance list from an event you are attending is a powerful tool to grow your network. Ideally, you will get the list ahead of time. E-mail the attendees and say, "I noticed that you are also attending the upcoming conference in Atlanta. Would you have some time there to meet?"

You can do this even after the event is over. An e-mail address with the subject line, "Follow-up on the Atlanta widget conference" is much more likely to get opened than an e-mail with the subject line, "Random stranger wants to talk with you." The mere fact that you were physically present in the same venue serves as an effective introduction to the person.

It's a mistake to send a sales pitch: "I wanted to contact you to tell you about what we sell." Instead, think of a way to give first and ask later. For example, you can say, "Incidentally, I blogged all of my notes on the widget conference at _____ . Perhaps you will find my notes helpful."

Whenever you attend an event, keep a list of all the attendees. Then you can send each of them a note after the event with a link to your blog notes from the presentation. This is also an excellent way to build relationships with the speakers at an event.

You can save all of your lists of attendees in an "Events" folder. Whenever you want to find other people interested in the topic of last year's conference in Dallas, or cannot remember the name of someone you met briefly in Tokyo, just look at the attendee list from the event.

What Do I Bring to the Table?

Relevance works both ways. At the same time that you are interested in meeting people who are high Relevance for you, you should be developing yourself to be a person of high Relevance for the types of people with whom you want to connect.

People typically develop their strongest relationships with people of a similar level to themselves.[232] If you are a financial advisor focused on building relationships with wealthy people, you will benefit from dressing and handling yourself like someone who is wealthy. Better yet, *be* wealthy. (Easier said than done.)

Many people are intimidated by building relationships with people far senior to themselves. They wonder: how can they bring any value to the interaction? Why should the "great and powerful Oz" have anything to do with little me?

The answer is that you have many ways to be of service to the senior executive:

→ **Help Mr. Big find a job for his child.**

→ **Introduce Mr. Big to new people;** he cannot possibly know all of the people you know in the sectors in which you are an expert.

→ **Introduce Mr. Big to new ideas and new technologies,** perhaps even social software.

If we had to summarize this chapter in two words, they would be: *you first.* Work on becoming more successful, more of a star, yourself. Then, and only then, other highly Relevant people will flock to you like bees to a flower.

20

Build Strong Ties

→ The shortest distance between two
people is solving a common puzzle.
—VANESSA DIMAURO, VICE PRESIDENT OF
STRATEGY AND RESEARCH, CXO SYSTEMS[233]

Many salespeople spend a tremendous time and energy playing golf and
drinking beers with customers. They believe that a personal "I like him"
relationship is key to closing the sale.

Neil Rackham, founder of sales consultancy Huthwaite, conducted a study
of whether salespeople who built good relationships would, in fact, really
make more sales:

> We found that sellers who dealt successfully with small retail out-
> lets in rural areas seemed to rely heavily on personal factors in their
> selling. . . . For example, the seller might ask, "How's Ann enjoying
> her riding lessons?" . . . In rural areas, where the size of the sale was
> small, successful sellers used more of these personal references than
> did sellers who were less successful.
>
> But it was a different story in the large urban stores, where the
> average sale was more than 5 times the size. *We found no relationship
> between success and reference to personal issues* [emphasis added].
>
> Even in the mere 15 years I've been studying selling, I've noticed
> a distinct change. Fifteen years ago buyers would tell me, "I buy from
> Fred because I like him." Now I'm much more likely to hear, "I like Fred,

but I buy from his competition because they're cheaper." It seems that personal loyalty is no longer an adequate basis for doing business.

I've heard many other professional buyers complain about sales-people who try to open calls by cultivating areas of personal interest. The last thing a busy buyer wants is to tell the tenth seller of the day all about his last game of golf. . . . Many buyers become suspicious of people who begin by raising areas of personal interest.[234]

Strength measures the closeness of the relationship between you and another person. Following are some of the characteristics that distinguish a strong from a weak tie; we list these as food for thought on how you can Strengthen your relationships.[235]

Aspects of the Relationship

→ **Age of the relationship.** The cliché that "old friends are the best friends" is supported by the academic research in this area.

→ **Frequency of contact.** The more contact people have online, the greater the impression they make on each other.[236]

→ **Emotional attachment.** Do you care about one another?

→ **Reciprocity.** Do you regularly do random acts of kindness for one another?

→ **Number of dimensions.** For example, if you are a colleague of Carol's, *and* you went to college with her, *and* you sing in a choir together, then you have a multi-dimensional ("multiplex") relationship.

→ **Common activities.** Whether or not two people have shared activities is a much better predictor of their becoming friends than whether or not they have common values.[237]

→ **Degree of closeness involved in an earlier encounter, however brief.** Stressful situations such as foxholes and work crises can establish extremely strong ties.[238]

Context of the Relationship

→ **Kinship.** Even if you do not see your cousin often, you still have a tie because of your common blood.

→ **Common language, values, and background.** It is much easier to bond with those similar to ourselves.

→ **Physical Proximity.** The likelihood that you will collaborate with someone drops very significantly if they are based more than just 50 feet away from you.[239]

→ **Number of common ties.** If you know multiple people in common, that Strengthens your tie.

→ **Barriers to entry of the context in which you meet.** The harder you work for something, the more you appreciate it, and the more appreciation you have for your comrades who passed the same tests. Fraternities haze and Microsoft has grueling job interviews for the same reason: they are quality tests, and they make people value the ties within those organizations much more highly. The application of this principle for virtual communities is the entrance requirement. The International Executives Resource Group is a highly effective group largely because it has high barriers to entry.

The Stronger your relationship, generally the more successful you will be in your business relationship together:

→ **You learn about more business opportunities** because people in your network are more likely to turn to you with leads.

→ **You get better deals.** In a study of Chicago banking, Brian Uzzi found that, "firms that embed their commercial transactions with their lender in social attachments receive lower interest rates on loans."[240]

→ **You close more deals.** In a study of network marketing home parties, "the degree of strength of the buyer-seller tie and buyer indebtedness to the seller, significantly affected the likelihood of purchase."[241]

→ **"Strong ties have greater motivation to be of assistance and are more likely to be available,"** observes Mark Granovetter.[242]

→ **Strong ties reduce transaction costs,** such as legal fees.[243]

→ **The people who trust your strong ties are more likely to trust you.**[244] If you are applying for a job to Nadine, and your common friend Matias refers you, Nadine's initial level of trust in you is much higher than it would be for a stranger.

→ **Lastly, strong ties are particularly important when you are in an insecure position.** For example, Ron Burt advises women in a male-dominated corporation to build a strong relationship with a senior strategic partner (not their boss), who can endorse them to the rest of their organization.[245] The woman needs the Strong tie with the senior executive in order to offset the fact that she is perceived as less Relevant.

We believe that building a Strong relationship is best achieved by working together toward a common goal. Sell a product and make sure that it's integrated into the customer's systems; take a class together; work on a project together; volunteer with the same organization; or even negotiate against one another.

Your close friend Jacques is a lawyer. However, you have never actually used him in his capacity as a lawyer. When Sarah asks you for a recommendation for a lawyer, your recommendation of Jacques will be weak at best . . . until and unless you use Jacques' professional services.

Returning to Neil Rackham's analysis: whether or not you should focus on personal interests during the sales process varies depending on the context. The same is true online. For example, Heidi Whitaker is a work-at-home mother who sells nutritional supplements and other wellness products from Synergy Worldwide, a multilevel marketing company. Her Ryze profile shows not product information, but resources about nutritional support for autoimmune disease, including a free newsletter and a free teleclass, in which "no product brand names will be mentioned or discussed."[246] She emphasizes building trusted personal relationships, including participating in "chatty" discussion forums:

> What has helped my business grow the most was joining a chitty-chatty group and doing very little to directly promote my business. Members came to know and TRUST the mom who is potty-training her toddler, homeschooling the older children, and madly in love with her husband. These network members are now my (true) friends. An outgrowth of this kind of relationship building has been them promoting me to others.
>
> In my business, "warm market" is critical. . . . More than half of my new business now comes from people I have met on Ryze.[247]

Influence: The Psychology of Reciprocity

Much of what we teach relies on the psychological principle of reciprocity: when you help people, they are more likely to help you. They may even feel obliged to help you.

Robert Cialdini's insightful book, *Influence: the Psychology of Persuasion,* offers extensive theoretical and empirical support for this principle.[248] Human societies train people to live by the rule of reciprocity, because this principle helps societies to function. People can make sacrifices for the group in the confidence that the group will, in exchange, take care of them.

For the sake of argument, let us analyze the worst that could happen if you are a very generous person. You help your friend Kevin get a job; you introduce him to his wife; you even offer your regular babysitting services when he is feeling overwhelmed by his new twins. And you are hoping he will use your investment banking services.

Suddenly, Kevin moves to Japan, and you never hear from him again. Kevin does not even respond to e-mails. You may feel that you have overinvested in Kevin. You may feel resentful that you never received anything from your many contributions. You may write us to request a refund for this book.

However, are you happy with yourself that you were a giving person? Do you think that you have contributed to your community by being such a giving person? Do Kevin's friends and community see you and admire your generosity?

Whether or not Kevin ever reciprocates, we would rather be a "lovecat"[249] than an alleycat.

Lovingkindness and Staying Connected

"Networking" has a bad name among some, in large part because it's perceived as being centered on how you can exploit others. On the contrary: true "networking" is finding how you can best help others. In Donna Fisher's book *Professional Networking for Dummies,* she defines "networking" as "people sharing and caring for one another."[250]

People resent being contacted only when you want to "use" them. They prefer at least the semblance (better yet the reality) of a long-term relationship. "[I]t takes about six or seven contacts with someone before they know who you are and before they have you in a marketplace niche in their mind," says career expert Lynne Waymon.[251] If you contact a person only when you have a request, he or she is likely to have forgotten you, as well as resent the fact that you have connected first with a "take" instead of a "give."

So your objective is to help people, support them, and also ping them periodically so that they have you in mind. Here are some ideas on how to do this[252]:

→ **Provide business leads.** E-mail your friend to point out people in online communities whom they should meet.

→ **Recognize and share successes.** Mail your group with the good news!

→ **Mentor a young person.** Make sure to register as an alumni advisor with your university.

→ **Send an invitation to join a virtual community** or participate in an online conference or blog.

→ **Send a thank you note for something the person sent you.**

→ **Contact the person to ask for advice on something** (for example, a company you are analyzing, marketing brochure you are finalizing, equipment purchase you are researching). This makes the person feel respected and authoritative, and it has built-in follow-up: you contact the person later to let the person know how the recommendation worked. Of course, the request should be sincere and appropriate.

→ **Send an e-mail with a link to an interesting article or Web site.** It's valuable to maintain a file of areas of common interest of your friends. For example, keep a short list of the e-mail addresses of all the people that you know who work in the pharmaceutical industry. Whenever you come across news or information relevant to the pharmaceutical industry, you can easily forward to those people with a simple cut and paste. You might also keep lists by interest: friends looking to get married, Democratic friends, Pakistani friends, etc.

→ **Observe what's important to them.** Send a St. Patrick's Day card to an Irish client or a Happy Chinese New Year card to a Chinese friend. These are far more noticeable and appreciated than a generic "Happy New Year" card.

→ **Speak their language.** If you have a Turkish friend, search online for "Turkish Happy Birthday," and you can then learn how to wish your friend *"Dogum gunun kutlu olsun!"*.

→ **Observe organizational/personal/company changes and send notes of congratulations.** Send a note regarding an award the person received. Write to say you enjoyed reading about his/her company profiled in a magazine.

→ **Send an announcement when your company or you is recognized in some way.** However, this tactic should not be over-used, to avoid excessive self-promotion.

→ **Report any major change in your situation:** marriage, promotion, or a new phone number.

→ **Send e-cards.** Blue Mountain (BlueMountain.com) and Yahoo! Greetings (Greetings.Yahoo.com) both provide free and low-cost options for sending cards; JacquieLawson.com offers a more expensive, higher-impact card. We always recommend customizing a card, paper or electronic, by writing a unique note on it. As a general rule, the more time and effort (not necessarily money) that you invest in a gift, the more it's appreciated. Since paper cards are labor-intensive to prepare and send, they have a greater impact than e-cards.

Sincere Interest

The best way to connect with people is to be sincerely interested in them. What is important to her? How did she arrive where she is today? Simply put, be curious.

A quick way to generate interesting conversations and become a better listener is to ask questions about the other person. People feel honored when someone shows a sincere interest in them. And you can only truly be of service to them once they tell you how. Searching online for a person's background will show that you take him or her seriously. "I noticed that you used to work for Altria; you must know my friend Jim." Be discreet; sharing everything that you learn may make the person feel as if you are a stalker.

This same approach works when talking with a potential employer or information source. Ask questions about their work and their industry. With the proper questions, you can accelerate the relationship-building process, and even determine if the person might be a prospective partner or customer without "pitching" yourself. Sharon Drew Morgen, author of *Selling with Integrity: Reinventing Sales Through Collaboration, Respect, and Serving,* recommends asking "facilitative questions." These questions provoke responses which provide you insight into the other person's values and thinking style. For example:

→ **For general relationship-building purposes:**

- **How do you decide which virtual communities to spend time in?** Which ones have you found useful—personally and professionally?

- **How will (current trend/news) impact your business?** How are you adapting to/taking advantage of that?

- **Can you give me some guidance as to how I can recognize a good customer for you?**

→ **With someone you have identified as a prospective partner:**

- **Do you currently partner with any other companies?** How is that working?

- **How do you go about choosing partners to work with?** Do you have a specific set of criteria you work from?

- **When would you be adding additional partners to the ones you are already working with?** Are you seeking partners in additional areas other than the areas your partners currently support you in?

→ **With someone who may be a potential customer:**

- **How do you currently handle X in your company?** How does that work for you?

- **When will you be seeking additional resources to help you manage that situation?**

- **How will you determine the criteria you will use to bring in a new vendor?**

If we have a choice between chatting in a chat room, and working with a virtual team of people raising money for a nonprofit we believe in, we'll take the latter every time. We'll be supporting a worthwhile cause, and we'll be making a very clear demonstration of our professional skills to potential clients. That sounds a lot more productive and exciting to us than asking about how Ann is enjoying her riding lessons.

21

Increase the Quality and Quantity of Information

When action grows unprofitable,
gather information; when information
grows unprofitable, sleep.—URSULA
K. LEGUIN, *THE LEFT HAND OF DARKNESS
(REMEMBERING TOMORROW)*[253]

A l Chase tells how he leveraged software and personal Information from the
client's virtual presence to land a major contract:

"I have been using LinkedIn as a virtual personal Web page for the
past six months, as well as for business development for my executive
search practice. I currently have 262 connections and 20 endorsements
from clients and candidates.

"Early in June, a prospective client contacted me who had found
my profile on LinkedIn. The client was motivated to call me because
of:

→ **The number and quality of my connections;**

→ **The number and consistency of my endorsers** and their comments about
my unusual approach to recruiting;

→ **The fact that the client and I were two degrees away from one another within LinkedIn,** separated by an attorney in Boston with whom we have both worked.

"After calling our common connection to learn more about me, the client contacted me to explore the possibility of engaging me to do a search for the General Manager of an entertainment complex to be built in the Northeast.

"We quickly determined that I had no prior experience in executing a high level search within this particular industry, and that I was competing with some of the large retained executive search firms in Boston for the right to conduct this search.

"My reading of the client's LinkedIn Profile led me to his Web page, where I learned that he had a background in choreography and dance. I used my knowledge of the world of dance to offer an analogy that prompted the client to consider engaging me for this search, despite my lack of prior industry experience. The client asked me to sign a Non-Disclosure Agreement and asked to meet me face-to-face.

"During the face-to-face meeting, I was able to present my approach to placing senior executives who are "Renaissance Souls" in companies where such a broad and classical approach to leadership is valued. At the end of the meeting, the client informed me that they would like to retain me for this search.

"Using a combination of LinkedIn and other personal networks, I was able to quickly engage with top leaders in the theme park industry, and learned that most of the Best Practices leaders in the industry would be speaking at a trade association convention in Singapore in mid-July. I proposed to the client that I attend to accelerate the search. I returned from Singapore with dozens of contacts within the industry, and several well-qualified candidates.

"One of those candidates whom I met in Singapore was engaged by my client to fill an operational role on the project, and another industry leader has been hired as general manager for the project."

Information is defined as the data you have about people in your network. Their coordinates are the fundamental Information you should have: e-mail, phone number, cell phone, home phone, family Information, and so on. Also invaluable is Information about how their business is progressing, what their likes and dislikes are, and so on.

Today, the single most important data points are the person's e-mail and cell phone. These are the coordinates which are least likely to change, and through them you can usually track the person down. We particularly recommend diligently recording all of the e-mail addresses you see for someone:

home, work, permanent, backup, etc. Inevitably, some of their e-mails will be discontinued, so it is critical to have a backup address.

Most people undercount the Number of relationships they have. They also usually cannot describe accurately the relationships they have: "as you move beyond your immediate circle, your accuracy . . . begins to fall off."[254] By using the tools we discuss in this chapter, you can have far better Information than the average, less-organized person.

Managing Your Contact Database

Andy Nunemaker is CEO of EmSystem, the world's leading developer of Web-based communications and resource management solutions for medicine and law enforcement. He keeps a detailed database of all of his contacts. Whenever he travels to a new city, he simply queries his database to see whom he knows living in that city. Then he can easily e-mail those people and suggest that they get together for a drink. In this way, he can keep in regular touch with people all over the world.

As the Number of people in your network grows, the importance of good organization tools and a comprehensive contact management system is critical. We strongly recommend purchasing a dedicated contact manager, such as ACT! by Best Software, Business Contact Manager by Microsoft, or GoldMine by FrontRange Solutions. Although Microsoft Outlook or another basic e-mail program may be sufficient to enter and retrieve data, it does not provide the sophisticated searching, analysis capabilities, and ease of customization of a true contact manager.

Any sophisticated contact manager allows you to customize the data fields. We recommend configuring your system to include fields for the following Information:

→ **Contact information**

- Employer, phone, address, e-mail, Web site

- Partner/spouse full name

- Children (listed in descending order by age)

- Category: Customer, Supplier, Lawyer, etc.

- Preferred communication methods (phone, e-mail, Short Message Service, other)

→ **Professional data**

- Résumé. Whenever your friend switches jobs, just cut and paste from the "Employer" field to the "Résumé" field. Over time, the "Résumé" field will develop into a full list of past employers.

- Special interests

- Accomplishments

- Affiliations (clubs, and so on.)

- Education

→ **Personal information**

- Birthday

- Where or how you met the person

- Connections (common affiliations)

- Religion (to determine appropriate holidays the person celebrates)

- Tier (discussed below)

Building and maintaining a comprehensive database enhances your ability to keep in touch with people and will also help you think about who you can introduce to whom. Any sophisticated contact manager includes the ability to make notes about people; for example, you promised to deliver 87 pallets by November 1. Keeping track of those business conversations is far more important than remembering to congratulate your customer on his fifth wedding anniversary.

You may wonder how you can gather all of the detailed Information above. You cannot meet someone and say, "Hi? What's your name? And your partner's name? Children's name? And by the way, would you mind telling me your social security number?"

The answer to this question: you will gradually pick up this Information as you spend time (face to face or virtually) with a person.

For example, you are working alongside Alexandra at PepsiCo. The Human Resources department organizes a birthday party for Alexandra on February 2. You make a note in your database, and next year you mention to Alexandra, "Isn't your birthday coming up?" We very strongly recommend that you update your contact manager every time you learn new Information about someone you know.

Address-book update services such as Plaxo and GoodContacts can help you keep the information in your contact manager current. You can maintain your own data, and all of your relationships will automatically get your new contact information whenever you change it. One caution: most of these services encourage you to send out messages to people who are not users of the system asking them to update their information for you. We do not recommend using this feature. Sending out canned messages asking people if they are still at the same address is perceived as a nuisance, not a relationship-building technique, and has caused some backlash.[255] Instead, we suggest double-checking that you have the right Information when you are directly talking or e-mailing with someone, so your updating fits smoothly into the conversation.

A portable contact manager (a personal digital assistant or a cell phone with a good contact manager built in) is an invaluable tool in managing your relationships. It makes it much easier to tell people, "You would really enjoy meeting my friend Sarayu," and then immediately give the person Sarayu's contact Information. If you are inundated with business cards, you may also want to consider buying an automated card scan device such as CardScan. We also recommend using a software tool such as AddressGrabber (from eGrabber Inc.), which quickly captures contact details from an e-mail, Web page, or a word file into your contact database.

Treat Strangers Well and Friends Even Better

You treat your close friends differently than your distant acquaintances; unless you are Prince Charles, you can only invite a limited number of people to your wedding. We suggest using your contact manager to manage these distinctions efficiently. Earlier you saw our suggestion that you create a "Tier" field in your contact manager. We suggest using that field to track how close you are to the people in your database (see Table 21-1). For example, using any sophisticated contact manager, it is easy to send only the people in Tiers 1 and 2 your wedding invitation.

TABLE 21-1. Categories of messages appropriate to send to different tiers

Tier	Category	Job changes/ professional updates	Holiday greetings	Birthday wishes	(Re-) introductory note/call
1	Family/best friends	X	X	X	—
2	Close friend	X	X	X	—
3	Casual friend	X	X	—	—
4	Casual acquaintance	X	—	—	—
5	Met once	X	—	—	X
6	Stranger: never met, spoke with, or e-mailed	—	—	—	X

The people in the first tiers will thank you for your consideration, when they receive your e-mails. By contrast, if the people in the lower tiers receive the more personal greetings, they may think of you as a spammer rather than as a business professional. If you send a "happy birthday" greeting, they may think of you as a stalker who is privy to too much personal Information. It's better to err on the side of sending fewer e-mails rather than more.

Database Maintenance

One out of five Americans moves every year.[256] If you do not work to maintain your database, its value will rapidly degrade. You can maintain the database by reading your school alumni magazine, as well as the general media. As you read about job changes, weddings, and births, simply enter the Information in your contact database.

Relationship capital management software is also a valuable source of current Information. When you are doing research on someone, just ask your intermediary links for the inside scoop. If you send an e-mail that bounces back, you can use services like ReturnPath.com and FreshAddress.com to find out the recipient's new address.

 If you want to be particularly diligent, subscribe to a newsclipping service, like Ewatch.com. Google also offers a free news-tracking service. Simply indicate to these firms the names of the people you most care about tracking, and the service will inform you when news comes out that covers those people. This provides you an excellent opportunity to write with congratulations when you learn about good news in the life of someone you know.

If there was a fire in your office, what would you grab as you ran out the door? For most people, the contact database is probably their single most important data file. Keep it current and organized, and you will be far more productive.

Multiply the Number of People in Your Network

> When online systems tell you that you can reach 98,000+ people, but you know you could not call on seven "friends" for advice or counsel, a conflict occurs. —JUSTIN HITT, ADVISOR, CENTER FOR STRATEGIC RELATIONS[257]

Mark Riser, a Partner with private equity firm Hamilton Robinson LLC, was able to back management in the buyout of a $35 million company by leveraging his network and the large Number of people in the Darden School online alumni community.

Hamilton Robinson LLC is a private equity firm founded in 1984 which works with financial and management partners to make investments in small to medium size growing businesses. Over the past decade, the firm and its principals have managed and organized transactions involving 33 companies, representing an aggregate value of approximately $850 million.

In July 2002, Mark Riser (Darden 1994) placed a request in the career services section of the Darden Alumni Web site noting Hamilton Robinson's desire to find "C"-level managers—CEO, COO, CFO, etc.—to back in buying out their business from the current owners. A business school classmate of Riser's saw the information, and contacted Mark Panozzo, a friend of that classmate.

Panozzo was the President of Black Clawson Converting Machinery LLC. Black Clawson is a 58-year-old industry leader in flexible Web converting and the plastics processing equipment worldwide. The company has 125 employees and $35 million in revenues.

Black Clawson was a family-owned business, and the then-owner was aging and seeking to sell the business. Panozzo contacted Hamilton Robinson to propose a buyout. In less than 10 months from Riser's initial outreach, Hamilton Robinson backed Panozzo and his team in a successful management buyout. Hamilton Robinson was able to make the deal happen in extremely short order, partly by their leverage of the Darden alumni network.

Number is the measure of your combined strong and weak ties, that is, how many people you know. A bigger Number is usually better. One study in Atlanta found that each employed person in your social network increased the annual income of the population studied by $1,400.[258] (Unfortunately, this is definitely not a generically applicable rule.)

Vanessa DiMauro, VP of Strategy and Research at CXO Systems, observes, "People confuse size with influence."[259] A quality network is one with many people who will actually take your call and potentially be helpful to you, not just people whose business cards you happen to have.

Write Early, Write Often

Writing articles for publication is an excellent way to build your Competence and Number in your field. The process of writing allows you to become an acknowledged expert and provides an excuse to meet the experts in your space. The general business publications (*Economist, BusinessWeek, Fortune, Forbes*) are difficult to penetrate. However, industry trade publications generally welcome quality contributions from industry insiders as opposed to journalists.

In the Ecademy virtual community, content publication by community members is a key strategy for building Competence and making new connections. In addition to blogs for all members, Ecademy encourages members to post longer content pieces as articles. The most recently published articles are listed on the Ecademy home page (as are recent blog entries), and the best articles each week are listed and linked to in a weekly e-mail newsletter sent to all Ecademy members.

You may wonder how you can write something for publication when you are already so busy with your work, family, and other obligations. The solution is twofold: repurposing and delegation.

→ **Recycle.** In the course of your work, you probably write many studies or reports. If you simply remove the confidential information, you will probably have a document that you can tailor for publication. The marginal cost to you is low; the marginal benefit, high. Of course, before publishing make sure that your employer does not oppose you publishing material that you developed for internal purposes.

→ **Leverage your junior staff (or perhaps ghostwriters).** After investing literally thousands of hours writing this book, we are much more sympathetic to the idea of hiring a ghostwriter!

Some ideas for writing include:

→ **Write a summary of best practices in your industry.** This gives you an excuse to interview the people in your industry with the best accounts receivable collection, the fastest turnaround time, and so on.

→ **Interview someone whom you have always wanted to meet.**

→ **Write about someone that you want to meet.** Publish it and then send it to him or her.[260]

→ **Create and edit a directory** for the members of a club in which you are active.

 You may want to consider submitting your pieces to Web sites where authors "deposit" articles to invest and where borrowers "take" the articles to read. Authors retain full rights to articles placed on article banks. A word of warning: do not give anyone unlimited permission to use your articles for any purpose they wish. That amounts to giving up your ownership of the piece.

Feed the Media Maw

One of the basic rules of building a highly visible public image for your organization or for you personally is to become the master of a domain. There is no expert police. If you call yourself an "expert," and have some relevant Competence, then the media will think of you as, "An expert in _____." Potential clients always want the #1 expert for a given situation, not the silver or bronze medalist.

The obvious way to bring your enterprise to the media's attention is by sending out press releases. However, the straightest line is not always the most effective one. Informal e-mails to a journalist who already knows you are far more effective than even the most eloquent press releases—as we will discuss below.

The two major providers of electronic press release distribution for mainstream media are PR Newswire (PRNewswire.com) and Business Wire (BusinessWire.com). These are both fee-based services which allow you to target your release based on geography, industry, and publication reader demographics. On the same day that Ken Lay resigned as CEO of Enron, he became an individual member of PR Newswire.[261]

Several free distribution services are available, but they do not have the reach of the fee-based services. PR Web (PRWeb.com) is the only one with any significant monitoring and usage by mainstream media. Your odds of getting major media coverage are lower with a service like this, but so is your cost.

BUILDING RELATIONSHIPS WITH JOURNALISTS

With the ready availability of mass communications, it has become very easy to reach the media on a large scale through e-mail blasts, media alerts, and wire services. However, just reaching them is not enough—you also have to reach them effectively and catch their attention in order to get coverage. We sometimes focus so much on the "P"—Public(ity)—that we forget that the "R" in PR stands for Relations(hips).

Build relationships with journalists *before* you want the coverage. Your goal should be to end up in their contact book as a source: someone they can rely on for responses, facts, introductions, and ideas. As with everyone else, remember to focus on the journalist's needs, not yours.

Some ideas for building relationships with journalists:

→ **If you are trying to develop a relationship with a particular journalist, read what he or she writes.** A sincere and genuine interest in what they do, as well as an understanding of their topic, their style, and their target audience, will greatly increase their receptivity to you. As a result, you will be able to bring more value to them.

→ **When a journalist writes a story in your area of interest, send him or her an e-mail of appreciation and perhaps offer additional story ideas, leads, or resources.** Following is a simple model of a note:

> I very much enjoyed your piece on new wireless Internet-access technology, because it gave me a lot of insight into the topic. I was fascinated to learn more about how rapidly this technology, combined with the ability to make phone calls over the Internet, would change the way that the traditional phone industry functions.
>
> As background, I am a consultant specializing in "push-to-talk" technology, which allows you to talk with people on your mobile

telephone without dialing a number. This is like instant messaging for cell phone users. I was the lead designer for this technology for Nextel. If you are interested in this topic in the future, please do not hesitate to contact me.

→ **Provide a lead for a hot story, particularly an exposé.** Journalists are always interested in story ideas relevant to their coverage area. An exposé particularly appeals to the crusading spirit of many journalists.

→ **Respond immediately to journalists' requests.** Even more so than most other people, a quick response carries a lot of value, because journalists are always under deadline. When a reporter contacts you, try to help. If you do not know the answer to a question, just say you do not know, but will get back to them with an answer or the name of someone else who can assist.

→ **Exposure builds on exposure,** so any visibility you can get will enhance your image as an expert and increase the likelihood of being contacted by other journalists. For example, contributing guest articles on prominent Web sites will build your relationship with the media. Journalists typically keep files of articles in their domain. Once you are quoted just once, you may appear in the sources file of many other journalists.

→ **Send the media invitations to events.** They like meeting your friends also! Invite journalists to join a board or committee, ask for advice, ask them to present awards, or to moderate an event. Free food and drink are an additional motivation for many underpaid journalists.

→ **The media (everyone) really appreciates knowing that they have influenced your life.** If their coverage helped you, let them know. Perhaps you got some new sales leads, or perhaps your mom was simply very proud of you. Either way, you are building a relationship at a personal level, even if you never meet the journalist face to face.

To contact a journalist excessively is highly counterproductive. Reaching out once or twice over several months is reasonable. A weekly e-mail will make them think you are either "another nutbag reader with little else to do"[262] or that you are trying too hard to position the journalist as your mouthpiece.

When looking for journalists with whom to create a relationship, do not limit your selection to major media outlets. Online, some of the seemingly second-tier outlets may be more effective in creating the exposure you are seeking. In particular, getting to know those journalists who run their own blogs will likely give you far more opportunities than focusing your efforts on major media outlets. Although coverage in a journalist's blog does not carry the same level of prestige as coverage in the main publication, it can have a powerful viral effect online.

Feed the Spiders

"The most fundamental way of finding people online is to help them find you," UCLA Professor Phil Agre tells his Ph.D. students. "In general, the more you spread around links to your home page, e.g., by always including it in your bio when you write magazine articles and the like . . . the more it will help you to connect with others."[263]

While we expect people's use of social network tools to grow rapidly, search engines will likely continue to be the way that Internet users seek out new information and even new people for quite some time. Referrals from search engines may only account for 10 to 15 percent of the total traffic to a Web site, but they typically account for more than 75 percent of new visitors to a site.[264] If you want to be visible to people who are looking specifically for you, your company, or the products and services you offer, being well positioned in the search engines is essential.

Search engines frequently change their ranking algorithms, making it extraordinarily complex to keep up with them all. Furthermore, your competitors (perhaps not literal business competitors, but other sites vying for high search engine rankings) are constantly changing their content and site design. An entire industry—"search engine optimization" or "SEO"—has grown up around the practice of trying to keep Web sites well-positioned in the search engines. SearchEngineWatch.com is one of the most thorough sites tracking this industry.

A high ranking for a popular keyword or phrase can drive thousands of visitors to your site. It's important that your site be ranked highly on all the major search engines for:

→ Your company name.

→ Any branded products or services you offer.

→ Your name.

→ The titles of any books you have written or speeches you give on a regular basis.

Why is this so important? So that people can find you with only a minimal amount of Information. Search engines are also extremely important for media visibility. According to a 2004 survey, 98 percent of journalists go online daily.[265]

Clear, well-organized sites with easy-to-follow navigation are what users want, and they are also what the search engines want. Search engines favor information that is highly visible and cannot be easily manipulated by the site's creator without affecting the appearance of the site, as well as "off-site" factors that are difficult for the site's owners to control or influence. Google offers some excellent advice to Webmasters: "Make pages for users, not for search engines."[266]

There are a few timeless principles that will help your site get ranked well:

→ **Get linked.** Link popularity (i.e., the number and quality of the sites linking to your site) is the major factor in search engine rankings. The search engines have software programs known as "crawlers" or "spiders" which read through Web sites and follow the links within them. The more links to your site that they discover (from quality sites), the higher your rankings. Wherever there is an appropriate opportunity, link. Include links in your signatures on discussion forums. Whenever you have articles published on other Web sites, be sure they link to your site. The links will drive relevant traffic themselves, in addition to the positive impact on your search engine rankings.

→ **Be distinctive, or better yet, unique.** If you are fortunate enough to have an unusual name (Ray Ozzie, Barack Obama), you are in good shape. If your name is Nancy White or John Smith, you are going to have to work harder. If someone with a similar name has already developed a strong Web presence, consider using a middle name or initial to differentiate yourself. When choosing a name for your company, products, and book or speech titles, uniqueness should be a high priority.

→ **Own the domain.** While owning the domain name that matches your company name, product name, or book title is no guarantee of a high ranking, it's certainly a major factor in search engine ranking algorithms. If you can get the domain name for your personal name, do so.

→ **Choose shorter domain names over longer ones.** If you do have a longer domain name, avoid using dashes, if possible. Just run all the words together (e.g., TheVirtualHandshake.com).

→ **Create dedicated pages.** Your profile or biography should have its own page, as should each branded product or service you offer. For example, if you give a speech entitled "The Hidden Power of Social Networks," that speech should have a dedicated page. That way, anyone wanting to link to it will clearly know which page to link to and what to name the link, another important factor described below.

→ **Place the key words high on the page.** Make the name or title the first visible text on the page, preferably in a large, bold font.

→ **Use the full name or title frequently throughout the page.** Do not shorten it for convenience in later references. For example, in the bio for Patti Anklam, do not refer to her as "Patti" or "Ms. Anklam," but as "Patti Anklam" whenever "she" is no longer appropriate.

→ **Use the full name in links to your dedicated pages.** For example, rather than having a link saying "About the Author," have it say "About Daniel Burstein."

This applies when you are linking to your site from other sites, as well. For example, in your profile page in a social network site, you may write, "Check out my new book, *The Hidden Power of Social Networks*." When you do, make the title the link, not the word "book."

Why Just Talk to One?

Why talk to just one person, when you can talk to a hundred? Some conversations should be private. But many conversations—particularly those regarding sharing knowledge or resources, or getting assistance with a problem—can be held, and in fact are better held, in a public setting.

Consider a sample request that a member recently sent to the International Executives Resource Group: "I am discussing joining two companies in a senior role in marketing: Pfizer and GlaxoSmithKline. Anyone in IERG that has info regarding the senior mgmt levels, or has worked for or with either of these companies, please drop me a line as I would like to discuss this with you ASAP (I have meetings next week)." This is a great way to gain valuable insight into potential employers.

Some might say that true altruism does not draw attention to itself. Even if you believe that, consider that if that one person had a problem or question, it is likely that another person in the community has had a similar problem or question. By helping the one person publicly, you help all the others who simply had not spoken up.

No matter your goal—altruism or exposure or both—you reach more people and can increase your Number by sharing what you have to offer in a public forum.

23

Double Your Diversity

> DIVERSITY: the art of thinking
> independently together.—MALCOLM S. FORBES

Steve Rubel, VP of Client Services at PR firm CooperKatz, shares how he used his blog and his Diverse network to land startup Topix.net as a client:

Rubel writes a blog called Micro Persuasion, which tracks how blogs and participatory journalism are changing the public relations practice. He periodically interviews people with insight into these topics. He makes a point of interviewing people with a range of backgrounds, which makes his blog more interesting and more visible. Although based in New York, he interviews people from around the country.

Before Rubel had the blog, the connections he made were mainly through his peers: other PR and marketing professionals. The blog has helped open the door to technology people, graphic artists, authors, and lawyers. He receives very diverse readers and e-mail; about one-third of his readers are from outside of the United States. He gets 20–30 e-mails/day through his blog and 2–3 media calls/week.

In April 2004, Rich Skrenta, Founder and CEO of Topix.net, contacted Rubel (whom he knew about through the blog) to discuss his new company. Topix is a highly-automated news aggregator, based in Palo Alto. Rubel interviewed Skrenta in a "Bloggerside Chat," which he posted.

Rubel observes that so much of the PR business is building credibility in the press, and the blog helps Rubel's credibility tremendously. Lots of journalists read the blog; they now see him as a journalist, not a PR flack. He reports, "Of the time I spend networking, 90 percent is online."

Rubel later met Topix's marketing director at the BlogOn conference. In November 2004, Skrenta was looking for a PR firm, and after a thorough evaluation he signed with CooperKatz.

"[When] we hired CooperKatz, the deciding factor was because of Steve's blog," Skrenta said. "It's not that we're pursuing a blog PR strategy, but because of what we're doing with disruptive online media."[267]

Rubel has now brought in three clients through the blog, generating 5–10 percent increased revenues for his firm. Ben Billingsley is running the account's day-to-day activities. Billingsley recently joined CooperKatz; he heard about the open position from Rubel's blog.

Diversity is the measure of the heterogeneity of your network. We specifically mean the extent to which your network is diverse across every possible measure. The most obvious is structural Diversity: geography, profession, hierarchical position, tenure, and industry. However, we also include demographic Diversity: age, sex, ethnicity, socioeconomic status, political orientation, and so on. Academic research in this area has found that both structural diversity and demographic diversity correlates with higher performance.[268] We use Diversity as a proxy for the number of structural holes in your network.

One significant advantage of a Diverse network is that you associate with people who think differently than you. Think of your network as a sort of "collective brain" that is constantly working on the task of solving problems for you. The more Diverse your network, the more possible solutions that collective brain will consider. This effect is so powerful that a Stanford University study by Martin Ruef showed that entrepreneurs who spend time in a diverse network are three times more likely to innovate than those in a uniform network.[269]

 We particularly recommend including both men and women at all levels of your network. Robert Putnam points out that women are much "more avid social capitalists" than men; they invest far more energy in relationship management.[270] The once-touted gender gap in Internet usage appears to have ended.[271]

Talk with Strangers

Peter Salovey, Dean of Yale College and a Professor of Psychology, teaches "Introduction to Psychology" at Yale. One of his favorite questions to ask students is, "Do you want to know whom you are going to marry?" The 18-year-olds are excited to learn the answer. Professor Salovey says, "Look at the person next to you."

Many students are disappointed at the type (and gender) of the person they are sitting next to. However, Professor Salovey's point is still valid. He is teaching that we tend to place ourselves next to and in the same environment as those who resemble ourselves. We are thus more likely to befriend those people, we are more likely to develop Strong ties to them, and even eventually to marry one of those people.[272] More generally, people are disproportionately likely to develop ties that are homogeneous by values (both conservative), interests (both golfers), affiliation (members of the same Rotary club), and participation (take a hip-hop dance class together).[273]

That said, we strongly recommend developing relationships with people who are foreign to you. As discussed in Chapter 2, a more Diverse network is a stronger network.

Professor Wayne Baker observes, "Without diversity, an organization ossifies like bone into rigid practices, customs, and attitudes. . . . That, in my opinion, is a chief cause of the problems of beleaguered corporate giants such as Sears. . . . For decades these dinosaurs had a policy of promoting from within, reproducing generation after generation of like-thinking, like-acting, inward-looking managers. . . . Inbreeding can be as bad for organizations as it is for families."[274]

The value of seeking Diversity is true both inside and outside an organization. Within a company, people tend to have their strongest ties with people at their same level in the hierarchy and in the same department. However, particularly as you move up the organizational ladder, a significant part of your job is building relationships across all the functional silos.

The farther two people are from each other, the less likely they are to work together.[275] To make connections with more people, we recommend eating in a different part of the cafeteria each day, or perhaps making a point of meeting in other peoples' offices instead of waiting for them to come to you.

Rob Cross, Assistant Professor at the University of Virginia's McIntire School of Commerce, writes,

Is there diversity in your network in terms of the length of time that you have known people? If you have known too many people for too long, you are probably hearing things you already know or, more insidious, knowingly or unknowingly using other people to get your own opinions confirmed. It is good to see new people cycling into (and out of) a person's network as his or her job changes. At the same time, if you have too many new people in your network, it may indicate a lack of sounding boards or confidants with whom you can discuss personal or inflammatory issues.[276]

Your Diverse Face-to-Face Network

A significant body of research has emerged to support the politically correct proposition that Diverse teams and companies outperform their homogenous equivalents. For example, "The Business of Diversity" report by consultancy Schneider-Ross found that 80 percent of respondents saw a direct link between good Diversity policies and improved performance.[277]

This is as true for your personal network as it is for a large company's. Make sure that you have critical categories well represented in your personal network. In particular, a healthy network includes people from all of the following areas[278]:

→ **Relevant members of your industry:** buyers, competitors, customers, suppliers, regulators.

→ **Community leaders:** elected local officials, leaders from major ethnic/religious communities (African, Catholic, Feminist, Jewish, Muslim, Protestant, and so on).

→ **Personal service providers:** auto mechanic, banker, real estate broker, a source for hard-to-get tickets, doctor, high-ranking police officer, executive recruiter, insurance expert, firefighter, travel agent.

→ **Most important, spouse and/or best friend.**

One of America's leading business networks for South Asians is TiE (The Indus Entrepreneurs, TIE.org). There are now 39 TiE chapters in nine countries. Although historically the group has focused on serving the Indian community, it has recently started to build alliances within the South Asian community and more broadly with other ethnic business networks.

Sridar Iyengar, president of TiE, said:

We will continue in the foreseeable future to be based significantly in [the Indian] ethnicity. But we're also . . . an open organization. . . ." Asked to comment on a recent event co-sponsored with Monte Jade (mjglobal.org), a Chinese-focused group, he said, "What happens is each one of the organizations started with some rationale of building a community. Generally, they perceive it along ethnic lines. Then after a while, as you look at the other organizations and you see them doing things that you can learn from, you try to explore what the linkages are. Business is business everywhere.[279]

Your Even More Diverse Virtual Network

Nancy White of Full Circle Associates (FullCirc.com) has leveraged her expertise and the Diversity of her network to expand her business internationally.

Full Circle provides strategic communication, virtual community development, facilitation, marketing, and project management services. In particular, the firm focuses on virtual community building. The firm is based in Seattle, Washington.

White had historically focused on working in the United States, mostly with non-profits. She also maintains a Web site full of resources she has created and links to others related to virtual communities and interaction, and she maintains an active presence on a variety of virtual communities.

While the groups in which White participates are bound together by their common interest in virtual communities, they are also extremely Diverse—geographically, socio-economically, and by industry. When the need for expertise in online facilitation arises in areas that do not have local experts on the topic, opportunities arrive in White's e-mail inbox unsolicited.

For example, she recently worked with Project Harmony, a nonprofit focused on community-building, to train their staff in online facilitation. She and her team then developed and facilitated a virtual conference on domestic violence in Russia and the Balkan states. This in turn has led to other international opportunities for White. It is highly unlikely that White would have gotten involved in a project so far away from her home base without leveraging her virtual presence.[280]

The most logical way to build the Diversity of your network virtually is to build relationships with people who are one step away from you. For example, let us say you are a female Chinese business process outsourcing (BPO) salesperson in San Francisco. Many of the members of your network are probably people in the same industry in San Francisco.

You can seek out groups of people who are one step away from you:

→ **By industry** (people in the outsourced manufacturing industry);

→ **By geography** (BPO salespeople in Sacramento); and/or

→ **By personal characteristics** (a group of male BPO industry executives; a South Asian-focused group like TiE).

You can search for communities of people of interest to you, perhaps by reviewing a community calendar. Alternatively, you can search online for specific people you would like to meet.

The power of this strategy is that you will have a lot in common with the people in these virtual communities or at these events. You will immediately have many topics to discuss with, for example, the Sacramento BPO executives.

Simultaneously, you will be highly visible at the event, because you are significantly different than most of the people there. As a result, you become a bridge across the structural hole between, for example, the Sacramento network and the San Francisco network. That is a powerful position: when the Sacramento people want to learn more about a potential San Francisco client, you become the logical person to call. Instead of fading in with the crowd, you become a uniquely well-positioned person.

It takes conscious attention to balance Diversity and Relevance. They are inversely proportional almost by definition. If you have identified a certain audience as having high Relevance, they probably are fairly homogenous. They are by definition not diverse in the dimension that you are targeting. If you are a personal coach focusing on helping lawyers be more effective, an audience of lawyers is highly Relevant. However, it does not contain anyone who can help you with, for example, your marketing challenges.

The definition of Relevance will change depending on your goals. However, Relevance is contextual—it depends on your current situation—while Diversity is not. This is why Diversity is so important. When your goals change, which they always do, a Diverse network has a greater likelihood of including people relevant to your new goals.

In addition, very few people have a single goal at any one time. In reality, you likely have many simultaneous goals: make more sales, find a babysitter for your child, find a new job, stay on top of industry news, and so on. No one person can help you with all of that; only a Diverse network contains people who can help in all of your manifold goals.

The classic example is job hunting. When people are job hunting, they meet many hiring managers, peers, and other unemployed people. Once they find a job, people typically fail to maintain those relationships, focusing instead entirely on those people that they perceive as immediately Relevant to their job.

When you are fully employed, you are just between job searches. The average American changes jobs ten times and switches careers three times over a lifetime.[281] When professionals enter the job market again, their networks are often insufficiently Diverse; they have to start from scratch to meet prospective employers.

Diversity is not just a politically correct notion; it is critical to a powerful personal network.

Part V

Turning Theory into Action: Online Networks in Your Job, Career, and Life

→ Good ideas are not adopted automatically. They must be driven into practice with courageous patience.—HYMAN RICKOVER

24

Ten Simple Steps to Radically Improve Your Network Online

→ We cannot seek or attain health, wealth, learning, justice or kindness in general. Action is always specific, concrete, individualized, unique.—JOHN DEWEY, *RECONSTRUCTION IN PHILOSOPHY*

When we were looking for a publisher for this book, one prominent academic publisher turned us down, saying it was "too practical." Far from being discouraged, we took that as a compliment! Our goal is not only to provide you with an understanding of the concepts of building a powerful social network, but also with the specific tools and steps with which to do so. While we've included detailed action steps throughout the book, we organized them conceptually rather than sequentially.

This section helps you develop a specific action plan to apply to your current situation. We start with basic steps that we think everyone should take, followed by specific tips on using these tools for job search, marketing, sales, business development, and volunteering. If you wear multiple hats—perhaps you are a CEO—we recommend reviewing all of the sections below.

The ten steps that we recommend everyone take are:

1. **Write down your goals** (Chapter 17). For each item on your list of goals, write down how virtual relationships can help you achieve it.

2. **Analyze your network** using the Seven Keys (Chapter 2):

   - How can you improve your Character and make it more visible?

   - How can you increase your Competence?

   - What is the best way to raise the Relevance of the people you know?

   - How can you build Stronger ties?

   - How can you increase your Information about the people you know?

   - How can you multiply the Number of people you know? Or, should you focus on building Stronger relationships with the people you know now?

   - How can you double the Diversity of your network?

3. **Make the mundane sublime** (Chapter 18). Master the basic office productivity tools. If you invest the energy to learn how to speed read, how to touch type, and how to use standard office productivity software comfortably, you will become far more productive.

4. **Become an Information sponge** (Chapter 21). Install professional contact management software. Record e-mails, phone numbers, the notes you take in meetings, and everything else you can about the people you know.

5. **Master your e-mail** (Chapter 14). Install a sophisticated e-mail reader and spam filtering and antivirus software. Set up mail filter rules to route mail into appropriate folders. Turn off automatic send/receive. Organize your e-mail folders, and keep your inbox empty.

6. **Share your knowledge wealth** (Chapter 18). Maintain a master file of documents, resources, Web links, etc., which have been helpful to you.

7. **Write your Recyclable Document** (Chapter 15). Centralize all of your recyclable e-mails and other text.

8. **Take control of your virtual presence** (Chapter 15). Make sure that when people look for you online, your image is both accurate and flattering.

9. **Join the virtual communities where your target market lives** (Chapter 8). Once you have joined one group, ask the members where else they connect with like-minded people. Be sure to look for smaller groups within larger sites.

10. **Take a leadership role** (Chapter 17). Write a blog to cover your domain, and perhaps create an online community around your unique interests.

If this entire book only convinces you to take these basic steps, we have succeeded in our own goal. You will significantly increase the value of your network, as well as your efficiency and your productivity.

25

Finding a Job

> Reporter: What kind of a governor would
> you be?
> Answer: I don't know. I've never played a
> governor.—RONALD REAGAN[282]

Executive recruiters love social software because it makes their job so much easier. Thirty thousand executive recruiters use LinkedIn.[283] In fact, using these technologies is Nitron Advisors' and Teten Recruiting's niche; we can find high-quality candidates for our clients much more quickly and efficiently than traditional research and recruiting firms. When a recruiter like us is looking online for a certain profile, our client will never have a chance to hire you if you do not have an effective virtual presence.

Beyond just findability, we emphasize that approximately half of all U.S. workers find employment through friends, relatives, and other social contacts, as opposed to help-wanted ads and other traditional measures.[284] Not only can you use social software to make yourself more findable, but you can also use it to build a stronger network for your job hunt.

Heather Hamilton, Senior Recruiter, Marketing Talent Acquisition at Microsoft, says that blogging has completely changed how people find jobs:

> "Blogging is a great opportunity in the staffing industry, both for
> the recruiter and the job seeker (or future job seeker). Blogs represent
> conversations and provide more info to a recruiter than a resume can.
> Through a blog, a recruiter can understand not just the experience of
> the candidate, but how they work, their passion, the quality of their

relationships with coworkers, their opinions. This creates a more dimensional snapshot of a candidate than a résumé. It is not unusual for a recruiter to do a Web search of a known candidate to identify their online presence. By creating a professional blog, the job seeker can brand themselves beyond what is represented in a typical résumé format.

"Where job boards provide a very transactional environment for active job seekers (active candidates search jobs and submit resumes, recruiters search resumes and contact candidates), blogs allow for more of a long-term approach for managing one's career and for recruiting talent. The best time to build a relationship with a recruiter is *before* you start looking for your next position. In an environment where large corporations can receive thousands of résumés a day, establishing a relationship through blogging (through your blog or the recruiter's blog) can greatly benefit the seeker because blogs establish a dialog, which can create an advantage over the thousands of other applicants vying for the recruiter's attention.

"For the recruiter, who likely specializes in recruiting a specific type of talent (marketing talent, in my case), the opportunity to identify likely candidates via blogging is huge. By engaging with a community of marketing professionals, I am able to interact directly with talent in my area of focus. I'm able to let the active seekers know whether I have something for them, and I am able to market our hot new jobs to active and non-active leads and candidates. Blogging truly creates a win/win opportunity for the professional and the recruiter."

Hamilton connects with marketing professionals via her own blog, Heather's "Marketing at Microsoft" Blog (blogs.msdn.com/HeatherLeigh).

How to Use Online Networks to Find a Job

 All of the techniques in this book help to make you a more productive professional with a more powerful network. If you follow these principles, and become visible in your industry because of your unique expertise, you will rarely have to look for a job. People will recruit you.[285]

We particularly recommend simply reaching out to people who are knowledgeable in your industry, building a relationship with them, and then asking for guidance. That is one of the best ways to find a position . . . before you need to find a position.

A key stage in the job search is to find companies which are hiring. In addition to noticing who has openings listed on job boards for your industry, we recommend looking for newly funded companies. Once you have found some promising companies, visit their Web sites. Notice who works there, especially in the department(s) to which you would apply. Your goal is to get a friendly introduction to one of those people. The tools discussed in Part II can help you to do that. Besides the "About Us" page, try looking in:

→ **Required regulatory filings** (the company's annual report).

→ **Other sections of the site** (The "news" or "press releases" section of the site).

When job postings are hard to find, that does not mean opportunities do not exist. Many times, you can create your own job description if you fill a need. Do not assume human resources personnel know how to do that. In fact, because recruiters are not involved day to day in the departments they hire for, they may not have a clue as to how you might meet a possible need. You need to get in front of the hiring managers, ideally as senior in the organization as possible.

Trade associations are a particularly useful resource. Though some premium features may require you to be a dues-paying member, Glenn Gutmacher of Recruiting-Online.com reports that many of his clients have found they can get access fees waived if they mention their student or unemployed status.

A common question is, "How do I approach people I find online?" One of the most important ways to use social software is to help you gain access to a company through a referral, a "name-drop." Gutmacher reports that résumés with a name drop get a response over twice as often as résumés without a name drop.

If you cannot get referred into the company, try to find bloggers at the company or other touch-points—people with whom you can build a relationship. If you still can't get a good lead into the company, we recommend a low-key, short introductory message, such as:

I thought that your recent list posting about [whatever topic] interesting. You may be interested in a pertinent article I recently wrote, which you can see at [http://www.recruiting-online.com/cxr2002bygg.doc]. I would be happy to talk about this further at your convenience.

I should mention that I am now looking for a new position in the Boston area. If you happen to have any ideas on upcoming events that I should attend or people I should contact in the region, I would be very grateful. You can read more about my background at [www.recruiting-online.com/glennbio.html].

This combines an initial "give" with your attempt to build Competence and a low-key request for names of contacts, employers, and events. Please note: you did not ask the person directly for a job. Never ask anything that can result in a "no" answer; keep the questions open-ended to foster more dialogue. Ideally, you will trade a few e-mails with lots of people and you will end up with a collection of informal mentors who keep their eyeballs open on your behalf.

Action Steps

1. **Build a compelling virtual presence** and a powerful online network using the techniques discussed in this book.

2. **Write an online-friendly résumé.** Résumés are often read on a word processing system different than yours, and fancy formatting makes them hard to read and harder to scan. Use simple text formatting in one font size, minimal table usage, no italics, no shadowing, no colors, and no graphics. Do not use the automatic bullets in your word processor; instead, manually type in asterisks. Make sure to include the keywords relevant for your profession, since recruiters need to be able to search for your résumé in their internal databases.

3. **Give your résumé a useable name in the format: "Smith-Caroline-Resume-2005.doc."** When the reader of your résumé saves the file, it will be easy for him or her to know later what is in that file. Vague names like "Dad's Resume.doc" make your reader's job much more difficult.

4. **Make sure your reader can read your résumé.** When you send a résumé, include it as an attachment in Microsoft Word or HTML format, and also include it in the body of the e-mail. Do not use PDF format (Adobe Acrobat), because most headhunters and corporations use résumé search engines that do not read that format.

5. **Visit Teten.com and Nitron Advisors' CircleOfExperts.com.** These Web sites include many resources for people seeking a new position.

6. **"Send is not the end."**[286] Follow up with phone calls and whatever else it takes to get into the firm you are targeting.

26

Marketing

→ There is more similarity in the marketing challenge of selling a precious painting by Degas and a frosted mug of root beer than you ever thought possible.—A. ALFRED TAUBMAN, OWNER OF SOTHEBY'S[287]

Max Blumberg started his career as a management consultant with Andersen Consulting (now Accenture). He then started and successfully exited from a £10 million-a-year technology distribution operation. Unsure what he wanted to do next, he started earning a Ph.D. in psychology and along the way discovered Ecademy.

"As a general entrepreneur," he says, "I had no idea how much I knew about marketing strategy and positioning until I started sharing my knowledge with other Ecademists and found them asking for more! I set up the Positioning Game club on Ecademy where members got into a queue in order for me to position their businesses in the club, live in front of anyone on the Internet who cared to watch. The queue grew and grew, and soon people at the end of the queue who knew that they would have a long wait became my first Ecademy clients."

He says that his first clients were owner-managed professional services and technology businesses, but that larger companies have started to take notice of his work. "The size of companies I work with has increased to operations with revenue in the region £2–6 million, referred mainly through contacts made on Ecademy."

While virtual relationships may not reach the massive numbers that advertising or national publicity does, it's very effective in reaching highly qualified prospective customers, establishing perceived Competence with them, and reinforcing your brand. It's also a powerful tool for market research. And it can even help you get that national publicity down the road.

How to Use Online Networks for Marketing

Here are some of the ways that you can use social networks to market you and your company:

→ **Research your market.** You have two ears and one mouth; listen more than you talk. Through participation in these communities, companies can learn about consumer interests and reactions with a candor rarely found in focus groups and surveys.

→ **Create Competence.** If becoming an expert in your field is part of your marketing strategy, social networks give you a much more accessible outlet than the media. You can speak up in a mailing list, discussion forum, or blog, and reach hundreds or thousands of people. Say something useful, original, and profound, and you will get quoted and linked to, reaching even more people.

→ **Build and reinforce your brand.** Every signature in an e-mail or on the Web, and every profile online, is an opportunity to reinforce your brand.

→ **Unveil a human voice.** Networked markets demand openness from the companies who want to sell into those markets. Organizations should have more people participating virtually than just professional marketers. A happy employee is a more powerful brand evangelist than almost anyone in Marketing. This is one reason why Microsoft has approximately 1,200 bloggers out of 55,000 employees.[288]

→ **Associate yourself with a not-for-profit cause.** People are much more willing to gather around a cause than a company.

→ **Microtarget.** If you have identified a particular narrowly-defined group to target, the odds are good that you can identify a virtual community where they are already gathered. Are you selling consulting services to independent bookstores? If it doesn't already exist, just create a virtual community for your target pool, seed it with your closest relationships, and watch it grow.

→ **Ignite word-of-mouth buzz.** If you have a new product or service, word-of-mouth—satisfied customers talking about you—is one of the most effective ways to establish your Competence. Word-of-mouth flows through social networks; Leaders of networks are excellent lighthouse customers. If the most prominent blogger in your field likes what you sell, you will create a powerful evangelist.

A common mistake many marketers make when dealing with online communication is in thinking that it can be turned on and off like an advertising campaign. Online networks are generally not very receptive to marketing messages from brand new members. You must earn the right to talk about your product through participation in and contribution to the community. Similarly, you cannot simply leave when the campaign is over, or you will be seen as shallow and a "user." People do not want to be used; please do not use people.

Action Steps

Here are steps you can take to leverage virtual relationships for marketing:

1. **Pull, don't push.** Focus on awareness, not persuasion. Your participation, your signatures, and your profiles will create awareness. Those who are interested will be attracted to you and will come to you for information and assistance.

2. **Create a standard template for e-mail and Web signatures for all your employees.** Reinforce your brand with every communication. It can be simple text, but it's easy enough to incorporate your company logo, as well. However, some people do not consider elaborate signatures appropriate for general correspondence.

3. **Cross-promote.** Link to your Web site in your e-mail signature. Link to your communities from your Web site. Link to your personal profile page from your community page. Link, link, link.

4. **Create a community around a cause or topic associated with your brand.** Music groups, films, authors, and many technology companies can often support a community around their brand. However, many other companies do not have that type of user base. Instead they can build a community around a cause, as Avon does with its Breast Cancer Crusade (www.Avon Company.com/women/avoncrusade).

5. **Be consistent, not persistent.** Long gaps in your participation will be noticed, and if your participation conveniently peaks for the two weeks before your marketing campaign, people will see it as manipulative.

Sales

There is no such thing as "soft sell" and "hard sell." There is only "smart sell" and "stupid sell."—CHARLES BROWER, PRESIDENT, BATTEN, BARTON, DURSTINE & OSBORN[289]

A very established partner at a top-tier strategy consulting firm had added a large bank to his target client list. His firm had no history of work with that bank, so he set an internal team in motion to learn all they could about the bank and its current challenges. Beyond this detailed external research and analysis, he also sent word around the firm to discover which of his 4,000 colleagues had relationships to staff at the bank. By polling the financial services practice group, sending a general request e-mail to all staff, and following up internally wherever possible, his team discovered 14 colleagues with significant relationships to the target bank.

One person on his team also did a search using a newly installed internal relationship capital management tool (in this case, from Contact Network Corporation). This search instantly found 63 colleagues with relationships to the target bank (including the 14 colleagues whom the team had spent hours tracking down). The software ranked each of the colleagues based on the strength of the relationship. The partner was able to tap his entire firm quickly and efficiently to find all relationships and cultivate these to gain a much deeper understanding of his target client, and then to get introductions to key people as he built new relationships in the process of introducing the bank to his firm's consulting services.

Amazon.com lists more than 13,000 book titles on a search for "sales".[290] What could there possibly be new to say about sales?

How to Use Online Networks for Sales

Virtual relationships can help you get more customers to the table faster, with more Information and stronger relationships once you get there. There are three fundamental ways you can leverage virtual networks to augment your sales activities and accelerate your sales cycle:

→ **Create allies.** Smaller organizations often benefit by allying with complementary, trusted partners who can be brought into deals when appropriate. Develop a network of trusted relationships to make it easier to find the right partner for a given situation.

→ **Find sales prospects, or people who might know sales prospects.** Use the Strength-building techniques that we discuss.

→ **Identify an internal champion.** Foundation Systems, a technology staffing firm, uses Leverage Software to identify and access relationships. CEO Jeannine Solanto reports in an e-mail, "I had been pursuing a $16 billion specialty retailer for months and my proposal was stalled. With Leverage Software, I discovered that my colleague knew an individual who worked at this retailer. That individual provided a trusted introduction to the deal influencer which accelerated the review process. As a result, I was able to exceed my prospect's requirements and quickly move the sales process to a closed contract. . . . We have received a quantifiable Return on Investment with Leverage Software, selling our solutions in a shorter period of time. Our sales cycles have decreased by 15–20 percent, on average." Receiving a Request for Proposal will only tell you what information your prospect is looking *at*, not what they are looking *for*, nor how they will make the decision. Use relationship capital management software to identify an internal champion.

Action Steps

As selling is really an extension of marketing, the first step is to follow the action plan in the Marketing section above. Beyond that, the following are additional action steps to take specifically to increase sales:

1. **Read the blogs of employees at your target companies.** Linking to them and discussing what they have to say is an excellent way to gain access to thoughtful people there.

2. **In the major virtual communities, search for people who are potential leads, or who are connected to leads.** An e-mail saying, "We should meet sometime; you might be interested in my company's services," will probably not be well received. Instead, look for people with whom you have commonalities: same alma mater, same mother country, same recreational sports, etc. Sales is one of the primary examples of a discipline where an indirect approach can work better than a direct one.

Let us make clear that this is not subterfuge—not a disguised motive. If you are not prepared to connect with these folks and sustain the relationships based on commonalities other than the fact that they might buy what you sell, *please* do not do this.

28

Business Development

> Would you take a new prospect into this customer's plant or offices to show off your partnership? If you can't get a good reference from this account—or if you aren't willing to ask for one—you need to re-examine the relationship.—ROBERT MILLER, *SUCCESSFUL LARGE ACCOUNT MANAGEMENT*[291]

In just four months of working with the Ecademy online network, Simon Rogers has uncovered more than £1 million in potential revenues for his company 2Delta, a reseller specializing in project management software.

2Delta's founders had extensive experience selling project management services into the financial services and telecommunications industries, but wanted to open new markets. They set up 2Delta as a door opener.

He sees Ecademy as a significant business accelerator: "It's early days, but this is start-up number five for me, and I know I am miles ahead of where I was with any of the others, and I built each of those businesses into £9 million annual revenue before selling them. I have high hopes."

His approach is to search for Ecademy members who have amassed many relationships, and then look at their background to understand where they have worked, what roles they have undertaken, and the organizations that they have been associated with. He then meets with them, explains 2Delta's proposition, how 2Delta is approaching its market, and what is in it for the Ecademy connector (20 percent of 2Delta's margin). Then, he asks them if they know anyone who might be interested.

This has led to introductions and presentations to:

2 local government councils,

1 regional police force,

4 international technology consultancies,

2 software houses,

2 reinsurance organizations,

1 national logistics organization,

1 major event organization (rock concert tours),

1 mobile telecommunications company,

1 pharmaceutical company, and

1 social/business network organization.

Each opportunity is worth £75,000 or more. After just four months in business, 2Delta has already closed four deals, including a 400-person "project-oriented" reinsurance organization that is "nicely into six figures."

When asked whether a social network like Ecademy works for people wanting to build a business, he answers, "Absolutely, but it needs to be 'worked' with a process and a view to sharing the rewards. I plan to make money for the people who help me. The word will get round that Rogers is a good man, that his proposition is a good one, that 2Delta delivers the highest quality service and has delighted clients, who give us all repeat business."[292]

How to Use Online Networks for Business Development

Business development and business networking are closely related activities:

→ **Business development is often a shared-risk proposition.** Business development is about partnerships. You are rarely "sold" in a business development context; there is much more of a sense of coming together. Suggestions of possible partnerships don't set off the automatic defense mechanisms that trigger when we detect that we are being sold or marketed to.

→ **Business development is often nonexclusive, or at least less exclusive, than sales or marketing.** In sales, the customer is usually only going to select one vendor for any given need. In business development, though, a company will frequently partner with multiple companies in a given market.

→ **The relationship is an end, not just a means.** In sales, for all the talk of "relationship selling," the ultimate goal is still a sale. For the business development professional, the relationship itself is an end.

Action Steps

The following strategy focuses on leveraging online network tools specifically for business development.

1. **Focus on what is in it for them, not for you.** Focus on how a relationship with you and your company can help your readers meet existing business goals.

2. **Participate in industry-related communities, forums, mailing lists, associations, and projects.** Your best opportunities will come from being visible in your industry. Standards bodies and professional associations are a big time commitment, but they create high visibility with a great deal of perceived Competence. The credentials are helpful both to your organization and to you personally in your career.

3. **Create a profile in sites that have a relevant audience.** Specify that you are interested in discussing business development opportunities and what kind you are open to. With whom do you want to connect? What roles? What industries? And what do you have to offer? Think not only in terms of your business development goals, but other assets—your contacts and expertise.

4. **Do not underestimate direct contact.** People are much more receptive to direct contact for business development than for sales.

29

Volunteering

> After I became a volunteer, I discovered
> that networking and volunteering are almost
> synonymous. A lot of what I've learned about
> selling, public speaking, raising money,
> working as part of a team, management, and
> organization—in other words, a lot of what I
> learned about everything worth learning in
> running a business—I learned by being a
> volunteer worker.—HARVEY MACKAY

Ash Nallawalla, a marketing consultant, writes:

"I live in Melbourne, Australia, so I was not hopeful of finding employment through the Software Product Marketing Group (SPM) [a Silicon Valley based group focused on helping software product marketers
get new jobs]. During early 2003, I became an active volunteer in SPM

Donna Fisher is a contributing author for this chapter. Her four books, *Power Networking, People Power, Power NetWeaving,* and *Professional Networking for Dummies*
have been translated into five languages, recommended by Time Magazine, and
used as reference books in corporations and universities. She is a contributing author for *Real World Communication Strategies that Work.* Donna speaks at corporate meetings, conferences, and conventions for clients such as Hewlett Packard,
JPMorgan Chase, Boeing, and Johnson & Johnson. Her Web site is DonnaFisher.com.

and was assigned to the Web Content group, which was then under the leadership of Mark Ogne. I set up QuickBase for SPM's project management needs and got to know some of the other volunteers.

"Mark had noted my skill at search engine optimization (which was a newly acquired skill unrelated to my primary field of CRM and lead management), and referred me to his client RingCentral, which was looking for this service. Mark had found an exciting new opportunity elsewhere, and his referral led to my current contract with RingCentral. Since April 2003, I have been performing a variety of marketing duties for this company across the Pacific.

"As luck would have it, Mark's new employer downsized him later that year, and he is now VP - Direct Marketing at RingCentral. He has also engaged two other SPMers on short engagements: Noreen Sullivan and Mazda Jamasbi.

"My unpaid volunteer work with SPM gave me the chance to get to know other professionals on the other side of the world. Not only did I learn a lot, but they got to see me in action, which led directly to some lucrative consulting engagements."

You no longer have to join a picket line (although you may still choose to) to take a stand and join with others to take action on causes you believe in. One of the best places to strengthen existing ties and create new ones is in volunteer organizations. You demonstrate your expertise and commitment to other like-minded people.

Particularly if you are looking for a job, what better way is there to get exposure than by showing what you do, rather than just telling about it?

Not-for-profit organizations all over the world are benefiting from recruiting virtual volunteers. Volunteers often find that they have more time to give because there is no travel time and they can often be more efficient in their own environment. Listed below are some of the most valuable categories of projects appropriate for virtual volunteering.

How You Can Volunteer with Online Networks

→ If you have writing skills:

- **Translating.** There is an increasing need to have Web sites, press releases, and other literature available in numerous languages.

- **Writing Web content.** Writing a quality Web site can make the difference in a cause getting public attention and support.

- **Proofreading.** Sites that want people coming back on a regular basis have to keep updating their information and must make sure everything is accurate and professional.

- **Writing e-mails.** You can be a valuable resource by helping to respond to the many e-mails that a nonprofit will receive.

→ **If you have research skills:**

- **Research grants, donors, etc.** You will be generating valuable information for a good cause.

- **Track legislation.** If you are fascinated by the ins and outs of government, you could be a valuable resource for a not-for-profit advocating legislation to further their cause.

- **Generating sponsor support.** Use your sales, marketing, and negotiation skills to get corporate sponsorships and alliances.

→ **If you have advisory skills:**

- **Professional advising.** If you have legal, financial, or management expertise, you could be a valuable on-call advisor or member of a virtual advisory board.

- **Mentoring.** Depending on your background and expertise, you might be a great mentor at an executive, management, or leadership level; or as a mentor for volunteers in the organization or the people served by the organization.

→ **If you have technical skills:**

- **Web development.** An effective Web presence is critical for any significant organization today.

- **Creating virtual forums.** Organizations need people who are tech savvy to host chat rooms, create virtual forums, develop blogs, and other Internet activities.

- **Database management.** You can help an organization be more efficient and effective with their database.

- **E-zine and newsletter development.** Making regular contact with members of a nonprofit's community of supporters is vital for its success.

- **Graphic design.** Graphics are critical to paint a powerful emotional picture of the problems and solutions addressed by a nonprofit.

Action Steps

Here are action steps to use online networks to create social change:

1. **Clearly identify your passion, desire, and arena in which you wish to make a difference.** Ask yourself if what you feel is totally unacceptable in the world. What do you feel passionate about? What is your vision of the future?

2. **Search for sites, organizations, and projects that are aligned with your focus.** Some sites available to assist you in your search for suitable organizations for your interest include Idealist.org and VolunteerMatch.org.

3. **Offer your support and services.** Let people know what you have to offer and how you want to contribute.

4. **Let others know about opportunities that people can support.** Pass along information to others in your network about events and opportunities.

5. **Create your own community promoting your cause and giving people a way to connect.** Creating a group within an existing social network will help you attract like-minded people and identify complementary organizations.

6. **Create links on your Web site to other sites that further social action.** At DonnaFisher.com, you can see a Links page that includes business links, a friend's link, and links to organizations that Donna believes in.

Some people choose not to donate their services because they believe that it somehow devalues them by "giving them away." In truth, there is nothing that demonstrates the value of your skills more than putting them to good use for a cause you believe in.

30

Afterword: How This Book Was Born

> As I grow older I pay less attention to what men say. I just watch what they do.—ANDREW CARNEGIE[293]

We leave you with the story of how this book came to be, because it incorporates all of the principles we've discussed in the book.

On December 10, 2002, Scott Allen posted a message on the Web Communities Yahoo! Group (Groups.Yahoo.com/group/webcommunities) soliciting success stories for a new book on building business relationships virtually.[294] While there were not a large Number of people on the list (about 200), it was a highly Relevant group for Scott's request. A few weeks later, David Teten contacted Scott with a private e-mail:

> Dear Mr. Allen,
>
> I saw your message on the Webcommunities list about online networks. Please tell me more about this project.
>
> The reason I ask is that I am thinking of writing a book in this general area also, and would like to see if we could be helpful to one another. Please see www.teten.com/David-Teten.htm for background on me.
>
> Thanks!

In minutes, Scott was able to review David's presentation and verify his Competence. David was working on a broader book about sales, raising capital, building a deal pipeline, and due diligence, which included coverage of online networks. After some discussion via e-mail and phone, we agreed it made more sense to collaborate than to compete.

We took an unusual approach with the book. The nature of the topic made it impossible and inadvisable to work in stealth mode. We have actively participated in the communities related to our topic, seeking out success stories and connecting with thought leaders. We've built Diversity across a broad spectrum—with academics, business leaders, and of course, the social software industry.

In June 2003, we released the first version of our e-book (a beta version) and started selling it on our Web site. The e-book evolved over the next year to become the core of the book in your hands. By putting it out there, we have received feedback, stories, endorsements, and peer review from hundreds of people, and demonstrated our Competence on the topic of online social networks.

In December 2003, looking for an agent to represent us, Scott connected with Christian Crumlish, an agent at Waterside Productions, via both LinkedIn and Ryze. Scott had learned from Christian's online profile that Christian had a particular interest in this topic. As it turned out, Christian had actually begun work on *The Power of Many,* a book which explores how ordinary people are using online networks (an excellent companion book to *The Virtual Handshake*).

As he was busy with his own project, Christian introduced us to his colleague, Danielle Jatlow, who agreed to represent us. Shortly after landing the deal with our publisher, Danielle decided to go to graduate school and connected us with her colleague, David Fugate, to work with us moving forward. We have yet to meet any of these people face to face.

During the course of writing this book, we have exchanged an enormous amount of Information—more than 8,000 e-mails (over ten a day) and at least several hundred phone calls, building a high-Strength relationship. We have definitely had significant challenges along the way, but those have also been a chance to test and know one another's Character.

As we put the finishing touches on the book to send to our publisher, we look forward to celebrating together when we meet face to face—for the very first time!

Appendices

APPENDIX A: The Network Valuation Formula^{SM}

Someone told me that each equation
I included in the book would halve
the sales.—STEPHEN HAWKING

David Teten developed the Network Valuation Formula^{SM} to express the Seven Keys to a powerful network in a concise way:[295]

Ch = Character, Co = Competence, R = Relevance, S = Strength, I = Information, N = Number, D = Diversity

$$\text{Network Value} = D * \sum_{n=1}^{N} (Ch_n * Co_n * R_n * S_n * I_n)$$

The "Σ" sign is a mathematical symbol called "summation" which means, loosely, "Addition of everything in the parentheses to the right, as we cycle through every value of the formula for $n = 1$, $n = 2$, $n = 3$, until $n = N$." The capitalized "N" is the Number of people in your network.

We mentioned in Chapter 2 your theoretical network of three friends: Armand, Brenda, and Chaim. The Value of your network is therefore (temporarily ignoring Diversity):

$($your Character in Armand's eyes $*$ your Competence in Armand's eyes $*$ Relevance of Armand to you $*$ Strength of your relationship with Armand $*$ Information that you have about Armand$)$

$+ ($your Character in Brenda's eyes $*$ your Competence in Brenda's eyes $*$ Relevance of Brenda to you $*$ Strength of your relationship with Brenda $*$ Information that you have about Brenda$)$

$+ ($your Character in Chaim's eyes $*$ your Competence in Chaim's eyes $*$ Relevance of Chaim to you $*$ Strength of your relationship with Chaim $*$ Information that you have about Chaim$)$

$$= \sum_{n=1}^{3} (\text{Character}_n * \text{Competence}_n * \text{Relevance}_n * \text{Strength}_n * \text{Information}_n)$$

We will assume that the Diversity of your Network is 2.5 on a scale of 1 to 4. Taking into account the Diversity of the network, the total Network Value is therefore:

$$= 2.5 * \sum_{n=1}^{3} (\text{Character}_n * \text{Competence}_n * \text{Relevance}_n * \text{Strength}_n * \text{Information}_n)$$

The Network Valuation Formula[SM] leads to a very different result than Metcalfe's Law and Reed's Law, two formulas frequently referenced in discussion of networks. We discuss this in depth at TheVirtualHandshake.com.

APPENDIX B: How to Use This Book to Grow Your Network

You can't build a reputation on what you're going to do.—HENRY FORD

Some ways that you could connect with us:

→ **E-mail us with your success stories, questions, and related articles and sites,** so that we can stay connected with you and pass along pertinent information to others. We very much value your feedback.

→ **Send your friends copies of this book.**

→ **Sign up for our affiliate program** and be part of our growing community. This is a way you can get paid to help promote the sale of this book and other information products on our Web site.

→ **Provide a quotable endorsement which we can publish on our Web site,** along with your name and a link to your Web site. Or, for even more exposure, publish a review of it on your Web site or newsletter and let us know about it.

The best way to reach us is through our Web site: TheVirtualHandshake.com.

Glossary

 You can see updated definitions at TheVirtualHandshake.com/ glossary

atom—A standard protocol for disseminating information via blogs.

biography analysis software—Software that collects and standardizes biographical information.

blog—Contraction of "Web log." A journal posted on the Web, usually arranged in reverse chronological order.

blogger—Someone who writes a blog.

blogging—The activity of updating a blog.

blogosphere—The community of all bloggers.

blogroll—The section of a blog which lists the sites that the blogger reads regularly. Doc Searls coined the term as a reference to "logrolling," defined as the exchange of favors or praise.

CAN-SPAM Act of 2003—U.S. antispam legislation. CAN-SPAM stands for "Controlling the Assault of Non-Solicited Pornography and Marketing."

Character—Your integrity, clarity of motives, consistency of behavior, openness, discretion, and trustworthiness.

chat—Real-time text communication, much like instant messaging, except that it usually indicates multiple participants meeting at a common virtual "place." Each participant's comments are repeated immediately and simultaneously on the screens of all other participants in the same chat room.

clique—A small group of people who are all tied to one another. Usually used with the implication that this small group is located within a larger group.

closed network—*See* closure.

closure—A network with closure is one "in which everyone is connected such that no one can escape the notice of the others."[296]

Competence—Your ability to "walk your talk" and do well the job that you claim to be able to do; your demonstrated capability. It includes functional knowledge and skills, interpersonal skills, and judgment.

contact management software—Software that helps you aggregate and analyze data about the people you know: not only name, phone, and e-mail, but also notes on personality, on your progress in selling to them, and so on.

crawler—A "robot" that searches the Web for new and updated Web pages. As the crawler finds pages, it places them in a central database, usually for the benefit of a search engine.

cross-posting—The act of posting the same message to more than one news group or list.

degree—In social network analysis, the number of steps between you and someone else. If you know Zeeshan, then Zeeshan is a first degree relationship. If Zeeshan knows Elizabeth, but you do not know Elizabeth, then Elizabeth is a second-degree relationship to you.

☞ **Diversity**—Heterogeneity of your network, by profession, age, sex, ethnicity, location, socioeconomic status, political orientation, and every other relevant measure. We use this term as a rough proxy for the number of structural holes in your network.

emoticons—Combination of characters meant to represent a facial expression. People use emoticons in electronic communications to convey meaning, just like people use voice tone in spoken communications. Some examples: ":-)" = smile, ";-)" = wink, ";-/" = wry smile, "!:-)" = imaginative.

enterprise whuffie—The reputation that employees can acquire by becoming known as experts in a given area. The term was possibly invented by Steve Gillmor.[297]

flame—A deliberately hostile and insulting message.

FOAF—Friend Of A Friend. A data file format that stores personal profile information and one's relationships to others. Developers are using it as the basis for early efforts at making this kind of information portable between various systems.

HTML—HyperText Markup Language, the code in which Web pages are written.

IM—*See* instant messaging.

☞ **Information**—The data that you have about the people you know.

instant messaging—Real-time text communication, generally person-to-person.

Internet Relay Chat—A free chat system that enables people anywhere on the Internet to join in live discussions.

Internet Service Provider ("ISP")—Company that provides Internet access to people or corporations.

IRC—*See* Internet Relay Chat.

ISP—*See* Internet Service Provider.

latent tie—A stranger that is relatively easy to convert into a weak tie.

link—1. In the context of social networks, the relationship between two people. 2. In the context of the World Wide Web, a piece of text or graphic that connects to another document (or section of the current document) or launches an action (such as executing a predefined search or sending an e-mail).

list serv—A server sold by L-Soft International, Inc.

list server—A program that forwards a message to all members of the list server's mailing list. The list server typically also generates an archive.

Metcalfe's law—The principle that the value of a communications system grows approximately as the square of the number of users of the system (N^2).[298]

multiplex—An adjective indicating that there is more than one type of relationship between two people.

netiquette—Etiquette of interacting with others virtually.

network—In the context of human relationships and this book, a network is the set of relationships that you need to get tasks done, to advance in an organization, and to grow as a person.

Network Valuation Formula[SM]—A formula developed by David Teten to analyze and value your social network (see Appendix A).

networking—Developing a significant Number of relationships for the purpose of supporting one another in achieving your group and personal goals. The word "networking" has also been widely adopted by the network marketing industry to refer specifically to the practice of network marketing. For example, one of the most popular magazines in the network marketing industry is titled "Networking Times."

networking groups—Organized groups where people get to know one another for business purposes. At their best, networking groups foster Strong relationships with Relevant and Diverse people. At their worst, they can be little more than strangers swapping business cards and asking each other for leads simply because they happen to be in the same room at the same time. We do not consider the latter "networking," but this is not an uncommon perception of it.

news aggregator—*See* news reader.

newsgroup—Collection of related messages (also known as articles) on a particular topic. Users post them to a news server, which then distributes them to other participating servers. Found primarily on the Usenet bulletin board system.

news reader—A Web site or software tool that allows the combination of data feeds from multiple blogs or Web sites into a single feed.

node—In a network, any point (e.g., a person) where two lines meet. If you know both Gilberto and Anthony, you are a node between the two of them.

Number—How many people you are linked to directly in your network, i.e., the combined number of strong and weak ties.

online community—*See* virtual community.

online social network—Any network of people which is entirely virtual (e.g., an online community which does not hold regular meetings) or partially virtual (e.g., the Bain & Company alumni network). People can build their personal networks online using any of the technologies we discuss in this book. For example, a group of bloggers discussing a particular issue constitute an online social network.

permalink—A permanent link on a blog which will link to a given post after that post is moved off the front page and into archives. Some blogs use the word "Permalink," but it is also common to use the time of the post or the "#" symbol.

RDF—"Resource Description Framework," standard data format for publishing and syndicating headlines and short content. Usually used for distribution of blog posts.

Reed's law—The principle that the value of large networks, particularly social networks, can scale exponentially with the size of the network (approximately 2^N).[299]

relationship capital management software—Software that helps you to track whom you interact with, and learn to which other people your network can provide you access. In other words, if you want to reach a particular target person who is a few degrees away from you, these tools help you figure out who can introduce you to her and provide background on her. Relationship capital management software typically allow you to analyze all of your relationships automatically by spidering through your e-mails, IMs, and other digital records.

Relevance—An acquaintance's value to you, defined as the acquaintance's ability to contribute to your specific goals, interests, and/or needs.

RSS—Originally "RDF Site Summary," but also commonly said to mean "Really Simple Syndication," a standard data format for publishing and syndicating headlines and short content. Usually used for distribution of blog posts.

RSS reader—News reader for RSS feeds.

signature file—Text that is automatically added to every online message you send. It usually includes your name, organization, e-mail, phone number, and frequently a physical address or Web site.

social capital—Social capital refers to the collective value of all "social networks" (who people know) and the inclinations that arise from these networks to do things for each other ("norms of reciprocity").[300] More formally, social capital is the sum of the resources, actual or virtual, that accrue to an individual or group by virtue of possessing a durable network of more or less institutionalized relationships of mutual acquaintance and recognition."[301]

social network—Any group of people acquainted with one another, ranging from casual acquaintances to close family bonds.

social network analysis (SNA)—"The mapping and measuring of relationships and flows between people, groups, organizations, computers, or other information/knowledge processing entities. The nodes in the network are the people and groups, while the links show relationships or flows between the nodes."[302]

social networking services—Services (primarily Web sites) that allow you to see more than one degree away (i.e., to see whom your relationships know).

social networking site—*See* social network site.

social network site—Virtual communities in which you can see more than one degree away from you (i.e., you can see whom your relationships know). These sites are a subset of virtual communities in general.

social network software—*See* social software.

social software—Web sites and software tools which allow you to discover, extend, manage, enable communication in, and/or leverage your social network. Some people use this term for the software used to run online communities and online dating sites, but we do not use that term for that purpose in this book.

spam—Unsolicited bulk e-mail (UBE), usually sent to thousands (or millions) of recipients. Also known as unsolicited commercial e-mail (UCE), although some spam is used for political advocacy or for chain letters. By definition, spam is sent without the permission of the recipients. In the context of virtual communities, "spam" refers not only to e-mails, but to posting any advertising in a discussion forum that does not expressly allow advertising.

spambot—A program used by spammers to automatically collect e-mail addresses from Web sites and add them to their database. These programs are the reason why we discourage you from placing your e-mail address on a public Web site.

spamming—The act of sending or posting spam.

spider—*See* crawler.

spoofing—The falsification of an e-mail header (originating address) so that the e-mail appears to have originated from someone or somewhere other than the real source.

⊖⊸ Strength—The closeness of the relationship between you and an acquaintance. This reflects the degree of trust and reciprocity in your relationship.

strong tie—Your family, close friends, and close professional colleagues. Typically, you have known these people for a long time, see them regularly, have a high level of emotional attachment, and frequently reciprocate advice, support, and other informal and formal "gifts."

structural equivalence—Two people are "structurally equivalent" if they have the same relationships to all other people within their organization. For example, two Vice Presidents of Purchasing for Ladies' Blouses working for Bloomingdale's are almost perfectly structurally equivalent. They have the same job title, same function, and interact with similar people almost every day.

structural hole—The weak connections between clusters of densely connected people. People with these connections can become brokers between the clusters.

TrackBack—A system of letting a blog owner know that you have quoted, referenced, or used his post for something in your post. This is called "trackbacking" or "pinging" his post. This is polite to the original source of your post; it expedites discussion; and it drives traffic to your blog.[303]

troll—A person who intentionally posts messages that create controversy or anger, without adding any value to the discussion.

trolling—The act of being a troll.

virtual community—A group of people that congregates and interacts with one another primarily or exclusively virtually.

weak ties—All of the people you know who are not "strong ties." Your weak ties are usually short term and instrumental, that is, you interact with them for a specific purpose.

web conferencing—A conference conducted online between two or more participants in different geographic locations. Participants typically use text, audio, and/or video to communicate in real time or asynchronously.

Weblog—*See* blog.

whuffie—Reputation currency, or digital reputation. You earn whuffie as people credit you for your accomplishments.

wiki—A collection of Web pages that are editable by any reader. Wikis use extremely simple linking and formatting commands rather than requiring people to learn HTML.

XML—Extensible Markup Language. XML is a text markup language used for interchange of structured data. It is similar to HTML, except that it can be customized (extended) as needed for a variety of applications.

Endnotes

1 John B. Horrigan, et al., "Online Communities: Networks that nurture long-distance relationships and local ties," Pew Internet and American Life Project, 31 October 2001 <www.pewinternet.org/pdfsPIP_Communities_Report.pdf> (10 February 2005).

2 Bureau of Labor Statistics, *Employee Tenure Summary*, 21 September 2004 <http://www.bls.gov/news.release/tenure.nr0.htm> (8 March 2005).

3 "Thirty Minutes Over Tokyo," *The Simpsons*, first broadcast 16 May 1999 by Fox Television. Directed by Jim Reardon and written by Donick Cary and Dan Greaney. Thanks to About.com Animated TV Guide's Nancy Basile for helping us track this down.

4 Deborah Tannen, *You Just Don't Understand: Women and Men in Conversation* (New York: HarperCollins, 1991), 275.

5 John H. Lienhard, *The Engines of Our Ingenuity* (New York: Oxford University Press, 2000).

6 Drawn from Bob Miles, "More About the Lunar Society" <jquarter.members.beeb.net/morelunar.htm> and Scholarly Societies Project, "Lunar Society of Birmingham" <www.scholarly-societies.org/history/1775lsb.html> (both 3 March 2003). Thanks to Michael Paul Reveal for calling our attention to the Lunar Society.

7 For a look at the early use of these tools, see Katie Hafner and Matthew Lyon, "Talking Headers," an excerpt from *Where Wizards Stay Up Late* (New York: Touchstone Books, 1996) <www.olografix.org/gubi/estate/libri/wizards/e-mail.html> (13 August 2004).

8 Pew Internet & American Life Project, "Content Creation Online," 29 February 2004 <www.pewinternet.org/PPF/r/113/report_display.asp> (10 April 2005), 2.

9 Robert Putnam, "Social Capital: What Is It?" <www.bowlingalone.com/socialcapital.php3> (20 January 2005).

10 Robert Putnam, *Bowling Alone* (New York: Touchstone Books, 2000), 106.

11 Wayne Baker, *Achieving Success Through Social Capital: Tapping the Hidden Resources in Your Personal and Business Networks* (San Francisco: Jossey-Bass, 2000), 9-18.

12 Baker also notes that high levels of social capital enable executives to successfully resist takeover attempts. However, we are hesitant to mention this as an advantage of social capital, since extensive financial industry research by Malcolm Salter and others has shown that a free market in corporate control has a positive effect on economic efficiency. Baker's point is that social capital can protect an individual's company from being taken over, but from a social policy point of view this restriction on market efficiency is counterproductive.

13 Putnam, *Bowling Alone*, 327.

14 This section is based in part on Mark Granovetter, *Getting a Job: A Study in Contacts and Careers*, 2nd ed. (University of Chicago Press, 1995), 53-55.

15 The academic term for a latent tie is "performative tie." See Sheen S. Levine, "The Strength of Performative Ties: Network Exchange in a Knowledge Intensive Firm," Working Paper, The Wharton School, 2004.

16 Robin Dunbar, "Neocortex Size as a Constraint on Group Size in Primates, *Journal of Human Evolution* 20 (1992): 469-493.

17 For a brief discussion of optimal group sizes when groups are used for different purposes, see <www.lifewithalacrity.com/2004/03/the_dunbar_numb.html >.

18 Mark Granovetter, *Getting a Job: A Study in Contacts and Careers,* 2nd ed. (University of Chicago Press, 1995).

19 Jay MacLeod, *Ain't No Making It: Aspirations and Attainment in a Low-Income Neighborhood,* 2nd ed. (Boulder, CO: Westview Press, 1985).

20 Suggested reading: Stephen P. Borgatti, "Structural Holes: Unpacking Burt's Redundancy Measures," *Connections* 20, no. 1 (1997): 35-38 <www.analytictech.com/connections/v20(1)/holes.htm> (25 October 2004).

21 Ron Burt, "The Network Structure of Social Capital," *Research in Organizational Behavior,* ed. Robert I. Sutton and Barry M. Staw (Greenwich, CT: JAI Press, 2000).

22 Linda Hill, *Power Dynamics in Organizations* (Cambridge, MA: Harvard Business School Publishing, 1994), 6-10.

23 The average relationship Strength *(S)* and the Number *(N)* of people in your network are inversely proportional. Mathematically,

$$\text{Total Time Available} = S_{average} \ast N$$

24 Geoffrey Hyatt, e-mail to David Teten (10 July 2004).

25 Ronald S. Burt, *Structural Holes: The Social Structure of Competition* (Cambridge, MA: Harvard University Press, 1992). This section also draws on S. P. Borgatti and P. C. Foster, "The Network Paradigm in Organizational Research: A Review and Typology," *Journal of Management* 29 (2003): 991-1013.

26 See Wayne Baker, *Achieving Success Through Social Capital: Tapping the Hidden Resources in Your Personal and Business Networks* (San Francisco, Jossey-Bass, 2000), 9-15.

27 Burt, "Structural Holes versus Network Closure as Social Capital."

28 Elizabeth Rosenthal, "Social Networks and Team Performance," *Team Performance Management,*. 3, no. 4 (1997): 288-294. This section also draws on Burt, "Structural Holes versus Network Closure as Social Capital."

29 See Shaul Gabbay, *Social Capital in the Creation of Financial Capital: The Case of Network Marketing* (Champaign, IL: Stipes Publishing, 1997).

30 John B. Horrigan, et al., "Online Communities: Networks That Nurture Long-Distance Relationships and Local Ties," Pew Internet and American Life Project, 31 October 2001 <www.pewinternet.org/pdfs/PIP_Communities_Report.pdf> (10 April 2005).

31 See Chapter 30.

32 Peter Steiner, "On the Internet no one knows you're a dog" (Cartoon), *The New Yorker* 69, no. 20 (5 July 1993): 61.

33 Search performed using Google, 5 September 2004.

34 As a rough estimate, 12 hours/day × 365 days/year × 30 years = 131,400 hours.

35 Jeffrey I. Cole, *The UCLA Internet Report: Surveying the Digital Future, Year Three* (Los Angeles: UCLA Center for Communication Policy, 2003), 22.

36 Jeffrey I. Cole, *The UCLA Internet Report: Surveying the Digital Future, Year Three,* 23.

37 Amanda Lenhart, Lee Rainie, and Oliver Lewis, "Teenage life online: The rise of the instant-message generation and the Internet's impact on friendships and family relationships," Pew Internet and American Life Project, 20 June 2001 <www.pewinternet.org/pdfs/PIP_Teens_Report.pdf> (7 September 2004).

38 Pew Internet and American Life Project, "Getting Serious Online," 3 March 2002 <www.pewinternet.org/report_display.asp?r=55> (20 October 2004), 3.
39 Wainhouse Research. Cited in "Virtual meetings-Being there," *The Economist,* 15 May 2004: 63.
40 International Telework Association and Council, "Work at Home Grows in Past Year by 7.5 Percent in U.S.," 2 September 2004 <www.telecommute.org/news/pr090204.htm> (28 September 2004).
41 Lee Rainie and John Horigan, "Internet: The Mainstreaming of Online Life," Pew Internet and American Life Project, 25 January 2005 <www.pewinternet.org/PPF/r/148/report_display.asp > (10 February 2005).
42 J. Bradford DeLong, "Seoul of a New Machine," *Wired,* September 2003 <www.wired.com/wired/archive/11.09/view.html?pg=5> (11 September 2004).
43 SpeedDating.com used to have an online dating service comparable to Match.com, but the site has been altered to focus on face-to-face speeddating.
44 ComScore Networks, "U.S. Consumer Spending for Online Content Totals Nearly $1.6 Billion in 2003," press release, 11 May 2004 <www.comscore.com/press/release.asp?id=455> (23 August 2004).
45 "Match.com Declared as Europe's Number One in Online Dating," 2 December 2004 <www.prnewswire.co.uk/cgi/news/release?id=135569> (20 January 2005).
46 Match.com, "Match.com Named As World's Biggest Dating Site," press release, 2 March 2004 <corp.match.com/index/newscenter_release_detail.asp?auto_index=19 > (15 January, 2005).
47 Match.com, "Match.com at a Glance" <corp.match.com/index/newscenter_press_glance.asp> (15 January, 2005).
48 Daniel S. Hamermesh and Jeff E. Biddle, "Beauty and the Labor Market," *American Economic Review* 84 (1994): 1174-1194.
49 Robert J. Brym and Rhonda L. Lenton, *Love Online: A Report on Digital Dating in Canada* (25 March 2001) <www.nelson.com/nelson/harcourt/sociology/newsociety3e/loveonline.pdf> (15 August 2004).
50 Robert J. Brym and Rhonda L. Lenton, *Love Online: A Report on Digital Dating in Canada* (25 March 2001) <www.nelson.com/nelson/harcourt/sociology/newsociety3e/loveonline.pdf> (15 August 2004).
51 Terry Perkins, "Anarchy Online: It's Alive #2," 8 December 2004 <rpgvault.ign.com/articles/571/571447p1.html > (10 February 2005).
52 Terry Perkins, "Anarchy Online: It's Alive #2," 8 December 2004 <rpgvault.ign.com/articles/571/571447p1.html > (10 February 2005).
53 Albert Mehrabian and Susan R. Ferris, "Inference of attitudes from nonverbal communication in two channels," *Journal of Consulting Psychology* 31 (1967): 248-252. In this analysis, Mehrabian drew on Albert Mehrabian and Morton Wiener, "Decoding of Inconsistent Communications," *Journal of Personality and Social Psychology* 6 (1967): 109-114.
54 Albert Mehrabian, "'Silent Messages'—A Wealth of Information About Nonverbal Communication (Body Language)," 23 February 2004 <www.kaaj.com/psych/smorder.html> (23 October 2004). Also see Richard Sproat, "Contributions of Different Modalities to Content," 13 May 2001 <www.linguistlist.org/issues/12/12-1332.html> (14 October 2004).
55 Nick Morgan, "When Body Language Lies," Harvard Business School Working Knowledge, 30 September 2002. <hbswk.hbs.edu/pubitem.jhtml?id=3123&t=organizations> (31 January 2005).
56 Robert J. Brym and Rhonda L. Lenton, *Love Online: A Report on Digital Dating in Canada* (25 March 2001) <www.nelson.com/nelson/harcourt/sociology/newsociety3e/loveonline.pdf> (15 August 2004).

57 J. A. Bargh, K. Y. A. McKenna, and G. M. Fitzsimons, "Can you see the real me? Activation and expression of the "true self" on the Internet," *Journal of Social Issues* 58 (2002): 33-48. We thank Lauren Bibeau for pointing us to this paper.

58 Putnam, *Bowling Alone,* 140.

59 See for example Tauber, Robert T. 1998. "Good or bad, what teachers expect from students they generally get!" ERIC document ED 426 985. Also, Bamburg, Jerry D. 1994. "Raising expectations to improve student learning," ERIC document ED 378 290.

60 Lee Sproull and Sara B. Kiesler, *Connections: New Ways of Working in the Networked Organization* (Cambridge, MA: MIT Press, 1991).

61 Tim Berners-Lee, "Web Accessibility Initiative" <www.w3.org/WAI> (30 December 2004).

62 Gregor Wolbring, Ph.D., Ryze private message to Scott Allen, 18 August 2004.

63 Clive Thompson, "The Honesty Virus," *The New York Times,* 21 March 2004 <www.nytimes.com/2004/03/21/magazine/21ESSAY.html> (22 August 2004).

64 Celeste Biever, "People Lie More on the Phone Than by E-mail," *New Scientist,* 12 February 2004 <www.newscientist.com/news/news.jsp?id=ns99994663> (15 October 2004).

65 Don A. Moore, Terri R. Kurtzberg, Leigh L. Thompson, and Michael W. Morris, "Long and Short Routes to Success in Electronically Mediated Negotiations: Group Affiliations and Good Vibrations," *Organizational Behavior and Human Decision Processes* 77, no. 1 (1999): 22-43.

66 M. W. Morris, J. Nadler, T. R. Kurtzberg, and L. L. Thompson, "Schmooze or Lose: Social Friction and Lubrication in E-mail Negotiations," *Group Dynamics* 6 (2002): 89-100.

67 Jonathon N. Cummings, Brian Butler, and Robert Kraut, "The Quality of Online Social Relationships," *Communications of the ACM 45:7,* 2002 <homenet.hcii. cs.cmu.edu/progress/cummings02-QualityOfOnlineRelationships.pdf> (10 February 2005).

68 Dina Mehta, "My Blog Is My Social Software and My Social Network," 27 January 2004 <radio.blogs.com/0121664/2004/01/27.html#a356> (14 October 2004).

69 Ann Majchrzak, Arvind Malhotra, Jeffrey Stamps, and Jessica Lipnack, "Can Absence Make a Team Grow Stronger?," *Harvard Business Review* (May 2004). Also see Arvind Malhotra, "Using Far-Flung Virtual Teams for Managing Knowledge in Global Companies," *Vantage Point,* Fall 2004 <www.kenan-flagler.unc.edu/news/ alumniMag/2004Fall/global.html> (11 November 2004).

70 Putnam, *Bowling Alone,* 176.

71 Howard Rheingold, *The Virtual Community: Homesteading on the Electronic Frontier,* rev. ed. (Cambridge, MA: MIT Press, 2000).

72 Peter Caputa, personal e-mail to David Teten, 17 August 2004.

73 Jack Schofield, "Social Climbers," *The Guardian,* 8 May 2003 <www.guardian. co.uk/online/story/0,3605,950918,00.html> (23 August 2004).

74 Stowe Boyd, *Social Tools: Ready for the Enterprise?* (Arlington, MA: Cutter Consortium, 2003).

75 Stowe Boyd, "Are You Ready for Social Software?" *Darwin,* May 2003 <www. darwinmag.com/read/050103/social.html> (11 August 2004).

76 Boyd, "Are You Ready for Social Software?"

77 Inspiration for this chart comes partly from earlier charts by Geoff Hyatt and Stowe Boyd.

78 Adapted from "Many-to-Many Social Software Timeline" <www.socialtext.net/ m2m/index.cgi?social_software_timeline> (21 August 2004).

79 Bill Clinton, quoted in "White House Announces Next Generation Internet Initiatives," 11 October 1996 <www.sdsc.edu/SDSCwire/v2.21/internet2.html> (14 February 2005).

80 Sean Michael Kerner, "U.S Adults Search for Info on Colleagues and Employees," ClickZ Network, 25 October 2004 <www.clickz.com/stats/sectors/software/article.php/3426021> (15 January 2005).

81 Sean Michael Kerner, "U.S Adults Search for Info On Colleagues and Employees,"

82 Lance Ulanoff, "No More Online Identity Crises," *PC Magazine*, 8 December 2004, <www.pcmag.com/article2/0,1759,1737415,00.asp> (15 January 2005).

83 David Weinberger, "Biography" <www.hyperorg.com/speaker/bio.html> (2 August 2004).

84 Pew Internet and American Life Project, "Content Creation Online," 29 February 2004 <www.pewinternet.org/reports/pdfs/PIP_Content_Creation_Report.pdf> (5 March 2004), 2.

85 Creative Commons Attribution 2.0 license <creativecommons.org/licenses/by/2.0> (5 March 2005).

86 Andrius Kulikauskas, "An Economy for Giving Everything Away," 2002 <www.ms.lt/en/workingopenly/givingaway.html> (5 September 2004).

87 Andrius Kulikauskas, in "Licensing Issues," CollabWiki <collab.blueoxen.net/cgi-bin/wiki.pl?LicensingIssues> (5 September 2004).

88 Jim Cashel, quoted in Jenny Ambrozek and Joseph Cothrel, "Online Communities in Business: Past Progress, Future Directions," 7th International Conference on Virtual Communities (July 2004) <www.sageway.com/ocibreport.pdf> (10 February 2005).

89 Chris Pirillo, "About LockerGnome: The Story" <www.lockergnome.com/about/story.phtml> (21 October 2004).

90 John B. Horrigan, et al., "Online Communities: Networks That Nurture Long-Distance Relationships and Local Ties," Pew Internet and American Life Project, 31 October 2001 <www.pewinternet.org/pdfs/PIP_Communities_Report.pdf> (10 February 2005), 11.

91 Idelle Davidson, "The Craigslist Phenomenon," *Los Angeles Times*, 13 June 2004.

92 Clifford Stoll, quoted in Belinda Frazier, "Linux as SCO Forum," Linux Journal, 1 (November 1995) <http://www.linuxjournal.com/article/2608> (14 February 2005).

93 Danielle Bailey, posting to Using Ryze Effectively Network, 12 August 2004 <www.ryze.com/postdisplay.php?confid=586&messageid=613850> (12 August 2004).

94 The Radicati Group, as reported by John Dickinson, "Radicati Forecasts Huge Growth in Enterprise Instant Messaging," *Enterprise Apps Pipeline*, 15 July 2004 <nwc.enterpriseappspipeline.com/howto/23901036> (12 August 2004).

95 Li, *Profiles*, 7.

96 Stowe Boyd, *Research Brief: The Case for Real-Time Response and Resolution* (Reston VA: Corante Research, 2004).

97 Kim Ki-hong, "New Forms of Online Communication Spell End of Email Era in Korea," The Chosun Ilbo, 28 November 2004 <english.chosun.com/w21data/html/news/200411/200411280034.html> (15 January 2005).

98 Eulynn Shiu and Amanda Lenhart, "How Americans Use Instant Messaging," Pew Internet and American Life Project, 1 September 2004 <www.pewinternet.org/PPF/r/133/report_display.asp> (26 September 2004).

99 David Pulaski, "nPost.com Interview with David Pulaski," 9 March 2004 <www.npost.com/interview.jsp?intID=INT00076> (12 August 2004).

100 Mary Madden, cited by Robyn Greenspan in "Chatters Quieting Down," 24 December 2003 <www.internetnews.com/stats/article.php/3292301> (10 August 2004).

101 Rob Frankel, personal e-mail to Scott Allen, 3 August 2004.

102 John P. Davis, Shelly Farnham, and Carlos Jensen, "Decreasing Online Bad Behavior," 2002 <research.microsoft.com/scg/papers/Bad%20Behavior%20CHI%202002.pdf> (15 August 2004).

103 Intertangent Technology Directory, "Brief History of VoIP" <www.intertangent.com/023346/Articles_and_News/1477.html> (15 August 2004).

104 Michael Powell, quoted in Daniel Roth, "Catch Us If You Can," *Fortune,* 9 February 2004, 66.

105 Stuart Henshall, "The Disruptive Nature of Skype," 19 February 2004 <www.henshall.com/blog/archives/000715.html> (15 August 2004).

106 Skype Web site, <www.skype.com> (5 April 2005).

107 Wainhouse Research, *Rich Media Conferencing 2004, Vol. 3: Audio, Video & Web Conferencing Services* (Brookline, MA: Wainhouse Research, October 2004) <www.thinkofit.com/webconf/wr-rmc/wr-rmc2004-v3.pdf> (10 February 2005).

108 Computer Industry Almanac, cited in "Population Explosion!" <www.clickz.com/stats/big_picture/geographics/article.php/5911_151151> (21 September 2004).

109 Kester Mann of EMC, quoted in "Mobile Subscriber Numbers Exceed 1.5 Billion," 23 June 2004 <www.3g.co.uk/PR/June2004/7947.htm> (21 September 2004).

110 Editor, "The March of the Mobiles," *The Economist,* 25 September-1 October 2004, 15.

111 Dr. Edward Tenner, quoted in Matt Richtel, "All Thumbs, Without the Stigma," *The New York Times,* 12 August 2004 <www.nytimes.com/2004/08/12/technology/circuits/12thum.html> (30 December 2004).

112 Howard Rheingold, "Smart Mobs Book Summary" <www.smartmobs.com/book/book_summ.html> (16 August 2004).

113 Eric Bender, "Social Lives of a Cell Phone," *Technology Review,* 12 July 2004 <www.technologyreview.com//articles/04/07/wo_bender071204.asp> (10 February 2005).

114 Michael Jones, personal e-mail to Scott Allen, 19 October 2004.

115 Kurt Vonnegut, "Thoughts of a Free Thinker," *Palm Sunday* (New York: Delacorte, 1981), 180.

116 Kimberly R. Swinth, Shelly D. Farnham, and John P. Davis, "Sharing Personal Information in Online Community Member Profiles," 2002 <research.microsoft.com/scg/papers/sharing%20personal%20information%20in%20online%20community%20member%20profiles%20-%20with%20names.pdf> (9 August 2004).

117 Lee Rainie and John Horigan, *Internet: The Mainstreaming of Online Life,* Pew Internet and American Life Project, 25 January 2005 <www.pewinternet.org/pdfs/Internet_Status_2005.pdf > (10 February 2005), 64.

118 John B. Horrigan, et al., "Online Communities: Networks That Nurture Long-Distance Relationships and Local Ties," Pew Internet and American Life Project, 31 October 2001 <www.pewinternet.org/pdfs/PIP_Communities_Report.pdf> (10 February 2005).

119 This section draws in part from Helen Baxter, "An Introduction to Online Communities," 11 June 2002 <www.knowledgeboard.com/cgi-bin/library.cgi?action=detail&id=1270> (23 October 2004).

120 David P. Reed, interview by David Weinberger, 19 January 2001 <www.hyperorg.com/backissues/joho-jan19-01.html#reed> (27 February 2004).

121 Lee LeFever, "Comparing Social Networking to Online Communities," 7 December 2004 <www.commoncraft.com/archives/000834.html> (15 January 2005).

122 Glenn Gutmacher, "Virtual Networking," *CareerXroads: The 2003 Directory to Job, Resume and Career Management Sites on the Web,* 8th ed., ed. Gerry Crispin and Mark Mehler (Kendall Park, NJ: MMC Group, 2003), 33-38 <out of print, see: www.recruiting-online.com/cxr2003bygg.doc>.

123 As of 10 February 2005.

124 As of 10 February 2005.

125 Mark Pincus, transcribed by David Teten, New York, 10 February 2004. Mr. Pincus was speaking as part of a Business Development Institute panel on "Social Networking: What's Next?"

126 Pew Internet and American Life Project, "The State of Blogging," January 2005 <www.pewinternet.org/pdfs/PIP_blogging_data.pdf> (2 January 2005).

127 Adapted sufficiently so as not to cause the author embarrassment from an actual 2004 blog post. "LMAO" is a common Web acronym for "laughing my ass off."

128 Lee LeFever, "What Are the Differences between Message Boards and Weblogs?" 24 August 2004 <www.commoncraft.com/archives/000768.html> (15 January 2005).

129 Pew Internet and American Life Project, "The State of Blogging," January 2005 <www.pewinternet.org/pdfs/PIP_blogging_data.pdf> (2 January 2005).

130 Matthew Herper, "Best Medical Blogs," *Forbes,* 3 September 2003 <www.forbes.com/sciences/2003/10/03/cx_mh_1003medblogs.html> (17 August 2004).

131 comScore Media Metrix, Press Release, 17 February 2004 <www.comscore.com/press/release.asp?press=427> (5 March 2004). The "Top 50 Properties" chart lists About/Primedia as #7, but this includes Primedia's other media properties. The "Ad Focus Ranking" chart breaks it down by individual domain. In it, About is ranked #31. Removing the six advertising servers ahead of it puts About at #25 as a destination site.

132 comScore Media Metrix, Press Release, 17 February 2004 <www.comscore.com/press/release.asp?press=427> (5 March 2004).

133 Source unknown.

134 Emilio J. Castilla, Hokyu Hwang, Ellen Granovetter, and Mark Granovetter, "Social Networks in Silicon Valley," *The Silicon Valley Edge: A Habitat for Innovation and Entrepreneurship,* ed. Chong-Moon Lee (Palo Alto: Stanford University Press, 2000), 218.

135 NITLE Blog Census, "Market Share" <www.blogcensus.net/?page=tools> (4 March 2004).

136 Pew Internet and American Life Project, "The State of Blogging," January 2005 <www.pewinternet.org/pdfs/PIP_blogging_data.pdf> (2 January 2005).

137 Clay Shirky, "Power Laws, Weblogs, and Inequality," 8 February 2003 <www.shirky.com/writings/powerlaw_Weblog.html> (6 October 2004).

138 John Hawkins, "The Three Cardinal Sins of Blogging," 27 April 2003 <www.rightwingnews.com/archives/week_2003_04_27.PHP#000905> (24 October 2004).

139 Christopher Locke, Rick Levine, Doc Searles, and David Weinberger, *The Cluetrain Manifesto,* 2000 <www.Cluetrain.com> (6 October 2004).

140 See MovableType.org/trackback/beginners for a detailed explanation of TrackBack.

141 Lee LeFever, personal e-mail to Scott Allen, 6 August 2004.

142 Lee LeFever, "Case Study: Using a Weblog to Achieve #1 Rankings in Google," 8 December 2003 <www.commoncraft.com/archives/000443.html>, CommonCraft (22 October 2004).

143 Michael Perrone, personal interview with David Teten, November 2004. Also Christopher S. Stewart, "Networking Web Sites That Get Your Foot in the Door," *The New York Times,* 25 January 2004 <www.nytimes.com/2004/01/25/jobs/25onlinenet.html> (23 August 2004).

144 Andrew Weinreich, interview by David Teten, New York, 15 July 2003.

145 Konstantin Guericke, Vice President of Marketing for LinkedIn, "LinkedIn Fact Sheet," personal e-mail to David Teten and Scott Allen, 12 February 2004,

146 Eliyon, *Home Page,* 10 April 2005 <www.ZoomInfo.com> (10 April 2005).

147 Tacit Software, "Case Study: Aventis," 2004 <www.tacit.com/customers/casestudies/aventis.html> (23 August 2004).

148 Entopia, *Application Services: Entopia Social Network Mapping,* 10 February 2005 <www.entopia.com/products/k-bus/application/networks.html> (10 February 2005).

149 We have not been able to find an authoritative source confirming that Mark Twain said this.

150 The Rolling Stones, "You Can't Always Get What You Want," *Let It Bleed,* 1969.

151 Caroline Haythornthwaite, "Strong, Weak, and Latent Ties and the Impact of New Media," *The Information Society,* 18 (2002): 385-401.

152 Myles Weissleder, personal e-mail to David Teten, 10 February 2005.

153 Scott Heiferman, "nPost.com Interview with Scott Heiferman," 20 April 2004 <www.npost.com/interview.jsp?intID=INT00099> (23 August 2004).

154 Adam Osborne, quoted in Otto Friedrich, "The Computer Moves In," *Time,* 3 January 1983 <www.time.com/time/archive/preview/0,10987,953632,00.html> (7 February 2005).

155 Ken Jordan, Jan Hauser, and Steven Foster, "The Augmented Social Network," First Monday, 14 July 2003 <www.firstmonday.dk/issues/issue8_8/jordan> (7 September 2004).

156 Peter Quintas, personal communication with Scott Allen, 5 June 2004.

157 Daniel J. Boorstin, *The Image: A Guide to Pseudo-Events in America* (New York: Vintage Books, 1992), 186.

158 "Netiquette for the Radio Control Soaring Exchange" <www.eclipse.net/mikel/rcse/netiquette.htm> (30 December 2004).

159 Report of the National Commission on Writing, *Writing: A Ticket to Work . . . Or a Ticket Out: A Survey of Business Leaders* (New York: College Board, September 2004), 5.

160 George Bernard Shaw, "Maxims for Revolutionists: The Golden Rule," in *Man and Superman* (1903).

161 Inspired by Kant.

162 Jessica Lipnack, Jeffrey Stamps, George Goldsmith, and Cory LeFebvre, *Working with a Virtual Team,* version 2.0 (Cambridge, MA: Harvard Business School Publishing, 2003), 21.

163 This section draws on William S. Frank, "SUBJECT: The Only Way to Address E-mail" <www.careerlab.com/art_e-mail_addresses.htm> (20 October 2004).

164 *DoubleClick 2003 Consumer E-mail Study* <www.doubleclick.com/us/knowledge_central/documents/research/dc_consumere-mailstudy_0310.pdf> (25 October 2004).

165 Ruben Gonzalez, "A crazy twist of fate for an introvert. . . ," 8 December 2002 <www.ryze.com/postdisplay.php?messageid=10760&confid=94> (22 June 2004).

166 Fred Whitson, "Setting up distribution channels," About.com Entrepreneurs Forum, 14 February 2004 <forums.about.com/ab-entrepreneur/messages?msg=2897.1> (22 August 2004).

167 Sharon Gaudin, "Nine Out of 10 U.S. E-mails Now Spam," eSecurityPlanet.com, 8 June 2004 www.esecurityplanet.com/trends/article.php/3365341 (25 October 2004).

168 Rebecca Blood, "Weblog Ethics" <www.rebeccablood.net/handbook/excerpts/Weblog_ethics.html> (25 October 2004).

169 Some guidelines adapted from Rebecca Blood, "Weblog Ethics."

170 This is done in HTML with the use of the <STRIKE> tag. For example:<STRIKE>An expatriate South African living in Austin</strike> A native Texan with a love of South Africa . . . will produce what appears in the example.

171 *New York Journal-American,* 21 January 1960. Cited in Simpson, James B., ed. *Simpson's Contemporary Quotations* (New York: Houghton Mifflin, 1988).

172 Ark Group Ltd., *E-mail Management: Are You in Control? Survey Results.* North Sydney, Australia, 2003.

173 Darren McKewen, "The Barrage of Workplace E-Mail Is Burdening Managers and Staff," *CareerJournal, 26 July 2004* <www.careerjournal.com/hrcenter/briefs/20040726-bna.html> (1 August 2004).

174 *Managing Incoming E-mail: What Every User Needs to Know,* by Mark Hurst <www.goodexperience.com/reports/e-mail> (25 October 2004).

175 David Allen, *Getting Things Done* (New York: Penguin Books, 2001), 128. Full disclosure: David Allen is Scott Allen's uncle.

176 David Allen, *Getting Things Done,* 131.

177 Return Path, "Return Path Re-Launches New and Improved E-Mail Change of Address Service," 20 October 2003 <www.returnpath.biz/aboutus/newsroom/press/release.php?id=16> (25 October 2004).

178 Ross Mayfield, "Why I'm Switching to Gmail," 12 May 2004 <ross.typepad.com/blog/2004/05/why_im_switchin.html> (22 August 2004).

179 Don Tapscott, quoted in Kevin Maney, "In the future, you'll pluck your info from thin air," *USA Today,* 20 July 2001 <www.usatoday.com/money/covers/2001-07-20-bcovfri.htm> (30 December 2004).

180 Ajit Jaokar, "How can people take you seriously when your profile includes...," 5 June 2004 <www.ecademy.com/node.php?id=24404> (25 July 2004).

181 Virginia Shea, *Netiquette,* 1994 <www.albion.com/netiquette/rule2.html> (23 October 2004).

182 Source unknown.

183 As of 24 October 2004.

184 A July 2004 search on one popular social networking site turned up three Silicon Valley technology CEOs who listed "sex" as one of their interests. While most of these profiles did not include real names, they did include a link to their company Web sites, so the CEOs were hardly anonymous.

185 Traditionally credited to Abraham Lincoln.

186 Match.com, "Why Post a Photo?" <www.match.com/photomanager/interstitial_photo.aspx> (13 August 2004).

187 Esther Dyson, "Mirror of Our Lives," 31 March 2004 <www.edventure.com/esther/article.cfm?Counter=4572142> (28 August 2004).

188 Merav Knafo, co-founder of LookBetterOnline.com, personal e-mail to Scott Allen, 12 August 2004. We acknowledge this is a potentially biased source.

189 H. Dean Hua, network posting <www.ryze.com/postdisplay.php?messageid=344566&confid=436> (12 May 2004).

190 Bob Burg, *Endless Referrals: Network Your Everyday Contacts into Sales* (New York: McGraw-Hill, 1998), 48.

191 Christopher Hurtado, OpenBC profile <www.openBC.com/hp/Christopher_Hurtado/> (10 February 2005).

192 Scott McNealy, addressing the 51st Conference on World Affairs, Boulder, CO, April 1999.

193 Polly Sprenger, "Sun on Privacy: 'Get Over It'," 26 January 1999, *Wired* <www.wired.com/news/politics/0,1283,17538,00.html> (23 October 2004).

194 Jeffrey Rosen, "With Liberty and Surveillance For All," *CSO Magazine,* January 2004 <http://www.csoonline.com/read/010104/rosen.html> (30 December 2004).

195 Kevin Bankston, "Online privacy and social networking sites," 19 February 2004, personal e-mail to Scott Allen (23 February 2004).

196 Electronic Privacy Information Center, "The Amy Boyer Case" <www.epic.org/privacy/boyer/> (24 October 2004).

197 Russ Cooper, quoted in Bob Sullivan, "Online Privacy Fears Are Real," *MSNBC,* 2004 <msnbc.msn.com/id/3078835> (10 February 2005).

198 Synovate, "Federal Trade Commission—Identity Theft Survey Report," September 2003 <www.ftc.gov/os/2003/09/synovatereport.pdf> (10 February 2005).

199 Stanton McCandlish, draws on *EFF's Top 12 Ways to Protect Your Online Privacy,* 2002 <www.eff.org/Privacy/eff_privacy_top_12.html> (19 October 2004).

200 Ross Mayfield, "Next Next Generation," 21 February 2004 <ross.typepad.com/blog/2004/02/next_next_gener.html> (24 October 2004).

201 MIT News. "Grad students uncover mountains of private data on discarded hard drives," 29 January 2003 <Web.mit.edu/newsoffice/tt/2003/jan29/diskdrives.html> (19 October 2004).

202 Peter Weddle, interview with David Teten and public speech, 8 April 2003, New York.

203 Roger Clarke, *Very Black "Little Black Books,"* 1 February 2004 <www.anu.edu.au/people/Roger.Clarke/DV/ContactPITs.html> (19 October 2004).

204 Dennis Wilen, quoted in *Salon.com,* "The Ryze surprise," 2 October 2002 <www.salon.com/tech/feature/2002/10/02/ryze> (19 October 2004).

205 Sean Ness, quoted in *Salon.com,* "The Ryze surprise."

206 Andrew Kraft, quoted in *Salon.com,* "The Ryze surprise."

207 Chris Kelly, personal e-mail to Scott Allen, 3 June 2004.

208 D. H. Lawrence, "Morality and the Novel," in *Phoenix: The Posthumous Papers of D. H. Lawrence,* ed. Edward D. McDonald (New York: Viking Press, 1936), 530. Quoted in *The Columbia World of Quotations* (New York: Columbia University Press, 1996).

209 Abraham Lincoln, *Lincoln's Own Stories,* ed. Anthony Gross (Netherlands: Fredonia Books, 2001).

210 Attributed to Murray Raphel.

211 Stephen Covey, *The Seven Habits of Highly Effective People* (New York: Simon & Schuster, 1989), 18.

212 Left-hand column is based loosely on Donna Fisher, *Professional Networking for Dummies* (New York: Wiley, 2001) and Donna Fisher, *People Power* (Austin: Bard Press, 1995).

213 This was his standard closing sentence when reporting the news for radio station KFOG in San Francisco.

214 Daniel Goleman, *Emotional Intelligence: Why It Can Matter More Than IQ* (New York, NY: Bantam, 1997).

215 Widely attributed to Kissinger, although we were not able to locate the exact source.

216 Scott Stratten, "My Ryze.com year in review," 29 July 2004 <www.ryze.com/postdisplay.php?messageid=585844&confid=279> (14 October 2004).

217 Robert J. Sawyer, "On Writing: Show, Don't Tell," 1995 <www.sfwriter.com/ow04.htm> (18 October 2004).

218 Anne Baber and Lynne Waymon, *Smart Networking* (Dubuque, IA: Kendall/Hunt, 1997).

219 Searches performed on Google, 15 August 2004.

220 Martin Ruef, quoted in Mary Petrusewicz, "Note to Entrepreneurs: Meet New People," *Stanford Report,* 21 January 2004 <news-service.stanford.edu/news/2004/january21/innovate-121.html> (29 August 2004).

221 Controversy <www.mikemilken.com/biography.taf?page=controversy>, 15 October 2004.

222 David Whelan, "Google Me Not," *Forbes,* 16 August 2004 <www.forbes.com/home/free_forbes/2004/0816/102.html> (28 October 2004).

223 Attributed to Molly Ivins.

224 These are not fictional examples. Teten Recruiting has seen job applicants make all of these errors, and worse.

225 Brian Koslow, *365 Ways to Become a Millionaire (Without Being Born One),* (New York: Plume Books, October 1999).

226 Steve Gillmor, "Weaving Social Nets for the Enterprise," eWeek, 10 February 2004 <www.eweek.com/article2/0,4149,1523237,00.asp> (16 October 2004).

227 Cory Doctorow, "My Blog, My Outboard Brain," *O'Reilly Network,* 31 May 2002 <www.oreillynet.com/pub/a/javascript/2002/01/01/cory.html?page=last&x maxdepth=0> (10 February 2005).

228 Susan Feldman, "The high cost of not finding information," *KM World,* March 2004 <www.kmworld.com/publications/magazine/index.cfm?action=readarticle& Article_ID=1725&Publication_ID=108> (25 October 2004).

229 N.D. De Graff and H.D. Flap, "With a Little Help from My Friends," *Social Forces* (67: 453-472).

230 American idiom.

231 Auren Hoffman, "Advantageous E-mail—How to Sell via E-mail," *ParMedia,* 16 November 2004 <parmedia.org/newswire/display/107/index.php> (10 February 2005).

232 Fischer, C.S. *To Dwell Among Friends.* University of Chicago Press, 1982.

233 Phone interview with David Teten, 15 July 2004.

234 Neil Rackham, *Spin Selling* (New York: McGraw-Hill, 1988), 140.

235 This list is based on research by Wayne Baker, Robert Putnam, Mark Granovetter, and others. For a discussion of measures of tie strength, see P.V. Marsden and K.E. Campbell, "Measuring Tie Strength," *Social Forces* 63 (1984): 482-501.

236 Y. Liu, *The Effects of Frequency and Duration of Messaging on Impression and Relational Development in Computer-Mediated Communication: An Exploratory Study* (Annual Conference of the International Communication Association, Washington, DC 2001).

237 Carol Werner and Pat Parmelee, "Similarity of Activity Preferences Among Friends: Those Who Play Together Stay Together," *Social Psychology Quarterly* 42, (1979): 1, 62-66.

238 Thanks to Ross Wirth for pointing out this item.

239 Jessica Lipnack and Jeffrey Stamps, *The Age of the Network* (New York: Wiley, 1996): 47.

240 Brian Uzzi, "Embeddedness in the Making of Financial Capital: How Social Relations and Networks Benefit Firms Seeking Financing," *American Sociological Review* 64 (1999) 481-505.

241 J. K. Franzen and H. L. Davis, "Purchasing Behavior in Embedded Markets," *Journal of Consumer Research,* 1990, 17:1-12.

242 Mark Granovetter, "The Strength of Weak Ties: A Network Theory Revisited," 113. In P. V. Marsden and Nan Lin (eds.), *Social Structure and Network Analysis* (Beverly Hills, CA: Sage, 1982).

243 Putnam, *Bowling Alone,* 136.

244 Brian Uzzi, "Social Structure and Competition in Interfirm Networks: The Paradox of Embeddedness," *Administrative Science Quarterly* 42 (1997): 35-67.

245 Burt, *Structural Holes,* 156.

246 Heidi Whitaker, Ryze home page <www.ryze.com/go/20again> (12 August 2004).

247 Heidi Whitaker, "re:_Brian and Gisela (Question for Scott) Is there such a thing as being TOO friendly?," message post on the Using Ryze Effectively Network, 11 July 2004 <www.ryze.com/postdisplay.php?messageid=545064&confid=586> (12 August 2004).

248 Robert Cialdini, *Influence: the Psychology of Persuasion* (New York: Quill, 1998).

249 Tim Sanders, *Love Is the Killer App: How to Win Business and Influence Friends* (New York: Three Rivers Press, 2003).

250 Donna Fisher, *Professional Networking for Dummies* (New York: Wiley, 2001), 1.

251 Lynne Wamone, quoted in ExecuNet, *ExecuNet's Career Guide. Networking Knowledge: Techniques and Strategies to Help You Build Your Lifetime Network* (Norwalk, CT: ExecuNet Inc., 2002). To our knowledge, there is no particular academic research supporting or refuting this claim.

252 Includes some ideas from Harvey Mackay, *Dig Your Well Before You're Thirsty* (New York: Doubleday, 1999).

253 Ursula K. Leguin, *The Left Hand of Darkness (Remembering Tomorrow)* (New York: Penguin, March 1969), 42.

254 Rob Cross and Andrew Parker, *The Hidden Power of Social Networks* (Boston, MA: Harvard Business School Press, 2004), 4.

255 Paul McNamara, "Had enough of Plaxo, et al.," Network World, 8 December 2003 <www.nwfusion.com/columnists/2003/1208buzz.html> (23 August 2004).

256 James M. Jasper, *Restless Nation: Starting Over in America,* (Chicago: University of Chicago Press, 2000), 72.

257 Justin Hitt, Private e-mail to David Teten, 1 February 2005.

258 Gary P. Green, Leann M. Tigges, and Irene Browne, "Social Resources, Job Search, and Poverty in Atlanta," *Research in Community Sociology* 5 (1995): 161-182.

259 Interview with David Teten, 15 July 2004.

260 Thanks to Billy McDermott for this tip. Billy met Scott Allen via this technique.

261 Dave Armon, interview by David Teten, New York, 14 January 2005.

262 Anonymous journalist, interviewed by David Teten, New York, 15 September 2003.

263 Dr. Phil Agre, "Networking on the Net," 11 June 2003 <polaris.gseis.ucla.edu/pagre/network.html> (30 December 2004).

264 Danny Sullivan, "The Search Engine Index," 10 September 2003 <searchenginewatch.com/reports/article.php/2156471> (8 October 2004).

265 Grant Crowell, "Public Relations Via Search Engines," 30 June 2004 <searchenginewatch.com/reports/article.php/3375321> (8 October 2004).

266 Google.com, "Webmaster Guidelines" <www.google.com/Webmasters/guidelines.html> (8 July 2004).

267 Keith O'Brien, "Topix.Net taps CooperKatz based upon blog relationship," *PRWeek,* 1 December 2004 <www.prweek.com/news/news_story_free.cfm?ID=229564&site=3> (20 January 2005).

268 Jonathon Cummings, "Work Groups, Structural Diversity, and Knowledge Sharing in a Global Organization," *Management Science* 50 (3): 352-364. Also see Barclays, "Press Release: Diversity drives business performance in both public and private sectors."

269 Martin Ruef, quoted in Mary Petrusewicz, "Note to Entrepreneurs: Meet New People," *Stanford Report,* 21 January 2004 <news-service.stanford.edu/news/2004/january21/innovate-121.html> (29 August 2004).

270 Putnam, *Bowling Alone,* 95.

271 Hiroshi Ono and Madeleine Zavodny, "Gender and the Internet," *Social Science Quarterly* 84 (March 2003): 111-121.

272 Matthijs Kalmijn, "INTERMARRIAGE AND HOMOGAMY: Causes, Patterns, Trends," *Annual Review of Sociology* 24 (August 1998), 395-421.

273 Peter V. Marsden, "Core Discussion Networks of Americans," *American Sociological Review* 52 (1987): 122-131.

274 Wayne Baker, *Networking Smart: How to Build Relationships for Personal and Organizational Success* (New York: McGraw-Hill, 1994), 148.

275 Tom Allen, *Managing the Flow of Technology* (Cambridge, MA: MIT Press, 1977).

276 Rob Cross, *Personal Networks and Leadership Development,* <gates.comm.virginia.edu/rlc3w/sna11.htm> (28 March 2004).

277 Barclays, *Barclays Web site,* "Press Release: Diversity drives business performance in both public and private sectors," 10 June 2002 <www.newsroom.barclays.co.uk/news/data/720.html> (6 August 2003).

278 Based in part on a list in Mackay, *Dig Your Well Before You're Thirsty.*

279 San Jose Mercury News, "Hot Topics: Q&A: Sridar Iyengar on the Indus Entrepreneurs." (25 April 2003), *San Jose Mercury News* <www.siliconvalley.com/mld/siliconvalley/business/special_packages/5714785.htm> (20 October 2004).

280 Full Circle Associates, *Project Harmony Domestic Violence Online Conference,* 14-20 March 2002 <www.fullcirc.com/community/phdvconferencereportfull.htm> (20 October 2004).

281 Robyn Greenspan, "Big Increase in Job-Seeking Surfers," *InternetNews.com,* 31 July 2002 <www.internetnews.com/stats/article.php/1437221> (22 October 2004).

282 Ted Rueter, *The 267 Stupidest Things Republicans Ever Said* (New York: Three Rivers Press, 2000), 20.

283 Konstantin Guericke, personal e-mail to David Teten, 13 February 2005.

284 Mark Granovetter, *Getting a Job: A Study of Contacts and Careers,* 2nd ed. (Cambridge, MA: Harvard University Press, 1995).

285 Portions of this section draw on Glenn Gutmacher, "Virtual Networking."

286 Marc Cenedella, "The Top 10 Blunders Of Online Job Hunters," *CareerJournal.com,* 16 August 2004 <www.careerjournal.com/columnists/perspective/20040816fmp.html> (10 February 2005).

287 BBC News, "History of a Conspiracy," www.news.bbc.co.uk/1/hi/world/americas/1694100.stm (20 April 2005).

288 Debbie Weil, "Microsoft's Employee Guidelines for Successful Blogging," 25 January 2005 <blogwrite.blogs.com/blogwrite/2005/01/microsofts_empl.html > (10 February 2005).

289 Charles Browder, quoted in James B. Simpson, *Contemporary Quotations* (Binghamton, NY: Vail-Ballou Press, 1964), 83.

290 Amazon.com, search in Books section on keywords "sales" (10 February 2005).

291 R. Miller, S. Heiman, and T. Tuleja, *Successful Large Account Management* (New York: Warner Books, 1991), 78.

292 Simon Rogers, personal e-mail to Scott Allen, 7 September 2004.

293 Andrew Carnegie, in *And I Quote: The Definitive Collection of Quotes, Sayings, and Jokes for the Contemporary Speechmaker*, rev. ed. (New York: St. Martin's Press, 2003), 6.

294 Scott Allen, "Looking for success stories about online business networking," 10 December 2002 <groups.yahoo.com/group/Webcommunities/message/484> (21 August 2004).

295 Inspired by David Maister, Charles Green, and Robert Galford, *The Trusted Advisor* (New York: Free Press, 2000).

296 Burt, "Structural Holes versus Network Closure as Social Capital."

297 Steve Gillmor, "Weaving Social Nets for the Enterprise," *eWeek,* 10 February 2004 <www.eweek.com/article2/0,4149,1523237,00.asp> (16 October 2004).

298 David P. Reed, "That Sneaky Exponential: Beyond Metcalfe's Law to the Power of Community Building," Spring 1999 and update <www.reed.com/Papers/GFN/reedslaw.html> (20 January 2005).

299 *Ibid.*

300 Putnam, "Social Capital: What Is It?"

301 Pierre Bourdieu and Loïc J.D. Wacquant, *An Invitation to Reflexive Sociology* (University of Chicago Press, 1992), 119.

302 Valdis Krebs, *An Introduction to Social Network Analysis,* 23 July 2004 <orgnet.com/sna.html> (23 July 2004).

303 Commoncraft, *TrackBack Described in Plain English* <www.commoncraft.com/archives/000568.html> (22 October 2004).

Index

Acknowledgments

All works of art should begin . . .
at the end.—EDGAR ALLAN POE

Unless we explicitly state otherwise, all case studies in this book are about real people. In the interests of full disclosure, the authors have had consulting relationships or partnerships with Spoke, LinkedIn, and Ryze.

Thank you to the many people who provided invaluable counsel and shared their tips, stories, feedback, and endorsements with the authors. Without you, this book would not have been possible. We would especially like to thank the management of the many companies that have given us access into their thinking: Albourne Village, aSmallWorld, Classmates, Contact Network Corporation, Corp-Net, Ecademy, Eliyon, Eloqua, Entopia, eWomenNetwork, FriendsReunited, International Executives Resource Group, International Virtual Women's Chamber of Commerce, Jigsaw, Knowmentum, Leverage Software, LinkedIn, LinkSV, Media Bistro, Meetup, MiPasado, Monster, openBC, ReferNet, Ryze, SilkRoad technology, Socialtext, Spoke Software, Sullivan Executive, Tribe.net, Visible Path, ZeroDegrees, Ziggs, and countless other mailing lists and niche sites.

We would also like to thank the following for their insightful comments and contributions on both our book and Web site: Paul Arnold, Carolyn Burke, Craig Calle, Christopher Carfi, Peter Caputa IV, Jonathan Donner, Andy Halliday, Dave Harris, Stephen Harris, Greg Head, Justin Hitt, Bruce Hoppe, Amy Hovis, Geoffrey Hyatt, Steve Jackson, Dan Koifman, Andrius Kulikauskas, Chris Kelly, Daniel Kreiss, Lee LeFever, Sheen Levine, William McDermott, Andrew McInnes, Sharon Drew Morgen, Mark Organ, Dani Shefer, Katja Vehlow, and Ross Wirth. A special thanks to Donna Fisher for her inspiration, collaboration, and support. Jayne Allen, Russell Cheng, and Joe Shapiro were very helpful in gathering quotations. We also thank our agents, Danielle Jatlow and David Fugate, and the ever-patient team working with AMACOM: Ed Reilly, Ellen Kadin, and Joel Stein. All mistakes are ours.

Lastly, our wives deserve our gratitude and devotion for supporting us in the very lengthy process of writing this book. Of course, they already had our gratitude and devotion after being kind enough to marry us.

David Teten and Scott Allen
April 10, 2005

About the Authors

DAVID TETEN is a serial entrepreneur who builds businesses that leverage social software. He is CEO of Nitron Advisors (NitronAdvisors.com), an independent research firm which provides hedge funds, private equity funds, venture capitalists, and other professional investors with direct access to frontline industry experts. He is also Chairman of Teten Recruiting (Teten.com), an executive recruiting firm specializing in the institutional investor, investment banking, and strategy consulting industries. Both companies leverage social software to help clients recruit and partner with the best possible people. David owns and runs TheVirtualHandshake.com, a resource site and blog about social software. Previously, he was CEO of an investment bank specializing in Internet domain names, which he built to over 450 clients.

While working with Bear Stearns' Investment Banking division, he was a member of their technology/defense mergers and acquisitions team, which at the time was ranked #1 in defense/aerospace M&A. He lived and worked in Brazil and the United States while a strategy consultant with mars & co. David holds an MBA from Harvard and a BA from Yale. While still a college student, he ran an advertising agency and built a computer consulting group which served more than 35 clients.

David has spoken at many finance and technology industry conferences and at such universities as Columbia Business School, Princeton, the Technion, Wharton, and Yale. He has received coverage in the *Wall Street Journal, Bloomberg, Financial Times, Red Herring, Tornado-Insider, Internet.com,* and other leading publications in nine countries. He speaks passable Hebrew and rusty French. David met his wife on the Internet; they live in Manhattan with two laptops. He writes his "Brain Food" blog mainly in English (Teten.com/blog). Contact: Handshake@Teten.com.

SCOTT ALLEN is a 20-year veteran entrepreneur and information technology executive and now provides strategic marketing consulting services to a select group of clients. He has run his own software company, consulting practice, and several online businesses. In his corporate roles, he has served as VP of Professional Services and VP of Product Management for Mongoose Technology (which creates software for online community management) and has implemented solutions for IBM and Amazon.com, among others.

Scott is a leading expert on building quality business relationships online, having offered training programs on the use of social software and online communities to create a powerful personal presence and professional network on the Internet. He has used online networking to find employees, find a new job, identify and develop business partners, and even to initiate a multi-million-dollar corporate merger.

He has been quoted in ABCNews.com, *Inc. Magazine, Christian Science Monitor, Sales and Marketing Management, Worth,* and other major publications. As the Entrepreneurs Guide on About.com, he provides over 30,000 monthly visitors with guidance and resources to help them start and develop their new businesses. His websites are www.TheVirtual Handshake.com/scott-allen and Entrepreneurs.About.com. He lives in Austin, Texas with his family and a diverse network of animals. Contact: Scott@TheVirtualHandshake.com.

David Teten and **Scott Allen** jointly write a monthly column for FastCompany.com and are contributing authors to *Blog!: How the World of Blogs and Bloggers Is Changing Our Culture,* by Dan Burstein & David Kline (CDS Books, 2005).